Economic Problems of the 1990s

Economic Problems of the 1990s

Europe, the Developing Countries and the United States

Edited by
Paul Davidson and J. A. Kregel

Edward Elgar

© Paul Davidson, J. A. Kregel 1991

All rights reserved. No part of this publication may be reproduced, stored in a retrieval system, or transmitted in any form or by any means, electronic, mechanical, photocopying, recording, or otherwise without the prior permission of the publisher.

Published by
Edward Elgar Publishing Limited
Gower House
Croft Road
Aldershot
Hants GU11 3HR
England

Edward Elgar Publishing Company
Old Post Road
Brookfield
Vermont 05036
USA

British Library Cataloguing in Publication Data

Economic problems of the 1990s: Europe, the developing
  countries and the United States
  1. Economic conditions.
  I. Davidson, Paul *1930–* II. Kregel, J. A. (Jan Allen)
  1944–
  330.9049

Library of Congress Cataloguing in Publication Data

Economic problems of the 1990s: Europe, the developing countries, and
  the United States/edited by Paul Davidson and J. A. Kregel.
    p.   cm.
  Includes index.
  1. European Economic Community countries – Economic conditions. 2. Economic forecasting – European Economic Community countries. 3. Europe, Eastern – Economic conditions – 1989– 4. Economic forecasting – Europe, Eastern, 5. United States – Economic conditions – 1981– 6. Economic forecasting – United States. 7. Developing countries – Economic conditions. 8. Economic forecasting – Developing countries. 9. International economic relations. I. Davidson, Paul. II. Kregel, J. A.
  HC241.2.E295 1991
  330.9'048–dc20   90-27100
                                                                                CIP

ISBN 1 85278 459 8

Printed in Great Britain by
Billing & Sons Ltd, Worcester

Contents

List of Figures and Tables   vii
Introduction   ix
List of Contributors   xiii

Part I Economic Development, Debt and International Finance

1. The Terms of Trade of Primary Commodities, Debt and Development   3
   A. P. Thirlwall
2. Banking on Capital Flight   31
   William Darity, Jr
3. Hyperinflation and Stabilization in Brazil: The First Collor Plan   41
   Luiz Carlos Bresser Pereira and Yoshiaki Nakano
4. A Post Keynesian Approach to Inflation, High Inflation and Hyperinflation   69
   Fernando J. Cardim de Carvalho
5. What International Payments Scheme Would Keynes Have Suggested for the Twenty-first Century?   85
   Paul Davidson

Part II East and West European Reconstruction

6. A German Perspective of a European Single Market and EMU   107
   Stephen F. Frowen
7. Alternative Economic Analyses of German Monetary and Economic Unification: Monetarist and Post Keynesian   122
   J. A. Kregel
8. Should There be a Marshall Plan for Eastern Europe?   134
   Irma Adelman

Part III The United States

9. Low Saving Rates and the 'Twin Deficits': Confusing the Symptoms and Causes of Economic Decline   161
   Robert A. Blecker
10. Efficiency, Rent-seeking and Privatization: Ten Propositions   194
    John D. Donahue

11. Public and Private Sector Relationships in the Age of Privatization *Ronald C. Moe*	219
Name Index	233
Subject Index	235

Figures and Tables

FIGURES

1.1	Movements in the net barter terms of trade	8
1.2	Terms of trade of non-oil primary commodities of LDCs vis-à-vis manufactures	9
1.3	Relation between industrial terms of trade and growth rate of industrial output	15
3.1	Four weeks' inflation	59
9.1	Growth of real disposable income and consumption per capita	169
9.2	Inflation-adjusted personal saving rates	171
9.3	Alternative measures of the real value of the US dollar	181

TABLES

1.1	Tests of the Prebisch asymmetry hypothesis	11
1.2	Terms of trade effects on real income growth	19
1.3	Components of the change in debt–service ratio of developing countries	22
3.1	Public sector accounts	42
3.2	Yearly inflation rate	44
3.3	Monthly inflation rate	44
3.4	Public sector's interest payments	45
3.5	Fiscal adjustment estimated by the plan	51
3.6	Money supply	55
3.7	Financial assets	55
3.8	Indicators of economic activity in 1990	58
3.9	Monthly inflation rate	60
9.1	Average US saving and investment rates in mid-to-late cyclical expansions	167
9.2	Average annual growth rates of real after-tax income and consumer expenditures	170

9.3 Non-financial corporate profits in mid-to-late cyclical
    expansions 172
9.4 Current account, saving-investment and budget balances for
    the US, Japan and West Germany 177

Introduction

A popular weekly US news magazine opened the sixth decade of this century with the title 'The Soaring Sixties' emblazoned on the cover. The new decade was seen with confident and optimistic expectations for a world economy which had successfully completed the post-war reconstruction in Europe and was looking to stable and continuous expansion of output and employment.

These expectations were met during the first half of the decade, but by the end of the period things were beginning to unravel. Before the end of the decade the US was mired in a regional war in Southeast Asia. The US economy was showing the first signs of what came to be called 'stagflation' as economic growth faltered and prices started to escalate.

The 1970s saw a further deterioration of international economic conditions. First, the Bretton Woods system of international finance collapsed with the declaration of the inconvertibility of the dollar in August of 1971. Then the second major blow to the international economy of the free world was the 'oil crisis' linked to the Arab–Israeli war in 1973. The problems were exacerbated by the second oil shock in 1978–9.

As a result there was a period of more than a decade where there was an interruption in the strong expansion of employment and output that had characterized the post-war reconstruction period and also produced radical changes in international financial markets. During this period the seeds for the creation of the less developed countries' (LDC) 'debt problem' were sown, while the developed world experienced repeated bouts of domestic financial instability and what appeared to be the risk of escalation into high inflation or even hyperinflation.

Accordingly the policies of the 1980s were primarily concerned with attempting to combat the maladies that had manifested themselves in the 1970s and the first priority was given to ending the drift towards high inflation rates in the developed world. While progress was made on the inflation front, the measures introduced to counter inflation created a number of other equally disturbing problems, such as the twin deficits: the huge external account deficit and the structural federal budget deficit of the US. These deficit problems were balanced by the emergence of Japan as a major international creditor and dominant economic power rivalling the US and of Germany as the dominant economy in the European Economic Community. Although from 1983 through the rest of the decade economic conditions of growth and employment improved throughout the developed free world's international economy – with growth rates returning to levels closer to those expected in the 1960s and almost equal to those achieved in the immediate post-war recovery – the basic economic problems that had been created in the 1970s and early 1980s continued. The fragility of the economic recovery and the continued presence of the underlying imbalances were confirmed in 1987 by the first major stock market break since the Great Crash of 1929, and its smaller-scale repetition two years later.

Partially as a result of the renewed economic expansion of the industrialized economies in the 1980s, and partially as a result of internal inertia and inefficiency, the Soviet economy and most of the Eastern European command economies began to experience problems similar to those which had afflicted the free world's industrialized economies, such as excessive international debt burdens and inflation and unemployment (although officially 'repressed' or 'disguised'). As a result these command economies stagnated. The introduction of 'glasnost' and 'perestroika' was an attempt to develop a simple restructuring of the Soviet economy, but it also led to political freedoms and the recognition of the glaring necessity of proposing major economic reforms capable of rejuvenating what had previously been rigidly controlled command economies. These rapid changes, and the increased demands for western aid and investment, added another set of economic problems to those already lying behind the recovery of the capitalist countries in the 1980s.

The world economy thus faced the 1990s with the Soviet system and Eastern Europe in collapse. Despite political commentators boasting that this demonstrated the superiority of US free market capitalism, the US financial system, with its savings and loans crisis, the collapse of real estate prices and the crash of the junk bond market, and the increasing likelihood of default by South American debtors, began to look as if it also could disintegrate at any time. In sharp contrast to these cases of the command economies and the US there was tremendous optimism surrounding the moves of the European Economic Community to introduce a truly free internal market by the beginning of 1993. Moreover the success of the Japanese 'lifetime' employment system and the German 'social market' economic systems, both representing what may be called a cultural middle ground between US free market capitalism and Soviet command socialism, seemed to be pointing a way.

The 1990s were thus announced as one of the most interesting experiences and problems facing economic forecasters, analysts and policy makers. To some viewing the progress of the European Community, the 1990s looked as if they would produce the promise earlier expected of the 'Soaring Sixties', while for others observing the rapidly developing financial, debt and international payments problems the 1990s seemed to provide a scenario which more resembled the preamble to the slump of the 1930s.

In view of the great theoretical and policy interest of the outlook for the decade of the 1990s, the *Journal of Post Keynesian Economics* and the College of Business Administration of the University of Tennessee, Knoxville organized an international workshop on 'The Economic Problems of the 1990s' at which over 60 economists from 14 different countries discussed more than 30 invited and contributed papers. This book presents a representative selection of those papers from three basic areas which emerged as being of greatest importance.

Part I deals with the problems of economic development, debt and the international payments system. In Chapter 1 Thirlwall looks at the impact of changes in the terms of trade on the development process. In Chapter 2 Darity looks at the impact of debt on developing countries and in particular at the consequence of capital flight. The discussion then moves to the more specific case of Brazil, with Bresser Pereira and Nakano's discussion of the first Collor Stabilization Plan and Cardim de Carvalho's analysis of the problem of hyperinflation. The discussion concludes with Davidson's proposals for a trade and payments system which might avoid the problems that were built up in the 1970s and 1980s.

Part II looks to the impending integration and reconstruction of Western and Eastern Europe, centred on the role of Germany. In Chapters 6 and 7 Frowen discusses the German view of the European Single Market and Kregel provides a comparison of Monetarist and Post Keynesian analyses of the impact of the economic and monetary union of the two Germanies, suggesting that the forecasts of the inflationary impact of unification are greatly exaggerated. In the provocative final chapter Adelman considers the question of a Marshall Plan for Eastern Europe, a possibility which she finally rejects.

The problems facing the US economy are the subject of Part III. Blecker deals with the problem of the twin US deficits which are the result of the economic recovery in the 1980s. The discussion closes by taking up a question of interest not only to the US, but to European countries seeking to reduce the role of government in economic activity. Donahue provides a guide to the areas in which privatization is and is not likely to be successful, while Moe argues that in a large number of cases the privatization that has been introduced in the US has been counter-productive to the efficient operation of government. The problems surrounding privatization emerge as being much more complex than simply arranging the simple dismission of public assets or the competitive letting of bids to private contractors.

The present collection does not intend to be exhaustive either as regards the problems discussed at the Workshop or the economic problems to be faced in the 1990s, for which much more than a small book would be necessary. Rather it intends to give a flavour of the discussion and the type of problems and the method of analysis employed by post Keynesian economists in dealing with economic policy issues and problems.

This volume is the result of the second in a series of International Workshops which was initiated when the creation of the J. Fred Holly Chair of Excellence in Political Economy at the University of Tennessee raised the possibility of a special conference. Papers from the first conference have been published as *Macroeconomic Problems and Policies of Income Distribution* (Elgar, 1989). As in the case of the first volume the editors would like to thank the College of Business Administration and the Department of Economics of the University of Tennessee for financial support for the Workshop, and Louise Davidson, the Editorial Office Manager of the *Journal of Post Keynesian Economics* for her tremendous organizational and editorial support.

P.D., J.A.K.
Knoxville

Contributors

Irma Adelman, Professor of Agricultural Economics, Giannini School, University of California, Berkeley.
Robert A. Blecker, Assistant Professor of Economics, American University, and Research Economist, Economic Policy Institute, Washington, DC.
Luiz Carlos Bresser Pereira, Professor of Economics, Getúlio Vargas Foundation, and Senior Researcher, Centro de Economia Política, São Paolo, Brazil.
Fernando J. Cardim de Carvalho, Associate Professor of Economics, Universidade Federal Fluminense, Niteroi, Rio de Janiero, Brazil.
William Darity, Jr., Professor of Economics, University of North Carolina, Chapel Hill.
Paul Davidson, J. Fred Holly Chair of Excellence in Political Economy, University of Tennessee, Knoxville.
John D. Donahue, Associate Professor, Kennedy School of Government, Harvard University, Cambridge, Massachusetts.
Stephen F. Frowen, Professor of Economics and Honorary Research Fellow, Department of Political Economy, University College London.
J. A. Kregel, Professor of Political Economy, University of Bologna and Adjunct Professor of International Economics, The Johns Hopkins University, Bologna Center.
Ronald C. Moe, Congressional Research Service, Library of Congress, Washington, DC.
Yoshiaki Nakano, Professor of Economics, Getúlio Vargas Foundation, and Senior Researcher, Centro de Economia Política, São Paolo, Brazil.
A. P. Thirlwall, Professor of Applied Economics, Keynes College, University of Kent, Canterbury.

PART I

Economic Development, Debt and International Finance

1. The Terms of Trade of Primary Commodities, Debt and Development

A. P. Thirlwall

This paper is a mixture of survey material and analytical frameworks for thinking about movements in the net barter terms of trade of primary commodities relative to manufactured goods and how these movements affect the growth performance of countries both directly and indirectly (for example by affecting the balance of payments or by worsening the debt burden of heavily indebted countries). Following a brief introduction, the paper is divided into five parts. Firstly, there is an up-to-date survey of movements in the terms of trade of primary commodities and of less developed countries (LDCs). Secondly, I address the issue of the determinants of terms of trade movements, drawing on my formalization of Kaldor's two-sector agriculture/industry model which captures both neoclassical and structuralist explanations of terms of trade movements (Thirlwall, 1986). Thirdly, a model of balance of payments constrained growth is presented which enables the effect of terms of trade movements on economic growth to be quantified. Fourthly, the interrelationship between primary product price changes and international debt problems is examined. Finally, some policy implications are drawn.

INTRODUCTION

Terms of trade changes affect the real income of a country in two major ways: first, directly and second, indirectly working through their effect (favourable or unfavourable) on the balance of payments. Both effects can be clearly seen using national income and balance of payments identities. Consider first the equation for money national income:

$$P_d Y = P_d C + P_d I + P_d X - P_f EM \qquad (1.1)$$

where Y is real income, C is real consumption, I is real investment, X is export volume, M is import volume, P_d is an index of domestic prices (assumed, for simplicity, to be the same for all components of demand), P_f is an index of foreign prices, and E is the exchange rate measured as the domestic price of foreign currency. Dividing through by P_d gives:

$$Y = C + I + X - \frac{P_f E}{P_d} M, \qquad (1.2)$$

where $P_f E/P_d$ is a measure of the real terms of trade; that is, a rise in foreign prices relative to domestic prices and/or a rise in the domestic price of foreign currency reduces real income directly. A deterioriation in the terms of trade is formally equivalent to an autonomous rise in imports, which also reduces real income directly. $P_f E/P_d$ is also a measure of the real exchange rate and, if that depreciates, this also reduces real income directly. Often, however, countries deliberately attempt to depreciate their real exchange rate in order to raise exports and reduce imports. If exports and imports change sufficiently, the adverse effects of real exchange rate depreciation (or terms of trade deterioration) on the level of real income may be offset. This effect will be the stronger the more the level of output is held below its potential because of balance of payments constraints on demand. If a deterioration in the real terms of trade or the real exchange rate improves the balance of payments, both consumption and investment can rise without balance of payments difficulties arising. Income then rises by a multiple of the improvement in the balance of payments alone. It is an interesting empirical question what the direct and indirect effects of terms of trade movements have been on real income growth in developing countries, and a framework for answering this question is provided in Section III.

One reason why export prices may be falling is that labour productivity in the export sector may be rising, which releases resources for other purposes (including more exports). This, too, increases real income. This is one reason why other measures of the terms of trade – other than the net barter terms of trade – have been developed, such as the income terms of trade or the single factoral terms of trade. We shall limit ourselves, here, however, to considering and modelling only the net barter terms of trade.

I STATISTICAL EVIDENCE ON THE TERMS OF TRADE

The debate on movements in the terms of trade of primary commodities started in earnest with the work of Prebisch (1950) and Singer (1950).

Since then, there has been a virtually continuous controversy over what the evidence shows. Prebisch and Singer were in no doubt that there had been an historical trend deterioration in the terms of trade of primary commodities relative to manufactured goods. This conflicted with the classical supposition that the terms of trade were likely to improve for primary commodities owing to diminishing returns in primary production. This presumption was associated with economists such as J. S. Mill, Torrens and Ricardo, and then later with Keynes and Robertson. According to Mill (1848), for example, 'the exchange value of manufactured articles, compared with the products of agriculture and mines have, as population and industry advance, a certain and decided tendency to fall.' Keynes (1912) commented on the years 1900 to 1911: 'we are obtaining for our exports almost exactly the same prices as in 1900, but are paying for our imports appreciably higher prices than in 1900 ... the deterioration ... is due, of course, to the operation of the law of diminishing returns for raw products which, after a temporary lull, has been setting in sharply in quite recent years. There is now again a steady tendency for a given unit of manufactured product to purchase year by year a diminishing quantity of raw product. The comparative advantage is moving sharply against industrial countries.' Dennis Robertson (1915) alluded to the same tendency: 'the normal tendency for the ratio of exchange to alter against the manufacturing and in favour of agricultural communities was in force in the seventies, was suspended in the eighties and the nineties, and is now once more on the whole, triumphing'.

Prior to Prebisch and Singer, it appears to have been Kindleberger (1943) who first noted a *secular* declining terms of trade for primary producing countries. In a Supplement to the *American Economic Review* he wrote: 'inexorably ... the terms of trade move against agricultural and raw material countries as the world's standard of living increases ... and as Engel's Law of consumption operates'. Also the League of Nations showed in 1945 (based on the work of Mr Falke Hilgert) that in the 60 years prior to 1938, primary product prices had fallen relative to manufactures. This was reiterated by the United Nations in 1949, working on League of Nations data and data compiled by Mr W. Schlote on British export and import prices. Singer was the (anonymous) author of one of the 1949 UN Reports (United Nations, 1949). League of Nations data give a trend deterioration over the period 1876–1938 of 0.64 per cent per annum. Independent work by Arthur Lewis (1952) gives a trend deterioration for 1871–1938 of 0.46 per cent per annum. Prebisch based his own thesis on the index of UK commodity terms of trade constructed by Schlote which showed, as estimated by Spraos (1980, 1983), an average deterioration in the terms of trade of primary commodities of 0.95 per cent per annum over the period 1876–1938. Findlay (1981) claims that the Prebisch–Singer thesis (and the alleged continued deterioration post-1950) has been subjected to 'devastating criticism, without any effective reply'. This is no longer true. There was criticism of the estimation methods and of what the data showed, but all recent re-evaluations of the Prebisch–Singer thesis confirm the historical trend deterioration of the terms of trade of primary commodities up to the Second World War, and also up to the present day if a structural break for the war and its aftermath is allowed for.

The criticisms of Prebisch's work and conclusions were sixfold: first, that 1938 was a depression year and therefore the trend estimate was biased downwards; secondly, that Britain's terms of trade experience was not shared by other industrialized countries; thirdly, that the terms of trade measure ignores improvements in the quality of manufactured goods; fourthly, that the reciprocal of Britain's terms of trade cannot be taken as the terms of trade of developing countries since imports are measured cost, insurance, freight (cif) and exports free on board (fob) and during the period 1870–1900, at least, there was a dramatic decline in ocean freight rates; fifthly, primary products are also exported by developed countries so that primary product price deterioration is not evidence that the terms of trade of developing countries have deteriorated, and finally, that the net barter terms of trade is not an appropriate measure of the gains from trade since it does not take account of changes in the total volume of trade or the fact that a fall in prices might be the result of an improvement in productivity, releasing resources for other purposes.

Each of these criticisms has been examined carefully by Sarkar (1986) and rebutted with the aid of the extensive re-evaluations of the Prebisch doctrine by Spraos (1980) and Sapsford (1985). The terminal year of 1938 makes no difference to the conclusion. If 1929 is taken, before the collapse of commodity prices in the 1930s, a trend deterioration is still observed. The terms of trade of industrial countries other than Britain may not have improved but this is not evidence that the terms of trade of primary commodities did not deteriorate because Britain was unique in its trading relations with 'agrarian' countries, and the majority of trade in Europe and America was *intra*-industrial country trade. The argument about quality bias is probably exaggerated. The quality of primary commodities has also improved, and the quality of some manufactures has deteriorated. There appears to be no evidence of valuation bias due to a decline in ocean freight rates. A correlation between an index of tramp shipping freight rates and the terms of trade index shows a *negative* relation. It is true that developed countries export primary commodities, but in the period up to 1913 over 80 per cent of primary exports of industrialized countries went to other industrialized countries while over 80 per cent of primary exports of less developed countries went outside. Over 50 per cent of manufactures of industrialized countries went to less developed countries. Thus industrial countries should be net gainers from declines in the terms of trade of primary products, and LDCs net losers. These proportions are not very different today. Lastly, in answer to the sixth criticism, this requires a measure of the factoral terms of trade. Spraos has constructed an employment corrected double factoral terms of trade index and concludes that, for the entire commodity producing sector of developing countries, the double factoral terms of trade 'were effectively deteriorating over the period of the data'.

Recent research on the net barter terms of trade suggests the following: Spraos (1980) puts the historical trend deterioration 1876–1938 at just over one-half of the figure indicated by Prebisch's data – or 0.5 per cent per annum, having corrected the statistics for the changing quality of goods, shipping costs and so on. Extending the data to 1970, however, he concludes that there is no significant trend deterioration. Using UN World Bank data, 1900–70 also shows no overall trend deterioration. Sapsford (1985) shows, however, that it is the structural wartime break which makes the whole series look trendless. Dividing the series into two sub-periods – pre and post Second World War – shows a trend deterioration in both sub-periods (see Figure 1.1), and the estimated trend deterioration over the whole period 1900–82 is 1.2 per cent per annum, allowing for the wartime structural break.

Grilli and Yang (1988) reach the same conclusion on the basis of extensive examination and reconstruction of the data. Over the period 1900 to 1983 they put the percentage terms of trade deterioration of all primary commodities at 0.5 per cent per annum and 0.6 per cent per annum for non-fuel commodities (allowing for the wartime structural break). For individual commodities the trend deterioration is estimated as: food (-0.3 per cent p.a.); cereals (-0.6 per cent p.a.); non-food agricultural commodities (-0.8 per cent p.a.) and metals (-0.8 per cent p.a.). Only tropical beverages registered an improvement (0.6 per cent p.a.).

Scandizzo and Diakosavvas (1988) take 14 individual primary commodities and four commodity aggregates over the period 1900 to 1982 and find a linear trend deterioration in all but five cases. Where the trend was positive, it was not statistically significant. Nguyen (1988) has looked more carefully at the structural breaks in the terms of trade series. Using World Bank data, he estimates an average terms of trade deterioration for all primary commodities of 0.6 per cent per annum, and a 0.7 per cent per annum deterioration for 80 LDCs, but a piecewise model shows a signifi-

Figure 1.1 Movements in the net barter terms of trade (NBTT)

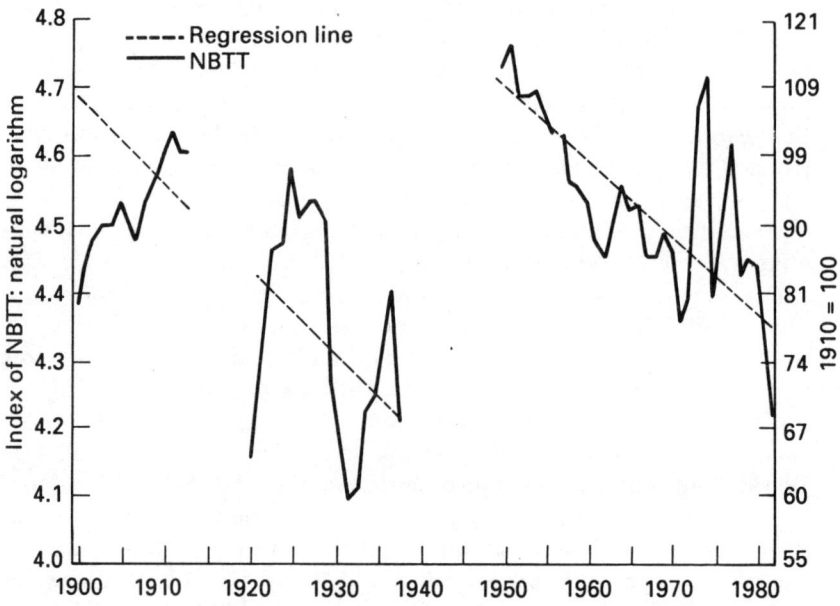

Source: Sapsford (1988). This NBTT was obtained by updating the UN series given by Spraos (1980) using UN *Statistical Yearbook* data and the IMF Research Department index of prices of non-oil primary commodities deflated by UN index of price of manufactures.

cant decline only for 1918–22 and 1975–85. From 1900 to 1918, the terms of trade improves, and no significant trend is observable between 1922 and 1975 (see Figure 1.2). The steep overall declines of 1918–1922 and 1975–1985 swamp the periods of improvement. Nguyen thus emphasises the important distinction to be made between factors which affect the terms of trade continuously (long-run 'structural' factors) and those which operate with great force but only sporadically. Steep declines seem to be the result of over-expansion of supply following previous price rises. This seems to have been the most recent experience. According to research at the World Bank (Morrison and Wattleworth, 1988), the massive decline in commodity prices and the terms of trade during 1984–6 was the result of substantial increases in world food supplies, as a lagged response to favourable prices and growing conditions.[1]

My own work with Bergevin (Thirlwall and Bergevin, 1985) concentrated on the post-war years, distinguishing between primary commodities exported by LDCs on the one hand and developed countries on the other,

Figure 1.2 Terms of trade of non-oil primary commodities of LDCs vis-à-vis manufactures, 1900–85

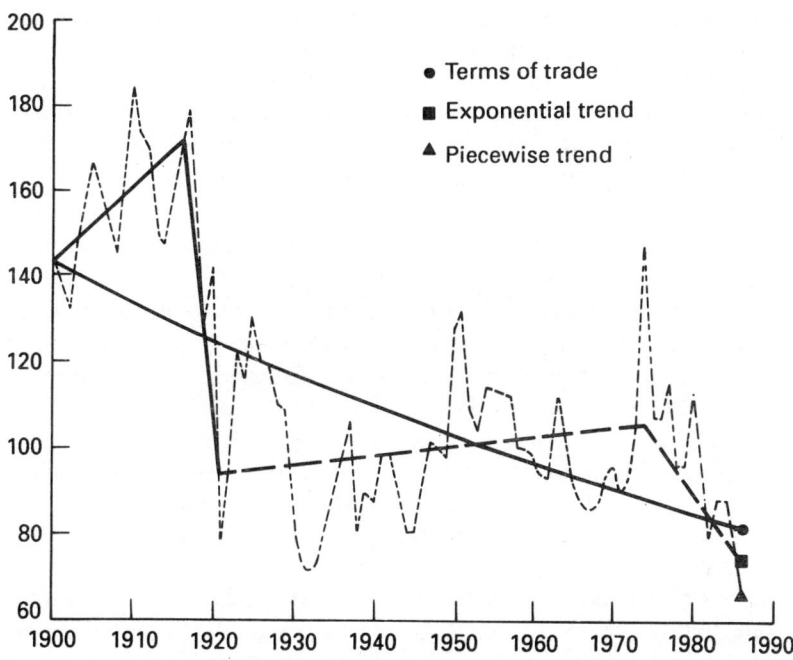

Source: Nguyen (1988)

estimating separately from 1960–72 and 1973–82 using quarterly data. For all primary commodities from LDCs the annual trend deterioration was 0.5 per cent from 1960 to 1972 and 0.36 per cent from 1973 to 1982 (excluding oil). For primary commodities from developed countries, the trend was not significant. Sarkar (1986) also looks in detail at the post-war years 1952 to 1980 (excluding fuel exports from 1971) and estimates a trend deterioration in the terms of trade of primary commodities of 0.89 per cent per annum. Sarkar also makes two other interesting calculations: one of export prices of LDCs relative to developed countries, and one of prices of exports from LDCs to developed countries relative to prices of imports from developed countries to LDCs (both excluding fuel). In the first case, the trend deterioration was 0.51 per cent per annum; in the second case, the relative deterioration was 0.93 per cent per annum. There seems little doubt that for the last 30 years, at least, the terms of trade of primary products of LDCs have deteriorated at roughly the average rate of decline estimated by Spraos (1980) for the period up to 1938.

Sarkar and Singer (1991) have also looked at the terms of trade of manufactures exported by LDCs relative to developed countries over the period 1970–87 and find a deterioration of approximately 1 per cent per annum. It appears therefore that the LDCs suffer double jeopardy. Not only do the prices of their primary products decline relative to manufactured goods, but also the prices of their manufactured exports decline relative to those of developed countries, reflecting, no doubt, the commodity composition of their exports – their lower value-added and lower income elasticity of demand in world markets.

The Cyclicality of Primary Product Prices and Asymmetries

Not only has there been a long-run trend deterioration in the barter terms of trade of primary commodities, but also primary product prices are more cyclical than those of manufactures. This causes further problems which will be considered in the final section of the chapter on policy implications. It is an interesting question, however, whether asymmetries in the cycles of primary product and manufactured goods' prices have been a source of trend deterioration as originally hypothesized by Prebisch: specifically, whether the elasticity of primary product prices with respect to manufactured goods' prices is higher on the downswing than on the upswing. My own research (Thirlwall and Bergevin, 1985) shows that, over the period 1960–82, the elasticity of primary product prices exported by LDCs with respect to the prices of manufactured goods was 2.4. Disaggregation by commodity group shows an elasticity of 1.25 for food, 1.3 for agricultural non-food products and 2.9 for minerals, including oil. For primary products exported by developed countries, the overall elasticity was 1.155. As an alternative test of cyclicality, the mean of the deviations of observations from the trend of primary product prices as a ratio of the mean of the deviations of observations from the trend of manufactured goods' prices gives a figure of 2.58 for LDCs and 1.26 for developed countries.

The asymmetry hypothesis can be tested directly by using a slope dummy variable for observations on price-changes when manufactured goods' prices have been falling. For each primary commodity grouping, the following equation was fitted over the period 1960–82:

$$\log P_p = \alpha + \beta_1 \log P_m + \beta_2 (d \log P_m) + \delta t + \mu_t,$$

where P_p is the price index of the primary commodity; P_m is the price index

Table 1.1 Tests of the Prebisch asymmetry hypothesis

Commodity	Developed countries $\hat{\beta}_1$	$\hat{\beta}_2$	R^2	Less developed countries $\hat{\beta}_1$	$\hat{\beta}_2$	R^2
All primary commodities	1.158 (7.00)	+0.105 (0.132)	0.971	1.305 (2.33)	−0.878 (0.176)	0.869
All primary commodities excluding petroleum				1.049 (6.03)	−0.262 (1.977)	0.941
Food	1.053 (5.38)	−0.582 (0.621)	0.957	1.251 (5.22)	−0.024 (1.39)	0.933
Agricultural non-food products	1.230 (7.80)	−0.011 (1.08)	0.958	1.337 (10.98)	−0.014 (1.38)	0.971
Minerals	1.526 (7.91)	+0.170 (1.60)	0.967	2.925 (11.36)	+0.046 (2.40)	0.977
Minerals excluding petroleum				0.549 (2.55)	−0.020 (1.35)	0.877
Non-ferrous base metals	0.402 (2.33)	−0.018 (1.51)	0.924	0.508 (0.186)	−0.038 (1.80)	0.805

of manufactures; t is time; μ_t is an error term and $d = 1$ when the price of manufactures has been falling, and zero otherwise. For the Prebisch hypothesis to be supported $(\beta_1 + \beta_2)$ must be greater than β_1, i.e. β_2 must be significantly greater than zero. The regression results, together with t statistics (in brackets), are shown in Table 1.1. Only for minerals (including oil) for LDCs is the asymmetry hypothesis supported. In all other cases the slope dummy either has a negative sign, or the coefficient is not significantly different from zero.

The only other research which has tested directly the Prebisch asymmetry hypothesis is that by Scandizzo and Diakosavvas (1988) who take the five major commodity groupings in Table 1.1 and 14 individual commodities over the years 1900 to 1982.[2] Only for agricultural non-food products, rice, cotton, rubber and copper, is the hypothesis supported, and only for agricultural non-food products and rubber is the elasticity in the downswing years substantially higher than the corresponding elasticity in the upswing years.

It is interesting to note that the Prebisch asymmetry hypothesis is also incidentally rejected by the work of Spraos (1983) for the historical period 1871–1938. He estimates a terms of trade equation first with time alone and then with time plus a cyclical variable and finds that the estimated trend coefficient is not influenced by the addition of a cyclical variable in the equation. If cyclical behaviour is symmetrical, this is to be expected. If cycles were affecting the trend, the trend coefficient in the second equation would be different from that in the first.

II CAUSES OF TERMS OF TRADE MOVEMENTS

Historically, four major schools of thought can be identified that have addressed the issue of terms of trade movements. First, there is the classical school, already mentioned, which emphasizes diminishing returns to land-based activities with the prediction that the terms of trade will move in favour of primary products. Technical progress and demand conditions are ignored. Secondly, there is neoclassical trade theory which emphasizes tastes, technology and factor endowments. The theory is clearly more embracive than classical theory, but also ambiguous. The terms of trade can go either way. In terms of the traditional analysis using offer curves, the terms of trade movements in a two-country, two-commodity model depend on the balance between the production and consumption of the two commodities, or in other words on the rate of increase in each country's import demand. Thirdly, there is the structuralist school which adds other considerations to neoclassical theory, particularly differences in the structure of product and factor markets between the production and sale of primary products and manufactured goods on the one hand, and between LDCs and developed countries on the other. The asymmetry hypothesis considered earlier is a part of the structuralist theory. Finally there is the theory of unequal exchange, primarily associated with the name of Emmanuel (1972), which argues that the terms of trade are inferior for poor countries because wages are lower than in rich countries, and lower than if the rate of profit was not as high as in rich countries: 'inequality of wages as such, all other things being equal, is alone the cause of the inequality of exchange'.

Taking an eclectic approach, the consideration of these historical theories leads to four broad explanations of terms of trade deterioration: firstly a lower price elasticity of demand for primary products than for manufactured goods, so that for given increases in supply the relative price of primary products falls; secondly, a lower rate of growth of demand for primary products relative to manufactures partly on account of a lower income elasticity of demand and partly because of the introduction of synthetic substitutes for primary commodities; thirdly, a more pronounced outward shift in the supply curve for primary products either because of faster technical progress or because productivity growth in agriculture is not offset by wage growth to the same extent as in industry; and fourthly, a greater degree of competition in the market for primary products (particularly in LDCs) which means not only that primary product prices are more volatile than manufactures but also that manufactured goods prices may be relatively more sticky downwards. As Singer (1987) has noted, many of these factors have as much to do with countries as with commodities themselves, which leads to the prediction not only that a decline in the terms of trade of primary products might be expected, but also that the decline might be faster for primary products exported by LDCs *vis-à-vis* developed countries and that the terms of trade of manufactures from LDCs might also be expected to deteriorate relative to manufactures from developed countries. Some evidence was given earlier that this has been the case. Grilli and Yang (1988) also find a close correspondence between the terms of trade of primary commodities relative to manufactures and the terms of trade of LDCs relative to developed countries.

Kaldor's Two-sector Model of Terms of Trade and Growth Equilibrium

Many models exist containing various combinations of the influences affecting the terms of trade discussed above (for example, Findlay (1981) and Evans (1987)). Here I should like to publicize Kaldor's (1979) two-sector model of world economic growth in which the terms of trade provides the equilibrating mechanism between the agricultural producing sector on the one hand and the industrial sector on the other. The model is not only interesting and important in its own right as a model of long-run development (Thirlwall, 1986),[3] but also it captures directly and indirectly most of the factors important in thinking about the terms of trade, such as diminishing returns in agriculture, the rate of technical progress in agriculture, the rate of technical progress in industry, wage movements in industry, and the income elasticity of demand between sectors.[4] Assume a closed economy with two activities, agriculture and industry. Agriculture produces wage goods, food or 'corn', and industry produces an investment good, steel. Industry sells steel to agriculture in exchange for food. How much steel is exchanged depends on the agricultural surplus and the terms of trade between agriculture and industry. Agricultural saving may be expressed as:

$$S_a = s_a Q_a, \qquad (1.3)$$

where Q_a is agricultural output, s_a is the propensity to save in agriculture and S_a represents the agricultural surplus. If p is the price of steel in terms of corn, then the amount of steel obtained by the agricultural sector in exchange for the agricultural surplus is:

$$I_a = S_a/p \qquad (1.4)$$

Equation (1.4) is a market clearing equation.

Now the growth of agricultural output may be expressed as the product of the investment ratio in agriculture and the productivity of investment in agriculture(σ):

$$\frac{\Delta Q_a}{Q_a} = \frac{\sigma I_a}{Q_a} \qquad (1.5)$$

Substituting (1.3) and (1.4) into (1.5) gives:

$$\frac{\Delta Q_a}{Q_a} = \frac{\sigma S_a}{p} \qquad (1.6)$$

Equation (1.6) not only gives the rate of growth of agricultural output but also the rate of growth of demand for industrial output at a given terms of trade (p). The equation traces out a hyperbole showing an inverse relation between the industrial terms of trade and the growth of agricultural demand for industrial goods (see Figure 1.3).

The level of consumption in the industrial sector depends on the real wage and the level of employment. It is assumed that all wages are consumed on food. There are assumed to be profitable investment outlets for all saving (that is, the surplus of steel).[5] Therefore:

$$C_i = k Q_i \qquad (1.7)$$

where C_i is consumption in industry; Q_i is industrial output and $k = wl$ is the wage bill per unit of steel output, where w is the real wage and l is labour input per unit of steel output (the reciprocal of labour productivity). For a given l, k is determined by the real wage.

The growth of industrial output can be expressed as the product of the investment ratio in industry and the productivity of investment (μ):

$$\frac{\Delta Q_i}{Q_i} = \frac{\mu I_i}{Q_i} \qquad (1.8)$$

Now I_i is equal to the total output of steel less the steel sold to agriculture:

$$I_i = Q_i - I_a \qquad (1.9)$$

From (1.4), $I_a = S_a/p$ and, since the agricultural surplus is sold to industry for workers' consumption, $S_a = kQ_i$. Therefore $I_a = kQ_i/p$. Substituting for I_a in equation (1.9) and for I_i in equation (1.8) gives:

$$\frac{\Delta Q_i}{Q_i} = \mu - \frac{\mu k}{p} \qquad (1.10)$$

Figure 1.3 *Relation between industrial terms of trade and growth rate of industrial output*

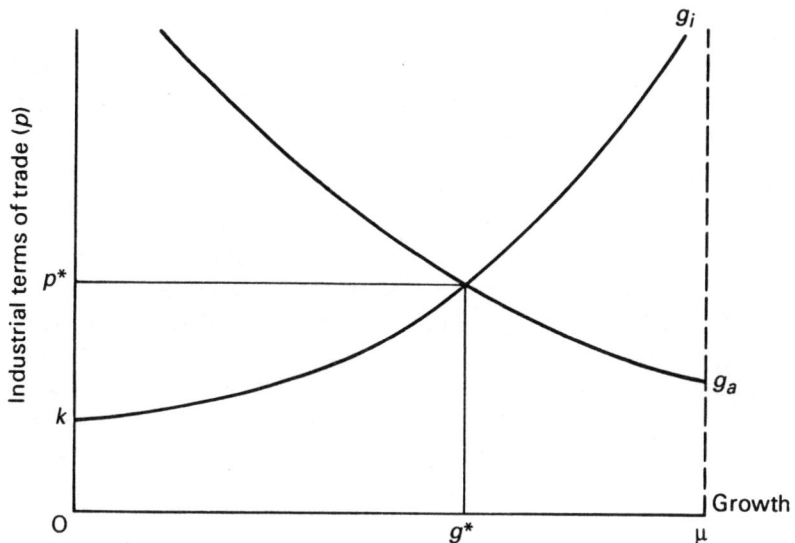

Equation (1.10) traces out a positive non-linear relation between the industrial terms of trade and the growth rate of industrial output. The curve has an asymptote, μ, and there is a minimum terms of trade ($p = k$) which gives the minimum price of steel in terms of corn at which there would be no surplus of steel for reinvestment and industrial growth would be zero. The curves of the two equations (1.6) and (1.10) are plotted in Figure 1.3. The stationary equilibrium growth rate of the system (g^*) and the equilibrium terms of trade (p^*) are found where the two curves cross. Formally, these equilibrium values are found by solving the pair of equations (1.6) and (1.10). This gives an equilibrium terms of trade:

$$p^* = k + \frac{\sigma s_a}{\mu} \qquad (1.11)$$

The industrial terms of trade will be more favourable, the higher the wage costs per unit of industrial output, the higher the level of productivity and the savings ratio in agriculture, and the lower the level of productivity in industry. Diminishing returns in agriculture will reduce σ and lower the industrial terms of trade. On the other hand, rising real wages in industry (by raising k) turns the terms of trade in favour of industry. Both effects may be offset (or more or less offset) by technical progress in agriculture and industry. Technial progress in agriculture (or land saving innovations) will raise σ and shift the g_a curve upwards. Technical progress in industry will raise μ and shift the g_i curve downwards. Long-term secular movements in the terms of trade are thus the outcome of four major forces: diminishing returns in agriculture, the course of real wages in industry, and the rate of technical progress in agriculture and in industry. These four forces are themselves the outcome of supply conditions in agriculture, inventions, and institutional arrangements and pressures (including the influence of trade unions and population pressures). Clearly there can be no 'iron law' of the terms of trade either deteriorating or improving in favour of agriculture or industry. What happens depends on the balance of these economic and social forces. A secularly deteriorating terms of trade for primary products, however, would suggest that technical progress has more than offset diminishing returns in agriculture, shifting outwards the g_a curve, while real wage growth has matched (or more than matched) productivity growth in industry, shifting upwards the g_i curve. Both forces would lead to a gradual rise in p, the industrial terms of trade.

III EVALUATING THE EFFECTS ON GROWTH OF MOVEMENTS IN THE TERMS OF TRADE

One framework for analysing the effects on a country's output growth of movements in the terms of trade is to model growth within a balance of payments framework where terms of trade changes can be shown to have direct and indirect effects on real income (Thirlwall and Hussain, 1982). The model is as follows. Since the balance of payments must balance, we can write:

$$p_{dt}X_t + C_t = P_{ft}M_tE_t, \qquad (1.12)$$

where C_t is the level of capital flows measured in domestic currency and P_d, P_f, X_t, M_t and E_t are as before (see equation (1.1)). $C_t > 0$ represents net capital inflows to 'finance' import payments in excess of export receipts. Taking rates of change of equation (1.12) gives:

$$\frac{E}{R}(p_{dt} + x_t) + \frac{C}{R}(c_t) = p_{ft} + m_t + e_t, \qquad (1.13)$$

where lower-case letters represent rates of change of variables, and E/R

and C/R are weights representing proportions of total receipts contributed by export earnings and capital flows, respectively, to pay the import bill. Let us now specify conventional (multiplicative, constant elasticity) export and import demand functions to derive expressions for x_t and m_t in equation (1.13). Let

$$X_t = (P_{dt}/P_{ft}E_t)^\eta Z_t^\varepsilon, \qquad (1.14)$$

so that

$$x_t = \eta(p_{dt} - p_{ft} - e_t) + \varepsilon(z_t), \qquad (1.15)$$

where $\eta\ (< 0)$ is the price elasticity of demand for exports, $\varepsilon\ (> 0)$ is the income elasticity of demand for exports, Z is the level of world income, and z is the growth of world income. Similarly let

$$M_t = (P_{ft}E_t/P_{dt})^\psi Y_t^\pi, \qquad (1.16)$$

so that

$$m_t = \psi(p_{ft} + e_t - p_{dt}) + \pi(y_t) \qquad (1.17)$$

where $\psi\ (< 0)$ is the price elasticity of demand for imports, $\pi\ (> 0)$ is the income elasticity of demand for imports, Y is the level of domestic income and y is the growth of domestic income. Substituting (1.15) and (1.17) into (1.13) and solving for y_t gives an expression for the growth rate consistent with a country's overall balance of payments of:

$$y_{Bt} = \frac{1}{\pi}[(1 + \psi + \frac{E}{R}\eta)(p_{dt} - p_{ft} - e_t) + \frac{E}{R}\varepsilon(z_t) + \frac{C}{R}(c_t - p_{dt})] \qquad (1.18)$$

Every country has a y_{Bt} consistent with the balance of payments identity in equation (1.12) and the national income identity in equation (1.1).[6] It is apparent that any country's growth rate associated with overall payments balance can be disaggregated into four component parts:

1. a pure terms of trade effect: $(p_{dt} - p_{ft} - e_t)/\pi$;
2. the effect of real terms of trade changes working through import and export price elasticities: $(\psi + \frac{E}{R}\eta)(p_{dt} - p_{ft} - e_t)/\pi$;
3. the effects of the exogenous growth of world income: $\frac{E}{R}\varepsilon(z_t)/\pi$;

4. the effect of real capital inflows/outflows: $\frac{C}{R}(c_t - p_{dt})/\pi$.

Crucial to the fitting of this model are well determined estimates of the income elasticities of demand for imports and exports. The contributions of each effect, including the two terms of trade effects, can then be evaluated. Some country evidence from fitting this model to a sample of developing countries will be given later.

Without capital flows, equation (1.18) becomes:

$$y_{Bt} = \frac{1}{\pi}[(1 + \psi + \eta)(p_{dt} - p_{ft} - e_t) + \varepsilon(z_t)] \qquad (1.19)$$

Solving for changes in the terms of trade (θ), we have:

$$\theta = \frac{\pi y_{Bt} - \varepsilon(z_t)}{(1 + \psi + \eta)} \qquad (1.20)$$

If the Marshall-Lerner condition is satisfied so that $\psi + \eta > -1$, equation (1.20) says that the terms of trade for a country will deteriorate if $\pi y_{Bt} > \varepsilon z_t$. For equal growth rates of a country and the rest of the world, the terms of trade will deteriorate if $\pi > \varepsilon$, that is, if the income elasticity of demand for a country's imports is greater than the income elasticity of demand for its exports. This is normally assumed for developing countries which export primary commodities and import manufactured goods. This result was originally derived by Johnson (1954). Notice, however, that the result is premised on the assumption of balance of payments equilibrium on current account (that is, no capital flows). It simply says that, if import growth exceeds export growth because of different income elasticities, the terms of trade *must* deteriorate if balance of payments equilibrium is to be preserved (assuming the Marshall-Lerner condition is satisfied). The deterioration may come about either through a fall in the ratio of domestic to foreign prices or through exchange rate depreciation ($e_t > 0$). The model can only be *part* of a causal theory of terms of trade movements and deterioration is certainly not inevitable if the underlying assumptions are different (for example, if there are net inflows of capital, or $y_{Bt} < z_t$ etc).

Some years ago (Thirlwall and Hussain, 1982) I applied equation (1.18) to data for a series of LDCs for which there were well determined estimates of the income elasticity of demand for imports. Components (3) and (4) of equation (1.18) were estimated,[7] leaving components (1) and (2) as the implied effect of terms of trade changes on the growth of income. The pure terms of trade effect of income growth was then estimated, leaving

Table 1.2 Terms of trade effects on real income growth (% per annum)

Country	Total effect (components (1) and (2))	Pure terms of trade effect[9] (component (1))
Brazil	+0.1	+1.1
Tunisia	+0.4	+4.6
Pakistan	−2.0	−4.1
Thailand	−0.5	+1.1
Sri Lanka	−0.6	−12.4
Costa Rica	−1.3	−0.4
Ecuador	−6.2	−0.5
Mexico	−4.2	−0.4
Honduras	−4.0	−1.6
Colombia	−1.0	+1.4
Morocco	−2.9	−0.7
Jamaica	−1.8	+0.6
Sudan	−3.1	−1.7
Philippines	−1.0	−3.1
Zaire	+0.6	+1.7
Portugal	+0.1	+0.8
Kenya	+2.1	−0.2
India	−1.3	−0.3
Turkey	−0.1	−0.9
Cyprus	+0.1	+2.7

the effect of real terms of trade changes working through import and export price elasticities as a residual.[8] The results are shown in Table 1.2.

For the majority of the 20 countries taken, the effect of terms of trade changes on real income growth has been adverse. The average effect for all countries was to reduce growth by 1.33 percentage points per annum. In 11 of the 14 countries where the total terms of trade effect is negative, the pure terms of trade effect is also negative. In cases where the total effect is greater than the pure (negative) terms of trade effect, this would imply that the price elasticity of demand for imports is perverse. Where the total effect is less than the pure (negative) terms of trade effect, the price elasticity of imports is normal but less than unity. On average, the pure terms of trade effect reduced growth by 0.62 percentage points per annum, but there is clearly a wide diversity of experience between countries. The framework outlined would seem to be a fruitful one for further research.

IV COMMODITY PRICES AND THE DEBT PROBLEMS OF DEVELOPING COUNTRIES

Commodity price falls and the debt problems of commodity-dependent exporting countries (mostly developing countries) are closely interrelated.

On the one hand, commodity price falls will (*ceteris paribus*) worsen the debt–service ratio of countries since the debt–service ratio is measured as the ratio of debt–service payments to export earnings. The risk of debt default is strongly correlated with the size of the debt–service ratio. Some calculations will be given later of the extent to which commodity price falls increased the debt–service ratio of countries over the crucial period 1980–5. On the other side of the coin, debt problems put downward pressure on commodity prices if debtor countries attempt to export more to meet debt service obligations without having to cut back imports. Terms of trade deterioration will be stronger, the greater the increase in the supply of exports, the lower the price elasticity of demand for exports and the less creditor countries which receive debt repayments spend on the exports of the debtors. The attempt by debtors to export more affects the terms of trade of *all* developing countries to the extent that they export the same or competitive commodities. Added to this downward pressure on the terms of trade is the tendency towards currency devaluation which will also directly lower the terms of trade. The countries then become caught in a vicious circle. Devaluation encourages domestic supply and reduces the prices of commodities still further, so that foreign exchange earnings may not improve, leading to further pressure for devaluation and so on (see Spraos, 1989). The necessity to reduce price to sell more is part of the transfer burden highlighted by Keynes (1929) in his attack on the excessive German reparations agreed at the Treaty of Versailles. The transfer burden is the export surplus that has to be generated to acquire the foreign exchange plus the possibility of a deterioration in the terms of trade if, in order to sell more exports, prices must be reduced. But even if prices are reduced, there is no guarantee that export earnings will increase if the price elasticity of demand is less than unity. In these circumstances, the transfer becomes impossible without a contraction of income to compress imports.

There is evidence of a concerted export drive by debtor countries to cope with debt difficulties (Sarkar and Singer, 1989). Between 1980 and 1987, the export volume of non-oil developing countries increased by 74 per cent, and the terms of trade of LDCs deteriorated by 34 per cent. There is also evidence that the higher the debt/GNP ratio, the faster the percentage decline in the unit value of exports and terms of trade. Sarkar (1989) shows this, taking 29 countries (including all 17 countries classified by the World Bank as highly indebted) over the period 1980–6. Spraos (1989) also shows this for 17 Latin American countries. He regresses changes in the terms of trade 1978/82 to 1983/7 against changes in the debt/GNP ratio 1975 to 1985 and estimates a slope coefficient of -0.093 which is significant at the 90 per cent confidence level.

The impact of the commodity price falls and/or export earnings on the debt–service ratio can be estimated by decomposing changes in the debt–service ratio into its component parts. The debt–service ratio (S) may be written as:

$$S = \frac{(i + a)D}{P_x X}, \qquad (1.21)$$

where i is the interest rate; a is the amortization rate; D is the volume of debt, P_x is the price of exports and X is the volume of exports. Taking discrete rates of change of equation (1.21) gives:

$$\frac{dS}{S} = \frac{di}{i}\left(\frac{I}{P}\right) + \frac{da}{a}\left(\frac{A}{P}\right) + \frac{dD}{D} - \frac{dP_x}{P_x} - \frac{dX}{X} \pm \text{Interaction Term}, \qquad (1.22)$$

where I/P is the share of interest payments in total debt–service payments, and A/P is the share of amortization payments in total payments. From equation (1.22) we can then decompose dS (the change in the debt service ratio) into five component parts:

1. the effect of interest rate changes: $\frac{di}{i}\left(\frac{I}{P}\right)S$;
2. the effect of changes in the rate of amortization: $\frac{da}{a}\left(\frac{A}{P}\right)S$;
3. the effect of changes in the volume of debt: $\left(\frac{dD}{D}\right)S$;
4. the effect of changes in export prices: $\left(\frac{dP_x}{P_x}\right)S$;
5. the effect of changes in the volume of exports: $\left(\frac{dX}{X}\right)S$.

A colleague and I (Gibson and Thirlwall, 1989) have done this decomposition for 96 countries over the period 1980–5 (and for the two sub-periods 1980–2 and 1982–5). The results are shown in Table 1.3. We are interested here in the effect of changes in export prices and export earnings. Unfortunately there are many countries for which export price indices are not available. Also the published price and volume data for exports (for example from International Financial Statistics) refer only to visible trade, whereas the denominator in equation (1.21) is *total* export earnings. In calculating the effect of changes in export earnings arising from price and volume changes, two calculations are therefore made: the first assumes that the recorded price index applies to all transactions, leaving the export

Table 1.3 Components of the change in debt–service ratio of developing countries, 1980–5

Country	Change in debt service ratio	Debt service ratio 1985	Interest rate	Amort-ization rate	Debt volume	Export prices (A)	Export volume (H)	Export volume (A)	Export prices (H)	Export earnings	Inter-action term
Somalia	34.0	38.4	3.6	17.4	12.9	—	—	—	—	9.9	−9.8
Sao Tome & Principe	31.3	36.2	5.3	−3.2	19.3	—	—	—	—	16.9	−7.0
Nigeria	29.4	32.1	−0.9	11.0	16.1	—	—	—	—	12.7	−9.5
Portugal	27.2	43.0	7.1	6.6	19.1	—	—	—	—	−4.4	−1.2
Yemen Arab Republic	27.0	33.0	2.2	7.6	13.7	—	—	—	—	8.6	−5.1
Burma	26.3	46.4	−3.5	−1.3	22.6	2.4	6.6	1.4	7.6	9.0	−0.5
Colombia	25.3	35.1	1.9	2.0	18.3	—	—	—	—	5.3	−2.2
Congo	25.0	33.8	5.1	13.5	11.1	—	—	—	—	−3.1	−1.6
Papua New Guinea	24.7	36.0	−2.2	0.8	24.9	—	—	—	—	1.1	0.1
Malaysia	24.6	29.2	1.6	10.5	18.7	3.3	−6.4	−2.6	−0.5	−3.1	−3.1
Argentina	24.5	53.0	8.2	−19.6	33.5	—	—	—	—	3.3	−0.9
Uruguay	20.5	36.3	2.1	−3.8	18.0	—	—	—	—	4.8	0.0
Niger	19.3	38.4	−10.3	−3.7	10.9	—	—	—	—	22.4	0.0
Madagascar	18.8	29.9	−1.8	−3.4	16.6	—	—	—	—	7.8	−0.4
Togo	17.7	25.8	5.7	7.3	−2.5	—	—	—	—	8.3	−1.1
Jamaica	17.3	32.9	−1.5	−0.1	16.2	—	—	—	—	2.8	−0.1
El Salvador	16.9	22.5	−0.4	4.3	11.0	—	—	—	—	4.0	−2.0
Greece	15.5	29.3	0.1	−4.3	16.2	−17.7	21.2	−3.4	6.9	3.5	0.0
Jordan	15.2	23.1	1.6	6.0	11.2	−2.9	0.0	−8.3	5.4	−2.9	−0.7
Guatemala	15.1	22.6	−2.1	−2.6	13.8	—	—	—	—	6.3	−0.3
Kenya	14.0	26.2	−1.4	5.4	4.7	−10.1	16.0	1.8	4.1	5.9	−0.6
Bolivia	13.7	44.1	−10.7	−6.0	17.5	4.5	8.4	11.1	1.8	12.9	0.0
Mali	13.2	16.8	2.2	4.9	6.6	—	—	—	—	1.4	−1.9
Ethiopia	12.5	18.3	−0.9	3.3	10.3	—	—	—	—	0.3	−0.5
Indonesia	12.4	25.1	−0.3	1.5	9.6	5.7	−3.9	−0.9	2.7	1.8	−0.2
Tunisia	12.3	26.8	−1.7	3.7	6.3	—	—	—	—	4.3	−0.3
Mexico	12.0	50.0	−1.2	−11.7	32.1	—	—	—	—	−8.3	1.1
Pakistan	11.7	31.7	0.2	9.4	5.2	−7.5	4.3	−8.3	5.1	−3.2	0.1
Hungary	10.9	24.7	−1.1	3.8	8.7	−3.3	3.0	−4.6	4.3	−0.3	−0.2
Thailand	10.8	25.4	−1.2	−0.7	15.6	0.2	−3.7	−7.6	4.1	−3.5	0.6
India	10.7	20.5	2.5	1.5	8.0	—	—	—	—	−1.0	−0.3
Uganda	10.7	17.4	3.7	4.5	3.7	—	—	—	—	−1.3	0.1
Costa Rica	10.6	38.0	1.6	−9.2	19.4	—	—	—	—	−1.3	0.1

Table 1.3 Components of the change in debt–service ratio of developing countries, 1980–5 – continued

Country	Change in debt service ratio	Debt service ratio 1985	Interest rate	Amort- ization rate	Debt volume	Export prices (A)	Export volume (H)	Export volume (A)	Export prices (H)	Export earnings	Inter- action term
Burundi	10.6	18.0	1.7	1.4	12.6	–	–	–	–	–5.5	0.4
Burkina Faso	10.1	16.8	–0.3	–0.4	5.9	–	–	–	–	5.4	–0.5
Cameroon	10.0	21.1	0.4	12.0	1.0	–	–	–	–	–4.9	1.5
Bangladesh	9.8	17.6	1.0	5.3	6.5	–	–	–	–	–2.9	–0.1
Malawi	9.0	29.3	–3.8	3.1	5.5	–13.5	17.7	1.3	2.9	4.2	0.0
Israel	8.9	28.5	2.8	–0.1	8.5	3.3	–5.6	–6.6	4.3	–2.3	0.0
Sri Lanka	8.6	14.9	2.1	0.8	7.9	–4.1	2.0	–3.5	1.4	–2.1	–0.1
Maldives	8.3	8.8	2.6	3.6	3.3	–	–	–	–	–1.5	0.3
Central African Republic	8.1	8.8	2.9	3.0	2.8	–	–	–	–	2.1	–2.7
Mauritania	7.8	18.9	0.8	4.2	8.9	–	–	–	–	–6.3	0.2
South Korea	7.3	21.3	–0.8	3.5	11.1	–5.5	–1.2	–10.2	3.5	–6.7	0.2
Fiji	7.2	10.6	1.4	1.9	3.6	–	–	–	–	1.0	–0.7
Egypt	6.8	25.5	0.3	–1.1	9.6	–	–	–	–	–2.1	0.1
Cyprus	6.7	12.1	0.0	1.4	6.9	–2.1	0.5	–0.5	–1.1	–1.6	0.0
Rwanda	6.6	8.9	0.4	2.6	3.8	–3.5	3.9	–3.6	4.0	0.4	–0.6
Algeria	6.5	33.1	1.0	9.1	–5.3	–	–	–	–	1.6	0.1
Chile	6.4	44.4	–1.1	–24.7	25.0	–	–	–	–	12.1	–4.9
Grenada	5.8	9.2	0.2	0.6	6.4	–	–	–	–	–1.6	0.2
Philippines	5.8	19.6	–0.8	–3.7	9.9	–11.5	11.7	0.5	–0.3	0.2	0.2
Swaziland	5.6	8.3	–0.1	2.8	0.5	–	–	–	–	2.7	–0.3
Mauritius	5.5	12.5	0.0	3.3	2.2	–	–	–	–	0.0	0.0
Benin	5.3	9.2	1.0	0.7	4.4	–	–	–	–	–0.6	–0.2
Tanzania	5.0	15.5	–4.5	–2.6	4.8	–	–	–	–	7.5	–0.2
Seychelles	4.8	5.0	1.6	2.4	2.0	–	–	–	–	–0.4	–0.8
Lesotho	4.7	6.1	0.1	1.2	3.3	–	–	–	–	0.7	–0.6
Ghana	4.5	12.2	–0.6	–1.3	0.7	–	–	–	–	5.7	0.0
Romania	4.1	13.6	2.3	4.8	–2.4	–	–	–	–	–0.8	0.2
Chad	4.0	7.5	1.3	5.0	–1.5	–	–	–	–	–1.8	1.0
Turkey	3.8	33.5	10.3	19.0	7.7	–	–	–	–	–32.4	–0.8
Botswana	3.8	5.5	0.8	1.2	2.7	–	–	–	–	–0.6	–0.3
Nepal	3.6	5.3	0.4	0.4	3.7	–	–	–	–	–0.9	0.0
Barbados	2.9	5.4	–0.1	–0.7	4.5	–0.6	–0.5	–4.9	3.8	–1.3	0.5
Western Samoa	2.7	20.7	–3.7	4.0	3.4	–	–	–	–	–1.1	0.1

23

Table 1.3 Components of the change in debt-service ratio of developing countries, 1980–5 – continued

Country	Change in debt service ratio	Debt service ratio 1985	Interest rate	Amort-ization rate	Debt volume	Export prices (A)	Export volume (H)	Export volume (A)	Export prices (H)	Export earnings	Inter-action term
Honduras	2.5	20.2	-4.4	-6.2	12.3	0.6	0.1	-0.4	1.1	0.7	0.1
Solomon Islands	2.5	2.6	1.5	0.5	1.4	–	–	–	–	0.0	-0.9
China	1.6	7.0	-0.4	-0.4	4.5	–	–	–	–	-2.3	0.2
Comoros	1.4	1.7	0.4	0.2	1.0	–	–	–	–	0.1	-0.3
Singapore	1.4	2.4	0.1	1.1	0.5	–	–	–	–	-0.3	0.0
The Gambia	1.3	2.5	-0.2	0.9	1.0	–	–	–	–	-0.3	-0.1
Bahamas	1.1	3.3	0.2	-0.3	1.9	–	–	–	–	-0.8	0.1
Malta	1.1	1.4	0.0	0.8	0.0	-0.1	0.4	-0.1	0.4	0.3	0.0
Ecuador	0.8	31.3	3.7	-13.2	14.6	5.6	-9.2	-14.3	10.7	-3.6	-0.7
Trinidad & Tobago	0.7	7.1	0.3	-4.6	3.7	-1.9	3.6	0.4	1.3	1.7	-0.4
Syrian Arab Republic	0.6	12.2	-0.7	-2.4	3.1	–	–	–	–	0.6	0.0
Panama	0.5	6.6	-0.8	-2.2	2.4	0.4	0.4	1.6	-0.3	1.3	-0.2
Oman	-0.3	4.8	-0.7	-4.4	6.2	0.9	-2.5	-2.4	0.8	-1.6	0.2
Haiti	-0.6	6.1	-0.7	-3.4	4.2	–	–	–	–	-0.6	-0.1
Dominican Republic	-1.4	18.1	-4.3	-7.6	11.2	–	–	–	–	-0.4	-0.3
Sudan	-1.4	11.2	-0.7	-6.4	6.5	–	–	–	–	0.1	-0.9
Liberia	-2.4	3.9	-3.3	-2.2	2.3	–	–	–	–	1.3	-0.5
Ivory Coast	-3.5	20.5	-3.3	-13.0	12.0	–	–	–	–	3.1	-2.3
Venezuela	-3.7	16.3	-3.8	-13.0	10.9	–	–	–	–	4.9	2.7
Paraguay	-4.3	13.8	-0.9	-6.2	11.1	-9.7	1.4	-7.8	-0.5	-8.3	0.0
Morocco	-5.4	30.6	-13.3	-10.6	18.1	–	–	–	–	1.1	-0.7
Nicaragua	-5.4	10.6	-8.5	-9.9	12.8	–	–	–	–	3.3	-3.1
Yugoslavia	-6.0	19.0	2.0	-9.5	2.9	–	–	–	–	-1.0	-0.4
Gabon	-6.2	10.6	-1.6	-1.0	-5.5	–	–	–	–	1.9	0.0
Zambia	-6.6	11.2	-6.6	-11.3	4.7	–	–	–	–	9.2	-2.6
Guyana	-7.5	9.4	-5.5	-9.4	3.6	–	–	–	–	5.8	-2.0
Sierra Leone	-8.2	6.2	-2.5	-10.6	1.2	–	–	–	–	5.5	-1.8
Senegal	-9.0	11.6	-5.7	-13.4	11.2	–	–	–	–	1.5	-2.6
Peru	-14.5	22.3	-11.1	-19.9	13.5	13.9	-7.8	0.6	5.5	6.1	-3.1
Brazil	-23.3	33.2	-9.2	-21.9	20.8	10.0	-20.3	-21.5	11.2	-10.3	-2.7
Column averages	7.6	20.1	-0.5	-0.8	8.7					1.1	-0.9

Note: A = actual; H = hypothetical

volume index as a residual; the second assumes that the recorded volume index applies to all transactions, leaving the price index as a residual. (All variables are measured as averages over the period under review in order to avoid index number problems associated with the use of either base or terminal year figures.) It is clear from Table 1.3 that the major cause of increases in the debt–service ratio over the period 1980–5 was the sheer increase in the volume of debt itself. There is, however, a wide variety of experience between countries. On the export front, there are some dramatic cases where the fall in commodity prices and/or export volume had the effect of raising the debt service ratio by 6 percentage points (p.p.) or more: for example, Somalia (9.9), Sao Tome and Principe (16.9), Nigeria (12.7), Yemen (8.6), Burma (9.0), Niger (22.4), Madagascar (7.8), Togo (8.3), Guatemala (6.3), Bolivia (12.9), Chile (12.1), Tanzania (7.5), Zambia (9.2), and Peru (6.1). Not surprisingly, there is a significant positive correlation between the share of primary exports in total exports and the contribution of changes in export earnings to changes in the debt service ratio ($r = 0.386$). The effect was greatest in Latin America and Africa where 42.5 per cent and 38.7 per cent, respectively, of the increase in the debt–service ratio can be 'explained' by falls in export earnings, the experience being particularly acute in the period 1980–2. There is a negative correlation between the contribution of export earnings' deterioration to the increase in the debt–service ratio and the contribution of interest rate and amortization rate changes to changes in the debt–service ratio ($r = -0.365$ and $r = -0.228$, respectively) suggesting that those countries most affected by a decline in export earnings received the least relief in the form of interest and amortization rate reductions. These results lead on to policy implications, and the need for reappraisal of policies relating to commodity price instability and the instability of export earnings.

V POLICY IMPLICATIONS

The cyclicality of primary product prices is not, of course, a new phenomenon. The syndrome of depression, falling commodity prices and debt difficulties for primary producing countries was exactly what the world economy experienced during the 1930s. Keynes (1938) noted in a paper delivered to the British Association for the Advancement of Science that for the four commodities of rubber, cotton, wheat and lead, the price had fluctuated by 67 per cent in the previous 10 years, and was led to remark: 'Assuredly nothing can be more inefficient than the present system by which the price is always too high or too low and there are frequent meaningless fluctuations in the plant and labour force employed'. Later, in his wartime proposal for 'Commod Control', Keynes expressed the view that 'One of the greatest evils in international trade before the war was the wide and rapid fluctuations in the world price of primary commodities ... It must be the prime purpose of control to prevent these wide fluctuations' (Moggridge, 1980).

The world economy in general, and the developing countries in particular, suffer several problems from the uncontrolled movements of primary commodity prices. First, they can lead to a great deal of instability in the foreign exchange earnings and balance of payments position of LDCs, which makes investment planning and economic management much more difficult than otherwise would be the case. Second, because of asymmetries in pricing behaviour, volatility imparts inflationary bias combined with tendencies to depression in the world economy at large. When primary product prices fall, the terms of trade of primary products tends to fall because the price of manufactured goods does not fall *pari passu*. But the demand for manufactured goods falls. Contrawise, when primary product prices rise, the terms of trade of primary products only improves temporarily because the prices of manufactures are quick to follow suit. Governments depress demand to control inflation and the result is stagflation. It can be shown that these price and terms of trade changes magnify normal multiplier effects on output, which is exactly what Keynes had in mind in 1942 when he proposed the establishment of buffer stocks (Commod Controls) to stabilize the prices of key commodities:

> At present, a falling off in effective demand in the industrial consuming centres causes a price collapse which means a corresponding break in the level of incomes and of effective demand in the raw material producing centres, with a further adverse reaction, by repercussion, on effective demand in the industrial centres; and so, in the familiar way, the slump proceeds from bad to worse. And when the recovery comes, the rebound to excessive demands through the stimulus of inflated price promotes, in the same evil manner, the excesses of the boom. (Moggridge, 1980)

Kanbur and Vines (1986) have shown large 'macro' gains to be derived from commodity price stabilization. On the assumptions that the 'north' spends 30 per cent of its income on primary products from the 'south', that primary product production fluctuates by 20 per cent, and that 'northern' governments cut expenditure when prices rise, they show that the variance of income is five times greater than in the standard case where price symmetry is assumed.

A third consequence of volatility is that the movements in the terms of trade may not reflect movements in the equilibrium terms of trade between primary products and manufactured goods in the sense that supply and demand are equated in both markets. In these circumstances, it can be seen from Figure 1.3 earlier that world economic growth becomes either supply-constrained or demand-constrained. At the equilibrium terms of trade, p^*, the growth rate of the system is maximized. If the terms of trade are out of equilibrium, say above p^*, the industrial sector has the capacity to grow faster than g^* but is demand constrained to a lower rate. If the terms of trade are below equilibrium, the demand growth for industrial output is faster than g^*, but growth is supply-constrained below g^*.

A fourth consequence of volatility, as we have seen, is that a collapse of commodity prices can cause severe debt service problems for countries that have previously borrowed heavily when prices were higher and export earnings were buoyant. When prices fall dramatically, there is no way in which debtor countries can service debts in *foreign* currency without a vast increase in export volume or a compression of imports. But when commodity prices are falling, world economic activity is invariably depressed, so that there is little or no scope for any increase in export volume. In 1981 and 1982, when commodity prices started to tumble, world economic activity contracted by 10.3 per cent over two years. There is then little alternative to import compression, which implies a sacrifice of growth and living standards. Falling commodity prices therefore inflict double damage on debtor countries. The terms of trade deteriorates and then, in order for debts to be repaid, medicine must be administered which inflicts further damage on the real economy.

To reduce the cyclicality of primary product prices, Keynes's wartime plan for global buffer-stocks still has a lot to recommend it. It was in 1942 that Keynes produced a detailed plan for what he called 'Commod Control' – an international body representing leading producers and consumers that would stand ready to buy 'commods' (Keynes's name for typical commodities), and store them at a price (say) 10 per cent below the agreed basic price and sell them at 10 per cent above. The basic price would be adjusted according to whether there was a gradual run-down or build-up of stocks, indicating that the price is either 'too low' or 'too high'. The finance for the storage and holding of 'Commods' would have been provided through his proposal for an International Clearing Union (ICU), acting like a world central bank, with which 'Commod Controls' would keep accounts. Keynes was convinced that such a 'Commod Control' scheme would make a major contribution to curing the international trade cycle. The injection and withdrawal of purchasing power by buying up 'Commods' when prices are falling and selling them when prices are rising would, he believed, operate much more effectively and immediately than public works. Keynes submitted his plan to the British War Cabinet, but it was not adopted as official policy because of opposition from the Bank of England and the Ministry of Agriculture for different reasons. The Bank thought the scheme too *'laissez-faire'* because it allowed for private trading, while the Ministry of Agriculture believed that only output restrictions could solve the problem of surpluses and that minimum prices would encourage production. The more modest proposal at Bretton Woods for an International Trade Organisation was negotiated but never got off the ground owing to the refusal of the US Congress to ratify it. At the present time, finance for the holding and storage of buffer stocks could be provided through the use of Special Drawing Rights (SDRs). The world has created new international money, but fails to use it for useful international collectively agreed purposes. If ever there was an instrument in search of a policy, it is SDRs!

From the point of view of developing country debt servicing, however, the promotion of export price stabilization may not be the solution. It is export *earnings* which are the key factor determining the ease with which debt servicing obligations can be met. Stabilizing export prices only stabilizes export earnings when the cause of the instability is variations in demand. When the product is subject to supply variations, stabilizing price will not stabilize earnings and may lead to greater instability. In this respect, schemes for stabilizing export earnings need improving.

A more serious problem with respect to export earnings is the fact that the export earnings of LDCs may no longer be unstable around a *growing* trend as they were in the 1950s and 1960s. Instead, the trend may be reversing itself. This brings us back to the question of the adverse movements in the terms of trade. These unfavourable trends cannot be tackled through export compensation schemes. They require a combination of buffer-stock schemes and export quotas to control the supply of commodities. Such schemes are not easily implemented and may be undesirable on efficiency grounds. These trends are a symptom of underdevelopment itself and ultimately will only be reversed by structural change. The development debate then becomes how to speed the process of structural change in the most expeditious and efficient way. This, however, must be the subject of another paper.

NOTES

1. In 1986, non-fuel primary product prices fell in real terms to their lowest level since the 1930s, and fell 36 per cent from mid-1984 to the third quarter of 1986.
2. Over this period there were 31 years in which manufactured goods' prices fell and 52 in which they rose.
3. See also Targetti (1985).
4. Differences in the income elasticity of demand for primary products relative to manufactures will not be modelled here because they complicate the model without adding to the basic insights. The effect can be shown heuristically. It is a property of the two-

sector model that, for a unique terms of trade equilibrium, the income elasticities must be the reciprocal of one another and that constant elasticities do not cause change in the terms of trade. A low income elasticity for primary commodities simply makes the terms of trade for primary products lower, in the same way that lower wages make the terms of trade lower in models of unequal exchange.
5. This can be justified on the grounds that, in most LDCs, at least, the natural growth rate exceeds the warranted rate.
6. The two equations are, of course, the same, since any excess of expenditure over income implies $P_f EM > P_d X$ which must be filled by net capital inflows (C). Thus $P_f EM - P_d X + C = 0$ is the equilibrium condition.
7. εz_i was proxied by x_i, thereby incorporating also the effects of relative price changes on export growth.
8. But see above footnote.
9. The terms of trade is calculated as the ratio of the country's export price index to its import price index, where all prices are measured in US dollars.

REFERENCES

Emmanuel, A. (1972), *Unequal Exchange: A Study of the Imperialism of Trade*, New York: Monthly Review Press.

Evans, D (1987), 'The Long-Run Determinants of North–South Terms of Trade and Some Recent Empirical Evidence', *World Development*, May.

Findlay, R. (1981), 'The Fundamental Determinants of the Terms of Trade', in S. Grassman and E. Lundberg (eds), *The World Economic Order: Past and Prospects*, London: Macmillan.

Gibson, H. and A. P. Thirlwall (1989), 'An International Comparison of the Causes of the Change in the Debt Service Ratio 1980–85', *Banca Nazionale del Lavoro Quarterly Review*, March.

Grilli, E. R. and M. C. Yang (1988), 'Primary Product Prices, Manufactured Goods Prices, and Terms of Trade of Developing Countries: What the Long Run Shows', *World Bank Economic Review*, January.

Johnson, H. G. (1954), 'Increasing Productivity, Income-Price Trends and the Trade Balance', *Economic Journal*, September.

Kaldor, N. (1979), 'Equilibrium Theory and Growth Theory', in M. Boskin (ed.), *Economics and Human Welfare: Essays in Honour of Tibor Scitovsky* (New York: Academic Press).

Kanbur, R. and D. Vines (1986), 'North–South Interaction and Commod Control', *Journal of Development Economics*.

Keynes, J. M. (1912), 'Tables Showing for Each of the Years 1900–1911 the Estimated Value of the Imports and Exports of the United Kingdom at the Prices Prevailing in 1900 [Cd. 6314]', *Economic Journal*, December.

Keynes, J. M. (1929), 'The German Transfer Problem', *Economic Journal*, March.

Keynes, J. M. (1938), 'The Policy of Government Storage of Foodstuffs and Raw Materials', *Economic Journal*, September.

Kindleberger, C. P. (1943), 'Planning for Foreign Investments', *American Economic Review*, March.

Lewis, W. A. (1952), 'World Production, Prices and Trade, 1870–1960', *Manchester School of Economic and Social Studies*, May.

Mill, J. S. (1848), *Principles of Political Economy*.

Moggridge, D. (ed.), (1980), *The Collected Writings of J. M. Keynes, Vol. XXVII: Activities 1940–1946 Shaping the Post-War World: Employment and Commodi-*

ties, London: Macmillan.

Morrison, J. and M. Wattleworth (1988), 'Causes of the 1984–86 Commodity Price Decline', *Finance and Development*, June.

Nguyen, D. T. (1988), 'Trends in the Terms of Trade of Primary Commodities: Nature, Causes and Variation Across Countries', unpublished.

Prebisch, R. (1950), *The Economic Development of Latin America and its Principal Problems*, New York, UN. ECLA.

Robertson, D. (1915), *A Study of Industrial Fluctuations*, London: P. S. King and Son.

Sapsford, D. (1985), 'The Statistical Debate on the Net Barter Terms of Trade Between Primary Commodities and Manufactures: A Comment and Some Additional Evidence', *Economic Journal*, September.

Sapsford, D. (1988), 'The Debate Over Trends in the Terms of Trade', in D. Greenaway (ed.), *Economic Development and International Trade*, London: Macmillan.

Sarkar, P. (1986), 'The Singer–Prebisch Hypothesis: A Statistical Evaluation', *Cambridge Journal of Economics*, December.

Sarkar, P. (1989), 'Debt Burden, Export Prices and Real Exchange Rates of the Less Developed Countries: A Cross-Country Study 1980–86', unpublished.

Sarkar, P. and H. Singer (1989), 'Debt Pressure and the Transfer Burden of the Third World Countries 1980 – 86, unpublished.

Sarkar, P. and H. Singer (1991), 'Manufactured Exports of Developing Countries and their Terms of Trade Since 1965', *World Development*, February.

Scandizzo, P. and D. Diakosavvas (1988), 'Trends in the Terms of Trade of Primary Commodities 1900–1982: The Controversy and its Origins', unpublished.

Singer, H. (1950), 'The Distribution of Gains Between Investing and Borrowing Countries', *American Economic Review*, Papers and Proceedings (May).

Singer, H. (1987), 'Terms of Trade and Development', in *The New Palgrave Dictionary of Economics*, London: Macmillan.

Spraos, J. (1980), 'The Statistical Debate on the Net Barter Terms of Trade Between Primary Commodities and Manufactures', *Economic Journal*, March.

Spraos, J. (1983), *Inequalising Trade: A Study of Traditional North–South Specialisation in the Context of Terms of Trade Concepts*, Oxford: Oxford University Press.

Spraos, J. (1989) 'Debt and Terms of Trade: Causalities and Externalities', unpublished.

Targetti, F. (1985) 'Growth and the Terms of Trade: A Kaldorian Two-Sector Model', *Metroeconomica*, February.

Thirlwall, A. P. (1986), 'A General Model of Growth and Development on Kaldorian Lines', *Oxford Economic Papers*, July.

Thirlwall, A. P. and M. Nureldin Hussain (1982), 'The Balance of Payments Constraint, Capital Flows and Growth Rate Differences Between Developing Countries', *Oxford Economic Papers*, November.

Thirlwall, A. P. and J. Bergevin (1985), 'Trends, Cycles and Asymmetries in the Terms of Trade of Primary Commodities from Developed and Less Developed Countries', *World Development*, July.

United Nations (1949), *Relative Prices of Exports and Imports of Underdeveloped Countries*, New York: United Nations.

2. Banking on Capital Flight
William Darity, Jr*

Traditional analyses of capital flight have focused on individuals voting with their portfolios against conditions of political and economic instability in the countries from whose currencies and assets they seek escape. These persons are Brendan Brown's 'unknown investor[s]' rather than 'the fly on the wall in the Finance Minister's office'.[1] It gives the inquiry a decidedly non-conspiratorial bent, despite our intuitive sense that there must be at least surreptitious flash and drama associated with capital flight. Indeed a fly on the wall can have drastic consequences, as anyone who has seen the dark Pythonesque film *Brazil* – which is really about Britain in the not too distant future – can attest.

My intention in this chapter is to organize a systematic investigation into the conspiratorial aspects of capital flight – to confront economic theory with the conspiracy between drug traffickers, Third World elites, pariah governments, and First World bankers. Therefore concern is not limited to hot money flows in Brown's narrow sense of 'large-scale international movements of short term capital under a fixed exchange rate system driven either by speculation on an imminent devaluation (or revaluation) or by interest rate differentials apparently greater than exchange risk'.[2] For Brown conceives of a *stock* of hot money, a pool of funds ready to move at the instant when 'the news' changes to whatever site promises the arbitrageur the greatest return. But Brown neglects the factors that generate the *flow* of new hot money, the subject matter of two profound and disturbing studies by R. T. Naylor and Ingo Walter.[3] The discussion here will follow Naylor's and Walter's lead rather than Brown's.

Contemporary motivations for interest in capital flight and hot money movements stem from the implications for the developing country debt crisis and the related implications for IMF adjustment programmes.[4] Arguably capital flight reduces the prospects for repayment of the debt obligations of the borrower countries, by removing from domestic channels funds that could have contributed to investment and growth generating payment capacity.[5] Capital flight, while hindering domestic investment prospects, also undermines the efficacy of IMF exchange rate devaluation objectives.

From the standpoint of the creditor institutions, particularly the multinational commercial banks, capital flight is an intriguing mixed blessing. On the one hand, it reduces the creditworthiness of the borrower nation. On the other hand, US banks apparently already have offset at least one-half of their Latin loans with clandestine deposits from citizens of the borrower countries via a new asset introduced after 1981, the IPB or International Private Banking channel.[6] Not only do these deposits perform a potential offset function, but, in principle, they give the banks the added advantage of having 'true insurance' against repudiation of the debts. It amounts to a semi-visible handshake between Latin elite depositors and transnational bankers. The major Latin borrower nations are unlikely to repudiate the debt if their elites know that their foreign assets could be frozen in the face of such an eventuality.[7]

The customary response to the 'true insurance' argument has been that the banks 'apparently do not, to date, have the legal ability to use these deposits as collateral against outstanding loans.'[8] But in the absence of a direct legal test it is not obvious that this is the case, particularly if the principals who have made the deposits also play functional roles in the governments undertaking repudiation. Whatever the case may be, these depositors value secrecy, for reasons that will be made apparent below, and, even if the banks could not freeze their assets, merely exposing information about their accounts could be a sufficient threat to inhibit repudiation of the debt.

If revolutionary leaders come to power who do not have fortunes abroad in private banking accounts, the possibility of repudiation becomes more realistic. But even then, those with wealth on the right can punish the left-wing regime by pursuing even greater export of their wealth overseas, inducing a fiscal crisis for the new government.[9]

Identification of capital flight as opposed to the non-pejorative concept of 'capital flows' is difficult. Cumby and Levich equate all illegal movements of funds across a nation's border with capital flight.[10] This could involve tax evasion, the movement of funds abroad that were obtained through illegal activities such as weapons or cocaine smuggling, or circumvention of capital controls. The problem here is that the definition is conditional on what is illegal in a particular country.

Lessard and Williamson have suggested that capital flight can be viewed as any outflow of finance that is viewed as undesirable by national authorities.[11] There is an obvious arbitrariness with such a definition. But Lessard and Williamson also have chosen to define capital flight 'as resident capital that flees from the perception of abnormal risks at home' – the push of political and economic insecurities.[12] But when are risks 'normal' and when do they become 'abnormal'? Lessard and Williamson appear to be suggesting that there is a stable level of outflow of finance that is disturbed upward in abnormal times. Their second definition bears similarity to one advanced in the late 1930s by Charles Kindleberger: '... abnormal [flows] propelled *from* a country ... by ... any one or more of a complex list of fears and suspicions'.[13] Again, the push factors are decisive.

Michael Dooley has sought to shift from the abnormal versus normal distinction to an emphasis on comparative risk. In his estimation, capital flight is propelled by risk differentials between nations.[14] This brings in the push and pull factors simultaneously, but reduces the tale of finance in flight to something akin to a portfolio readjustment rather than an extraordinary rush of funds across the border.

There also is the Alesina and Tabellini definition that treats capital flight as a starkly political phenomenon; the segment of the population with wealth can 'vote' for or against a regime by choosing to keep their wealth at home or by choosing to send it hurriedly abroad.[15] If there is electoral politics the class with the numerical capacity to determine the regime in authority is unlikely also to be the class with the wealth that can dictate the pace of domestic accumulation; the latter can always hold a veto over social policy by undertaking a substantial and sudden migration of its funds.[16] This concept illuminates a stylized feature of the phenomenon discussed by Brendan Brown, the discontinuous, wave-like character of capital flight.[17]

Several operational definitions of capital flight have been employed. When applied, all of them demonstrate that with respect to the major Latin American borrower nations, especially Mexico, capital flight has been of such a magnitude that, if it could be appropriated toward such an end, debt burdens would be dramatically reduced. If the cumulative LDC debt, including both principal and interest payments, today is in the vicinity of $400 billion, estimates of capital flight from Latin borrowers in the interval 1976–84 range from $36 billion to $125 billion.[18] Even the low end estimate is three times the magnitude of the $12 billion that the Bush administration is now offering to forgive on US official loans to Latin nations. Manuel Pastor has estimated that the cumulative capital flight from Argentina and Brazil between 1973 and 1987 was more than 60 per cent of the change in external debt. Even more dramatic, Pastor estimates that capital flight from Venezuela over the same period was 132 per cent of the change in external debt![19]

The causal explanations for capital flight are usually tied to the standard explanations for private acquisition of foreign assets. First on the list is overvaluation of the domestic exchange rate coupled with expectations of a devaluation. Individuals holding domestic currency-denominated assets will suffer a loss if they stand pat in such a climate. Better to convert into foreign currency-denominated assets. A second explanation is the existence of financial repression in the home economy, the maintenance of ceilings on domestic interest rates. Domestic residents will seek to place their funds abroad, although the reversal of such a policy may trigger loan pushing by the multinational banks.[20]

A hyper-rational explanation that resembles Barro's so-called Ricardian equivalence theorem has it that the accumulation of external debt spurs capital flight. Domestic residents will anticipate future tax payments to finance the debt and will seek to get their wealth out of the country to escape the future tax obligations.[21] Or domestic residents could move their funds abroad to evade the existing tax structure rather than out of fear of a rise in taxes at a future date. It is especially hard for LDC governments to enforce tax policies on residents when information on their foreign income sources is not provided by foreign governments. Here is an element in Ingo Walter's analysis of the demand for secrecy on the part of individuals who place their funds abroad.[22]

But these are all fairly colourless explanations. Why label movements of funds under these conditions as 'capital flight' rather than 'foreign investment'? More enlivening is, in the somewhat sterile language of bank analysts, the transition that occurred in banking practice from 'asset management' to 'liability management'. Under the practice of asset management bankers seek safe loans. Under the practice of liability management the bankers make high-profile loans and then find the funds to honour their commitments. When the borrower spends the loaned funds, often unproductively, the bankers then rush to find the requisite liabilities as the general quality of their asset portfolio declines.[23]

It is the transition to liability management which has opened up the world of 'private banking', the increased emphasis of banks on obtaining profits through fees charged for the provision of special services to large – *very* large – depositors. It is through the lens of the rise of private banking activities to the forefront of commercial bank practice that the paradox can be uncovered of banks simultaneously promoting debt acquisition by countries and flight of capital from those same countries. Banks engaged in loan pushing and capital flight luring at the same time. Would they have lent so enthusiastically without the expectation that some significant proportion of the funds would 'return' to them in the form of deposits in IPBs?

Bank competition for large depositors is intense. The ability of banks to promise secrecy is crucial in a world where some of these large accounts function for laundering the money of major drug traffickers. The importance of secrecy is such that Walter argues that there are three dimensions to asset characteristics that are valued by investors. In addition to low risk and high return, high levels of secrecy are desired as well and *de facto* investors are willing to pay a secrecy premium on their accounts.[24]

Brendan Brown's 'unknown investor', shifting funds to arbitrage exchange rate or interest rate differentials, is not particularly interested in secrecy *per se*, unless confronted with capital controls. There is a symmetry involved in the 'unknown investor's' actions. His or her funds will move back to the home country when the relative price advantage dictates a reversal of the flows. And flows in either direction may not mean the full transferral of wealth to the more lucrative site because of the attempt to achieve portfolio diversification.

With respect to capital flight in the sense in which the term is used here such reciprocity does not exist. Substantial repatriation of funds to the developing countries does not occur instantaneously with each appreciation in exchange or interest. Nor are there parallel reciprocal flows of funds to those countries from the 'unknown investor' in the developed countries who is seeking portfolio diversification.

The importance of secrecy in these proceedings also explains why transnational banking cannot become an activity that operates entirely above the nation-state. The amount of secrecy a particular bank can offer depends on national policies with respect to disclosure, which in turn is a matter of international relations. The stability of a banking system's access to foreign depositors' accounts becomes a matter of national policy. In this arena Switzerland's and Luxembourg's banks can outdo those whose base of operations is in the US.[25]

New flows of hot money always pass into the multinational banking system for cleansing and, ultimately, access for usage. Whether it is a fly-by-night banking operation in a mid-Manhattan penthouse *à la* Uruguayan entrepreneur Sergio Hochman or a thoroughly unregulated bank on a Caribbean island that constitutes the point of entry, the funds move towards more secure and established institutions.[26]

Manuel Pastor has posed the puzzle of loan pushing-cum-capital flight luring as follows:

> [There] is one peculiar characteristic of much of the flight from Latin America: the movement of residents into foreign assets even as international bankers acquired Latin American assets through their extension of new loans. If the 'investment climate' in a country is negative enough to push out local capital, why would savvy international bankers extend their own capital in the form of loans?[27]

After raising the big question, Pastor offers 'small' answers: the guarantees given by Latin governments to foreign creditors that caused '"discriminatory treatment" of locally-held domestic assets' and the profitability of such two-way flows when Latin exchange rates were overvalued. Pastor does not address the larger answer, which has to do with the alteration in the institutional emphases of transnational banks, as their new orientation towards liability management has led them, competitively, to push loans and to build up their private banking activities.

Indeed frequently loaned funds themselves would pass back to the banks via official corruption in the borrowing countries. I have dubbed the variable that measures the percentage of borrowed funds for projects that go into the hands of national elites through corruption the 'Jain r' after work on this theme by Canadian finance professor Arvind Jain.[28] Richard Barnet's recent article on African economic problems suggests that the Jain r is 10–15 per cent on most large projects.[29] The Jain r is probably much higher for some autocracies. Mobutu in Zaire placed about $4 to 6 billion in his Swiss personal account in the 1970s, about equal to the country's net external borrowings, implying that r was equal to unity in Zaire.[30] The Jain r appears to approach one for Zambia as well.[31]

There are suggestions that sovereign loans for Nicaragua were often transferred directly into the dictator Somosa's account without ever passing into the national treasury. Before his overthrow in 1979 he exported at least $500 million outside the country into foreign accounts.[32] At the time of his death in 1975 the Ethiopian emperor, Haile Selassie, had over $15 billion in foreign assets, having made regular annual deposits of 500 kilograms of gold bullion in Switzerland.[33]

Elites can flee when necessary to live comfortably elsewhere; witness, for example, Jean Claude 'Baby Doc' Duvalier of Haiti. Zambia's Kenneth Kaunda may well be anticipating a lucrative existence in exile.[34] The burden of the debt is left to the regimes that follow them to fix. Occasionally the banks pay a price. The Californian Overseas Bank of Los Angeles, whose primary function was to launder stolen funds for Ferdinand and Imelda Marcos, was recently turned over to the Aquino government by a US District Court. The Aquino government is still trying to retrieve over $200 million that the Marcoses allegedly embezzled from the Philippine treasury in 20 years in power.[35] The recent acquittal of Mrs Marcos in her racketeering trial in New York City makes it less likely that the sum will ever return to the Philippines.[36]

Bankers have known about such corruption as a source of the flows of capital flight for a long time. Why would they make project loans to countries where the Jain r was so high that there was little likelihood that the funds would be invested productively? The 'big' answer, assuming that bankers are indeed 'savvy' fellows, is that they can get their pound of flesh coming and going. The funds raked off by corrupt elites will enter IPB accounts, a source of profitable customer service accounts. Banks receive fees, proportionate to the size of the account, for managing these personal funds. Indeed the funds obtained through corruption do not become mobilizable personal wealth until they are transferred by capital flight, making such accounts very much worth the while of elites from developing countries.[37]

The existence of such large deposits held by Third World elites will stymie efforts to repudiate the debt. As long as repudiation does not occur prospects for eventual payment of a significant (and still profitable) portion of the loans will remain, even if 40 to 60 per cent of the current outstanding debt is forgiven. Loan pushing also helped forge long-term customer relations for the banks with those individuals with whom they negotiated sovereign loans.

Capital flight is much more than mere portfolio readjustments. Its most important faces can be seen in the generation of additional wealth for the already affluent of the poorer nations and the legitimization of ill-gotten gains. It is through the mechanisms of capital flight that mob money was transferred to the state of Israel in the 1950s and 1960s and that Reverend Moon built up his Unification Church movement in the US in the 1970s.[38] The creation of new hot money flows can be found in illegal activities, such as the illegal drug trade and the illegal weapons business, but in the 1980s it can be found just as prominently in the process of commercial bank lending to the developing countries for projects. The theory of capital flight converges with the theory of international lending with a vengeance. In the process both are transformed from Brendan Brown's emphasis on the 'unknown investor' to an emphasis on dictators, criminals, and money launderers. These are some very large and human 'flies' indeed.

NOTES

* The author is grateful to Bobbie Horn, Paul Davidson, Jan Kregel and Hyman Minsky for helpful suggestions.
1. Brendan Brown, *The Flight of International Capital: A Contemporary History*, London: Routledge, 1988, p. 8.
2. Brendan Brown, 'Hot Money', *The New Palgrave: A Dictionary of Political Economy*, Vol. 2, edited by J. Eatwell, M. Milgate and P. Newman, 1987, pp. 671–2.
3. R. T. Naylor, *Hot Money and the Politics of Debt*, New York: The Linden Press/Simon & Schuster, 1987; Ingo Walter, *Secret Money: The World of International Financial Secrecy*, Lexington: D. C. Heath and Company, 1985.
4. Apart from the familiar Latin American cases, dramatic instances of capital flight on the African continent include Liberia, Nigeria, South Africa and Kenya. For Kenya's impoverished economy the adverse consequences are particularly drastic. See, for

example, Roger Thurow, 'Capital Flight Strains Kenyan Economy: Foreign Investors Cite Inefficiency, Rampant Corruption', *The Wall Street Journal*, 17 August 1989, p. A10.
5. This type of argument apparently presumes that capital flight would occur on the same scale without loan pushing and vice versa. This is tantamount to saying that the right hand does not know what the left hand is doing in international banking. Perhaps that is the case.
6. David Felix and Juana Sanchez, 'Capital Flight Aspect of the Latin American Debt Crisis', Working Paper 106, Washington University, St. Louis, August 1987.
7. William Darity Jr. and Bobbie L. Horn, *The Loan Pushers: The Role of the Commercial Banks in the International Debt Crisis*, Cambridge: Ballinger/Harper & Row, 1988, especially ch. 5.
8. Jonathan Eaton, 'Public Debt Guarantees and Private Capital Flight', *The World Bank Economic Review*, vol. 1:3, 1987, p. 380.
9. For an examination of these possibilities see Alberto Alesina and Guido Tabellini, 'External Debt, Capital Flight and Political Risk', *Journal of International Economics*, vol. 27: nos. 3 and 4, November 1989, pp. 199–220.
10. Robert Cumby and Richard Levich, 'On the Definition and Magnitude of Recent Capital Flight', in Donald R. Lessard and John Williamson (eds), *Capital Flight and Third World Debt*, Washington: Institute for International Economics, 1987, pp. 27–67.
11. Donald R. Lessard and John Williamson, 'Introduction', ibid., p. 2.
12. Donald R. Lessard and John Williamson, *Capital Flight: The Problem and Policy Responses*, Washington DC: Institute for International Economics, November 1987, p. 55.
13. Charles P. Kindleberger *International Short-Term Capital Movements*, New York: Augustus Kelley 1937, p. 158.
14. Michael Dooley, 'Comment', in Lessard and Williamson (eds), *Capital Flight and Third World Debt*, pp. 79–82.
15. Alesina and Tabellini, 'External Debt'.
16. For a related analysis see Veijo Kaitala and Matti Pohjola, 'Economic Development and Agreeable Redistribution in Capitalism: Efficient Game Equilibria in a Two-Class Neoclassical Growth Model', *International Economic Review*, vol. 31:2, May 1990, pp. 421–38.
17. Brendan Brown, 'Capital Flight', *The New Palgrave: A Dictionary of Political Economy*, vol. 1, edited by J. Eatwell, M. Milgate and P. Newman, 1987, p. 343.
18. Sunil Gulati, 'Capital Flight: Causes, Consequences and Cures', *Journal of International Affairs*, vol. 42, 1988/9, pp. 165–85. The upper end estimate is from Morgan Guaranty but, interestingly enough, Morgan modifies other estimates, generally based upon manipulation of national accounts data, by 'subtract[ing] the increments and add[ing] the decrements to the short term foreign assets of commercial banks from [the capital flight measure]'. Felix and Sanchez, 'Capital Flight', p. 4, observe: 'Since Morgan Guaranty is reputedly one of the largest holders of IPB deposits, its modification seems little more than a gratuitous slighting of the capability of Latin American banks for comparable chicanery.' Cumby and Levich, 'Recent Capital Flight', p. 34, are equally dismissive of Morgan's adjustment. 'Morgan Guaranty (1986) offers no justification for treating the banking system differently from other firms and individuals. None will be given here.'

Bankers seem predisposed to omit their own role in this game. In a recent paper, Suhas L. Ketkar and Kusum W. Ketkar estimate capital flight from Argentina, Brazil and Mexico between 1977 and 1986. While admitting that 'some accuse banks in the developed countries of enticing capital flight through the activities of their international private banking groups', they restrict their measures to changes in US bank deposits of non-banking entities in the debtor countries. Thus the interbank flows are deleted from consideration. Still they find evidence of substantial capital flight from the three countries in question, although the funds from Argentina and Brazil disproportionately first pass into Uruguayan financial institutions, while funds from Mexico pass into US banks. The former Ketkar is Vice President with the Economics Group at Marine Midland Bank in New York. Ketkar and Ketkar (p. 13) rationalize their omission of transfers by banking entities with the observation that 'The foreign asset buildup by banks is more likely to be associated with normal capital flight for trade financing, etc.' This ignores the role of trade financing in facilitating capital flight by mis-invoicing, under-invoicing of exports and over-invoicing of imports. See Ketkar and Ketkar, 'Determinants of Capital Flight from Argentina, Brazil, and Mexico', *Contemporary Policy Issues*, vol. 7, July 1989, pp. 11–29.

19. Manuel Pastor Jr., 'Capital Flight from Latin America', *World Development*, vol. 18, no. 1, January 1990, p. 3.
20. Darity and Horn, *The Loan Pushers*.
21. Eaton, 'Public Debt Guarantees'.
22. Walter, *Secret Money*.
23. Naylor, *Hot Money*, pp. 31–4.
24. Walter, *Secret Money*.
25. Bob Hagarty, 'Luxembourg Banks Face Tough Task of Preventing Money-Laundering', *The Wall Street Journal*, 16 March 1990, p. 4B. Also see Robert Guenther, 'Broken Trust: How a Private Banker Cost Wealthy Clients as Much as $50 Million', *The Wall Street Journal*, 22 May 1990, pp.A1, A14. Guenther reports on the fraudulent activities of a certain Mr Phacos, who ran a private banking operation for Manufacturers' Hanover. Writes Guenther, p. A1:

    Manufacturers' Geneva debacle is in part a result of the risks of private banking, or catering to the financial needs of wealthy clients, which has become one of the most lucrative and fastest growing fields in consumer banking. Switzerland in particular is a favored locale for private-banking operations because of the country's laws protecting customer privacy.

    But wealthy individuals' passion for secrecy can give bank creditors and officials nightmares if they don't take extra precautions. Many of Mr. Phacos' clients, for example, left explicit instructions that they not be sent monthly statements or confirmation notices on trades.

    Many wealthy individuals bar such written communication in order to hide assets from relatives or others in their home nations ...

    Thus individuals with IPB who may have acquired their funds dishonestly will want perfect honesty from their private banker.

26. On Hochman's operation which included, according to US federal prosecutors, the transfer of funds for Colombia's Medellin cartel, see John J. Fialka, 'Cleaning Up: How a Big Drug Cartel Laundered $1.2 Billion With Aid of U.S. Firms', *The Wall Street Journal*, 1 March 1990 p. A1. On the similar function performed by banks in the Bahamas see R. T. Naylor, *Hot Money*.
27. Manuel Pastor Jr., 'Capital Flight from Latin America', p. 7.
28. See especially Arvind Jain, 'An Agency Theoretic Explanation of Capital Flight', *Economics Letters*, vol. 28, 1988, pp. 41–5 and Arvind Jain, 'Dictatorships, Democracies and Debt Crisis', unpublished manuscript, July 1988.
29. Richard Barnet, 'But What About Africa?', *Harper's*, May 1990, pp. 43–52.
30. Walter, *Secret Money*, p. 46.
31. Kenneth Good, 'Debt and the One-Party State in Zambia', *The Journal of Modern Africa Studies*, vol. 27:2, 1989, pp. 297–313.
32. Ibid., p. 46.
33. Ibid., p. 46.
34. Jane Perlez, 'Failed Zambia Coup Weakens Leader', *The New York Times*, 1 July 1990 p. 3.
35. Associated Press, 'Phillipines Get Bank', *Durham Morning Herald*, 8 May 1990, p. A1.
36. Wade Lambert, 'Former First Lady of Philippines Gets Best Birthday Gift', *The Wall Street Journal*, 3 July 1990, pp. A3, A12. Lambert (p. A3) reports, 'Mrs. Marcos was

accused of using $200 million allegedly stolen from the Philippine government to buy jewelry, artwork and real estate in the U.S.' Apparently what had been hot money as it left the Philippines had grown very cold in the Manhattan real estate market.
37. This is what Hyman Minsky might call 'money management capitalism'.
38. R. T. Naylor, *Hot Money*, pp. 20–3, 152–6.

3. Hyperinflation and Stabilization in Brazil: The First Collor Plan

Luiz Carlos Bresser Pereira and Yoshiaki Nakano

At the beginning of 1990 the Brazilian economy experienced hyperinflation for the first time. The rate of inflation reached 56 per cent in January, 73 per cent in February and 84 per cent in March. On 15 March a newly-elected president took office and the next day announced an ambitious stabilization programme, including a profound monetary reform. Ninety days after, when this paper was finished, it was clear that the plan failed to meet the expectations of its authors: inflation was back, in a very similar way to that under the previous plans, and a recession had already begun, differently from the recessions experienced under previous plans.

In this paper, divided into eight sections, we will analyse (1) the conditions that gave rise to hyperinflation in early 1990; (2) the alternative programmes of stabilization that were being suggested; (3) the logic of the stabilization plan that was finally adopted; (4) the insufficiency of the fiscal adjustment; (5) the liquidity question; (6) the demand problem; (7) the causes of the resurgence of inflation with recession; and finally (8) additional issues.

I BRAZILIAN HYPERINFLATION

The general conditions that gave rise to hyperinflation in Brazil were similar to the ones that prevailed in countries that had experienced hyperinflation earlier. Brazil was not defeated in a war nor was she required to pay war reparations, but the foreign debt accumulated in the 1970s, the external shock of 1979 (second oil shock and interest shock) and the suspension of new external financing since 1982 had together produced similar consequences. The country that in the 1970s received around 2 per cent of gross domestic product (GDP) of foreign savings was now required to transfer real resources of 4 to 5 per cent to the creditor countries.[1] The reduction in domestic investment was basically pro-

Table 3.1 Public sector accounts (% GDP)

	Tax receipts	Personnel expenditure	Public deficit
1979	24.7	7.0	8.3
1980	24.7	6.3	6.7
1981	24.5	6.4	6.0
1982	25.0	7.0	7.3
1983	24.7	6.5	4.4
1984	21.4	5.5	3.0
1985	22.0	6.8	4.3
1986	25.0	7.2	3.6
1987	22.2	7.5	5.5
1988	19.8	7.2	4.3

Source: First two columns, IBGE (Instituto Brasileiro de Geografia e Estatística); last one, Central Bank.
Note: The first two columns refer to the public sector in the strict sense; the last one includes state-owned corporations.

portional to this transfer: the rate of investment, which was around 22 per cent of GDP in the 1970s, fell to around 17 per cent in the 1980s.

On the other hand, there are the fiscal consequences of the foreign debt. The debt, which in the mid-1970s was 50 per cent private and 50 per cent public, was almost fully nationalized during the 1981–3 adjustment: at the end of the 1980s, 90 per cent of the debt was the responsibility of the public sector. In the 1981–3 stabilization programme there was a strong effort to reduce the budget deficit, but this effort was defeated, first, by the high rates of interest paid by the state and, second, by the increase of the foreign and domestic public debt (see Bresser Pereira, 1990). With the interruption of foreign loans deficit financing depended increasingly on domestic indebtedness and seigniorage. The consequence was a fiscal crisis: the budget deficit remained high (see Table 3.1), public domestic debt increased to around 50 per cent of GDP, maturities of domestic debt turned incredibly short (most of the domestic debt start being financed in the overnight market). The last characteristic is the most important one when defining the fiscal crisis since it shows that the state had completely lost creditworthiness. The fiscal crisis immobilized economic policy, transforming government into a passive instrument of validation of inflation through fiscal deficits and inflationary financing.

The strong, yet incomplete, adjustment programme of 1981–3 and the 1983 real devaluation of local currency led, first, to a real reduction of real wages and to the aggravation of distributive conflict (given the widespread conviction that income distribution is deeply uneven in Brazil) and then to a wage–price spiral. This wage–price spiral was engineered by an informal but effective agreement among the labour unions and the firms of the modern and oligopolistic industries (Nakano, 1989).

The wage–price spiral has its origins in 1978–9, when the first big strikes since 1964 took place, but it only gained momentum in 1985, after the transition to democracy was completed. It did not lead to hyperinflation sooner for two reasons: first, the heterodox stabilization plans (1986, 1987, 1989) pushed down inflation for a while; second, given the high degree of formal and informal indexation, inflation in Brazil has a strong inertial component (Bresser Pereira and Nakano, 1987).

Inertial inflation tends to be rigid downwards, since future inflation is strongly linked to past inflation. But it also tends to hinder the acceleration of inflation, as long as it avoids or postpones the dollarization of the economy. In the 1923 German hyperinflation, for instance, the dollarization of the economy led to an exchange-rate/price spiral. Economic agents received payment in the local currency and immediately tried to buy dollars to protect their assets. As a consequence the real demand for dollars increased and real devaluations of the local currency took place continuously, leading to hyperinflation (Merkin, 1982). In contrast, in Brazil economic agents could protect their financial assets by buying indexed bonds, mostly Treasury bills financed daily in the overnight market. These bills (the LFTs – Letras Financeiras do Tesouro) represented a remunerated, interest-bearing, quasi-money, and thus a better alternative to buying dollars.

Actually to buy dollars was risky, first because the parallel exchange rate tended to be artificially high and, second, because it would fluctuate markedly. On occasion speculative attacks against the cruzado made the premium of the parallel market exchange rate over the official rate increase strongly. Inflation, however, would not follow immediately, given the low import coefficient of the Brazilian economy (less than 5 per cent of GDP) and the dual exchange rate market. The official exchange rate was under strict government control, protecting the trade balance from the wild fluctuations of the parallel exchange rate. It was indexed, following a crawling peg rule with daily devaluation. The parallel exchange rate was market-determined. After each speculative attack the premium would recede, imposing heavy losses on the last buyers.

The indexation of the economy delayed hyperinflation but did not avoid it. Inflation tended overall to accelerate, but its acceleration encountered levels or plateaus, and was interrupted by price freezes, starting in 1986 with the Cruzado Plan. However, after the breakdown of the Cruzado Plan and particularly of the Summer Plan (January 1989), inflation accelerated very rapidly, as these plans helped to disorganize the economy (see Table 3.2).[2] Confidence in the indexation system, which was already

Table 3.2 Yearly inflation rate

Year	%	Year	%
1970	19.3	1980	110.2
1971	19.5	1981	95.1
1972	15.8	1982	99.7
1973	15.5	1983	211.0
1974	34.6	1984	223.8
1975	29.4	1985	235.1
1976	46.2	1986	65.0
1977	38.8	1987	415.8
1978	40.8	1988	1037.6
1979	77.2	1989	1782.9

Source: General Price Index (IGP/FGV – General Price Index – Getúlio Vargas Foundation).

Table 3.3 Monthly inflation rate

	1986	1987	1988	1989	1990
Jan	17.8	12.0	19.1	36.6	71.9
Feb	22.4	14.1	17.6	11.8	71.7
Mar	−1.0	15.0	18.2	4.2	81.3
Apr	−0.6	20.1	20.3	5.2	11.3
May	0.3	27.7	19.5	12.8	9.1
Jun	0.5	25.9	20.8	26.8	
July	0.6	9.3	21.5	37.9	
Aug	1.3	4.5	22.9	36.5	
Sep	1.1	8.0	25.8	38.9	
Oct	1.4	11.2	27.6	39.7	
Nov	2.5	14.5	28.0	44.3	
Dec	7.6	15.9	28.9	49.4	

Source: IGP/FGV[3].

very low, collapsed with the Summer Plan, because conventional indexation is based on past inflation, and past inflation was no longer a good proxy for present inflation. With the bankruptcy of indexation the price system lost its basic anchor. Inflation began to accelerate in a spiral way (see Table 3.3).

As the financial market lost confidence in Treasury bills the government increased its interest rate. The result was the increase in budget deficit and a perverse additional loss of credit of the Treasury bills. On the other hand, the successive plans changed the inflationary behaviour of economic agents, introducing new destabilizing factors in the economy.

Table 3.4 Public sector's interest payments (% GDP)

	External debt	Domestic debt	Total	Public deficit
1983	3.70	3.01	6.71	4.4
1984	3.89	3.30	7.19	3.0
1985	4.47	3.44	6.91	4.3
1986	2.89	2.23	5.12	3.6
1987	2.62	2.17	4.79	5.5
1988	2.85	2.88	5.73	4.3
1989*	2.80	9.50	12.30	12.4

Source: Central Bank.
*The total figure for 1989 is taken from Central Bank of Brazil: *Brazilian Economic Program*, vol. 24, March 1990, p. 66. The interest on the foreign debt is estimated and, on the internal debt, a residue.[5]

They anticipated possible government actions, such as freezes or domestic debt repudiation, by increasing prices and promoting capital flight.

As inflation accelerated every month, expectations that it would continue to do so assumed a self-fulfilling character. The economy was headed towards hyperinflation, which materialized in early 1990.

The Summer Plan intended to be very orthodox in its monetary policy. Thus it raised the interest rate to extremely high levels. These reached 16 per cent a month in real terms during the first two months. Subsequently, as economic agents realized the unpleasant arithmetic involved (the high interest would be paid primarily by the state itself, increasing dramatically the interest component of the deficit), the rate of interest was reduced, but it remained very high.

At this moment the fiscal crisis of the state finally became evident to everybody. The government faced increasing difficulty in financing its deficit, whose interest component was now overwhelming (see Table 3.4). The suspension of payments of interest related to the foreign debt, in August 1989, helped very little, since the expectations of the economic agents were already clear: hyperinflation and some form of confiscation of the domestic debt were viewed as highly probable.

Throughout the year the economic agents lived under these two expectations, trying to anticipate the more likely government actions. They strove to protect their financial assets by selling their Treasury bills ('flying from the overnight'), but they had limited alternatives, since the price of others assets, including the dollar in the parallel market, increased considerably. The premium of the parallel market exchange rate over the official one, which used to be around 25 per cent, exceeded 150 per cent several times during the year.[4]

The money supply, which is usually endogenous, in this case was fully passive, increasing automatically as the nominal demand for money increased. When inflation is high and chronic (inertial) the money supply is endogenous, validating price increases, because the alternative of trying to keep it fixed while prices are soaring means a serious liquidity crisis. On the other hand, government is supposed to finance its deficit in the overnight market. Speculation with Treasury bills was very high. Financial intermediaries would often buy Treasury bills without having a final buyer for them. In such a situation the normal procedure would have been for the intermediaries to finance themselves in the money market. But, as they usually would not have sufficient credit for that, the Central Bank would repurchase the Treasury bills. This repurchase, which in the early 1980s was the exception, became the rule in 1986. Paradoxically this was a correct policy, since it reduced speculation and lowered the interest burden of the state. But the consequence was to make the money supply fully passive. Whenever economic agents fled from Treasury bills, leaving the financial intermediaries without reserves, the Central Bank automatically repurchased the bills without costs for the intermediary.

Hyperinflation was the necessary outcome of all these events: the official inflation rate (IPC – Consumption Price Index) was 53 per cent in December, 56 per cent in January, 73 per cent in February and 84 per cent in March. Actually these figures refer in each case to the previous month, given the system adopted to calculate the price index. Thus the new stabilization plan was decided after inflation had reached 84 per cent in February.[6]

II THE ALTERNATIVES

After the failure of the Summer Plan, the policy-making capability of the Sarney government was exhausted and immobilized. Everyone agreed that nothing more could be expected from it. All expectations were directed to what would be done by the new government that would be elected in December and would take office on 15 March 1990.

During 1989 the economic debate was intense. A consensus was formed about the severity of the crisis, its fiscal character and the need for a profound fiscal adjustment.[7] As the exchange rate, during and after the Summer Plan, was overvalued by around 40 per cent, a consensus was also established about the need for a devaluation of the cruzado. No agreement was reached, however, about two questions: whether a new price freeze and a moratorium of the domestic debt were necessary or not.

The debate about incomes policy divided economists into three groups:

(1) pure monetarist economists who believed that no incomes policy at all was indicated; (2) monetarists who, verifying the high economic or social cost of orthodox policies in a situation of chronic inflation, incorporated some of the neostructuralist ideas about inertial inflation (Blejer and Liviatan, 1987; Kiguel and Liviatan, 1988); and (3) neostructuralist (and post Keynesian) economists who believed that, besides fiscal and monetary policy, a profound economic reform should be combined with a stabilization programme in which a new freeze was a necessary first step.

The pure monetarist view was not considered or defended seriously in Brazil. Although preferring not to say so overtly, most monetarist economists know that, when inflation has a high inertial component, the economic and social costs of a monetary and fiscal shock when not combined with some kind of incomes policy are too high. They prefer to think in terms of liberalization after the shock.

The idea of a gradual deindexation of the economy, with decreasing targets of inflation, had more followers. Experience shows that, when inflation is chronic and reaches high levels, gradualist programmes are ineffective and only shock therapy can work (Yeager, *et al.* 1981; Dornbusch and Fischer, 1986; and the economists who, in Brazil, developed the theory of inertial inflation).[8] The unpopular character of freezes among the Brazilian elites, however, given the failure of the previous ones, was behind the attitude of rejecting a new freeze. On the other hand, theoretically, it is true that inertial inflation can be fought in a gradual administrative way. What was forgotten by these economists is that gradualism is only possible when inertial inflation is in its first stages; it is very difficult and implies an enormous social cost when inertial inflation is over one digit monthly; it is impossible when inflation is nearing hyperinflation.

The unfeasibility of gradualism when inflation is very high is related to the free rider issue. Let us suppose two situations: one where inflation is 4 per cent a month, the other, when it is 80 per cent. In both cases the decision is to reduce inflation gradually, over four months, dividing inflation by half each month and defining guidelines for this reduction. In the first case, the premium of the free rider for not following the guidelines is only 2 per cent, in the second case, 40 per cent; the risk is the same. If, instead of guidelines, the government decided to impose the gradual path, it would have the same difficulties arising from a freeze several times over. Actually these difficulties would be greater because it is easier to control a full freeze than a 'partial' one. In the first case the norm is very simple: prices are supposed to remain the same. In the second the rule may also be clear, but very difficult to be controlled by government officials and economic agents: prices are supposed to be increased according to a pre-established and decreasing rate.

The debate about the need for a moratorium on the domestic debt was focused on two issues: the size of the debt and its maturity. The proponents of a moratorium said either that the debt was the basic cause of the budget deficit, given the amount of interest to be paid, or that there was a great probability that economic agents, victims of monetary illusion, would expend their financial assets (invested in Treasury bills and in savings accounts) as soon as they ceased to see huge nominal increases in their indexed financial assets every month. In this case the reduced nominal rate of interest would lead economic agents to consume or to invest out of their financial wealth, provoking a great increase in aggregate demand just after the price freeze. The Cruzado Plan was presented as an empirical demonstration of this hypothesis.

The first argument on the size of the public debt is very fragile. After a while the domestic debt, although increasing, was not so high. Total Treasury bills represented 6 per cent of GDP in 1979 and near 13 per cent in 1989. To reach 50 per cent of GDP (the total public debt) we have to add around 12 per cent of GDP for domestic debt of state-owned enterprises and for states and municipalities, and 25 per cent of GDP total public foreign debt.

The interest burden on the domestic debt was indeed high. It was around 3 per cent of GDP before 1989. In that year, with the Summer Plan and the loss of control of the economy heading towards hyperinflation, real interest rates paid by the government exploded. The interest rate on the domestic debt jumped to 9.5 per cent of GDP (see Table 3.4).[10]

The true problem with the government debt was the very short maturity of the Treasury bills. They were almost fully financed in the overnight money market, showing that the state had lost creditworthiness – besides the loss of credibility of government. This fact was presented as a second argument in favour of a domestic moratorium. Indeed economic agents could decide to change into consumption or investments their liquid financial assets at the moment that its nominal valorization stopped. But this was just a possibility, not a necessity. After the 1987 freeze there was not a flight from the money market towards real assets. The costs and risks of such a flight are very high. If this flight occurs, as happened in 1989 for fear of hyperinflation and of a domestic moratorium, the cost and risk of buying overvalued real assets (dollar, gold, real estate) are very high. Actually in these circumstances the degree of economic freedom of economic agents in relation to their portfolios is rather small.

Taking this into consideration a group of economists, among whom we are included, rejected the idea of a domestic moratorium as a first step, not only because the measure was too risky (a no-return policy) but especially because it could endanger the creditworthiness of the state and the confidence in the financial institutions. If, after the decision on fiscal adjustment and on a new freeze, economic agents started to divest from their financial assets, causing an undesired and uncontrollable increase in aggregate demand, in spite of the adoption of a rigid but conventional monetary policy (high interest rate), it would be possible to add a domestic moratorium to the stabilization programme.

III THE LOGIC OF THE MONETARY REFORM

The stabilization plan – the Collor Plan – that was adopted by the new government in its first day in office (16 March 1990) included four sets of short-term measures: (1) a monetary reform, that included the blockage of 70 per cent of the financial assets of the private sector; (2) a fiscal adjustment; (3) an incomes policy based on a new price freeze; and (4) the introduction of a floating exchange rate. Its medium-term policies were liberalization of foreign trade and privatization.

The four sets of short-term measures were important, but the actual emphasis of the stabilization programme was on the domestic moratorium, which represented an attempt to control inflation through a radical monetary constraint.

The monetary reform had some similarity to the reforms made after the Second World War in Japan, Belgium, West Germany and other European countries. It included, however, specific features. Instead of establishing a conversion factor larger than one between the old money (the novo cruzado) and the new money (the cruzeiro),[11] around 70 per cent of M4 was blocked in novos cruzados (that could only be used to pay past debts), whereas 30 per cent was immediately converted into cruzeiros.[12] While in Germany the Reichmarks ceased to function as a currency, the novos cruzados, besides being used to pay debts previous to 16 March, are supposed to be redeemed in 12 tranches, with full monetary correction and 6 per cent annual interest rate, after 18 months.

This 30 per cent conversion in cruzeiros was the weighted result of the conversion of 20 per cent of all financial assets (money market, time deposits and even checking accounts balance) except savings accounts, where the conversion was limited to 50 000 cruzeiros. The same rules were valid for individuals and business firms, whereas in Germany, for instance, firms received, besides the Deutsche marks corresponding to the exchange factor, 60 Deutsche marks per employee (the same minimum amount that each individual would receive).

Why was the decision on such a radical domestic moratorium taken? We have already seen that, if the problem was the possibility of economic agents divesting from their financial assets, the moratorium could be decided immediately when this possibility materializes. We are convinced, however, that the fundamental reasons that led the new economic authorities to decide upon the moratorium were different. They were confronted by the unfeasibility of a drastic fiscal adjustment in a very short time. Besides, they supposed that the monetary crunch would defeat inflation.

This is the real logic of the domestic moratorium. The medium-term necessary fiscal adjustment that would be proportionate as small fiscal surplus would be around 7 per cent of GDP per year. This figure may be explained in two ways: in fiscal terms and in national account terms. In fiscal terms or in public sector borrowing requirements terms the operational public deficit of Brazil in 1987 and 1988 averaged 5 per cent. In 1989 there was an increase to 12.4 per cent.[13] But this figure overestimates the Brazilian permanent deficit, given the exceptionally high interest paid by the state that year. In national account terms we can come to a similar figure, considering that public sector savings are negative around 3 per cent and should be positive around 4 per cent of GDP to finance essential government investment programmes. According to this second reasoning it is clear that we are assuming that the fiscal adjustment cannot impose further reductions in public investment. Fiscal adjustment will have to be made by increasing taxes and cutting current expenditures.

The objective should be a small budget surplus, given that, during the transition to stability, the government would be forbidden to resort to domestic or foreign additional finance. After stabilization the budget surplus would provide government with some degree of freedom to stimulate aggregate demand and resume growth with stability.

It is quite clear today that, given the political and constitutional limitations it faced, the new government did not have the power to impose such fiscal adjustment in the required time. The Constitution establishes the principle of annuity for income taxes. In political terms, there is not enough support in Brazil, either in Congress or in the business elite, for sizable taxes increases.

IV INSUFFICIENT FISCAL ADJUSTMENT

It is not easy to calculate the size of the fiscal adjustment embodied in the plan. The government spoke about a 10 per cent adjustment, but this is clearly an overstatement. On the other hand, it is essential to distinguish permanent adjustment from once and for all adjustment. In Table 3.5 we present an estimate of the fiscal adjustment presented by the Ministry of the Economy (*Gazeta Mercantil*, 18.4.90).

Table 3.5 Fiscal adjustment estimated by the plan (% GDP)

Permanent adjustment		3.9
Revenues		
Consumption tax	0.6	
State-owned enterprises prices	0.5	
Tax evasion	0.5	
Expenditures		
Interest reduction	1.5	
Expenditure reduction	0.5	
Olivera–Tanzi effect	0.1	
Other	0.3	
Once and for all adjustment		6.0
Capital levy (IOF)	2.5	
Privatization certificates	2.0	
Privatization	1.5	
Total		9.9

It should be noted that almost two-thirds of the gains (6 per cent of GDP) refer, not to a permanent fiscal adjustment, but to once for all gains (particularly the IOF – Imposto sobre Operaçíes Financeiras – and the sale of public sector assets). These 6 per cent estimated gains are not yet assured. In relation to the permanent adjustment, the tax reform implemented by the Collor Plan will increase the federal government revenue by only 1·3 per cent of GDP in 1991. Although small, the reduction in expenditures is also not yet assured.

This fiscal adjustment is clearly insufficient. The new Ministry of the Economy already acknowledged this fact when it announced that a new fiscal package was under study to be sent to Congress. Anyway it is clear that the domestic moratorium played the role of a provisory substitute for the fiscal adjustment. Deciding on the domestic moratorium the government won time to lengthen its fiscal adjustment in the future.

It is important, however, to underline that a stock measure like this is not a real substitute for a flow fiscal adjustment, nor should it be confused with a monetary policy that effectively controls the flow money supply. The radical reduction of the stock of money could have had some flow (fiscal and monetary) consequences in terms of reduction in interest, but this did not happen. The domestic debt was blocked and slightly reduced, not cancelled.

There was some reduction in the stock of debt. Three days of banking holidays, when monetary correction was not counted on Treasury bills, represented almost an 8 per cent reduction. The capital levy (IOF) represented a reduction around 9 per cent of the stock of government debt. And some reduction was also achieved by less than proportionate correction for financial assets in March 1990 (BTN was limited to a 41 per cent increase).[14]

This limited debt reduction plus the forced reduction of the interest rate on the blocked public debt caused some interest reduction for the public sector. But it is quite clear that the domestic moratorium is not a substitute for fiscal adjustment.

To complement and to lengthen the fiscal adjustment is now an essential task for the economic authorities, since the success of the plan depends on not having to rely on inflationary financing. The public deficit was not the direct cause of Brazil reaching hyperinflation. Given chronic or inertial inflation, often the public deficit was a convenient manner of validating the money supply increase necessary to comply with the transaction demand for money (Bresser Pereira and Nakano, 1987, pp. 73–9). But once the time for stabilization comes, there is no other alternative to eliminating the public deficit.

V THE LIQUIDITY QUESTION

A stabilization programme usually involves a certain degree of recession of the economy, even if the previous inflation cannot be directly attributed to excess demand. Fiscal adjustment and monetary control have a recessive character. The control of wages requires some degree of slow-down of economic activity. The need of firmly fixing a nominal anchor (usually the exchange rate) requires a previous over-devaluation which induces contractionary forces. If a freeze is included in the stabilization plan, a weak aggregate demand will facilitate the subsequent price liberalization.

In the Collor stabilization programme there was assumed as an objective – or as a necessary consequence – a moderate recession. The general and correct idea was that it is impossible to stabilize an economy so deeply unbalanced without some sacrifice. The instrument to impose this sacrifice, however, was rather the reduction of money supply than fiscal adjustment. And this reduction was so radical, it hit the business enterprises so strongly, that it disorganized production and is leading the economy to a much deeper recession than expected or desired, without achieving the control of inflation.

In the first 60 days after the plan the attention of the public and the economists was very much directed to the 'liquidity question'. First, the sharp reduction of liquidity was said to be both the cause of the stabilization and the reason for recession. Second, when the money supply began to increase, it was made responsible for excess demand and/or the resurgence of inflation. Our view is, first, that recession was rather the result, at the supply side, of the disorganization of production, caused by the blockage of financial assets including the blockage of working capital, than the consequence of the reduction of liquidity provoking a fall in demand; second, that the increase in money supply that immediately followed was a clear demonstration of the endogenous character of money supply; and third, that the resurgence of inflation cannot be related to this increase. In this section we will discuss the first two points, the third will be discussed in section seven.

According to neostructuralist and post Keynesian economics the money supply is endogenous.[15] It is basically determined by the demand for money, accommodates the increase of GDP and validates the rate of inflation.

The government budgetary constraint, in a closed economy or in a highly indebted economy, requires that the fiscal deficit be financed by the net creation of government liabilities: increase in the money supply, dM, and issue of Treasury bills dB.

$$D = dB + dM$$

Conventional economics assumes that in this equation either dM or D are the exogenous variables. When D is the determinant factor, the increase of money supply is a residuum, given the government incapacity to finance fully the deficit with Treasury bills. If this is not necessarily true when moderate inflation prevails, it is clearly invalid when inflation is very high and chronic or inertial. In this case the money supply – and thus dM – is determined by the demand for money, and the increase in government indebtedness is the residuum. In Brazil, before the stabilization plan, the Central Bank projected the rate of inflation and, passively, established the required increase in the nominal supply that would keep it balanced with the demand for money or, in other words, that would avoid a liquidity crisis. This practice was adopted independently of the orientation of finance ministers and Central Bank governors.

Actually, in the case of Brazil, where, besides a chronic inflation the economy was fully indexed, the endogenous money supply should include a portion of the Treasury bills traded in the overnight market. The maturity of Treasury bills was one night. And government, in order to reduce its interest bill and to induce financial intermediaries to buy the Treasury bills, warranted the automatic and daily repurchase of Treasury bills that did not find buyers among the public. In this way the interest rate was fully determined by the Central Bank, and the money supply was fully endogenous.

As a consequence the overnight deposits represented a quasi-money, besides a remunerated money. The potential money supply was near to M4, since all financial assets were extremely liquid, but actual money supply was really formed of M1 plus a part of the overnight deposits. The conventional concept of money supply makes it equal to M1. In equilibrium we have,

$$M^d = Yp/V = M1$$

where M^d is the demand for money, Yp nominal increase, V the income velocity of money, and $M1$ the money supply.

In a situation of high inflation, V would increase sharply while the conventional supply of money would be much smaller. The actual velocity of money, however, does not increase so much as it seems, because the actual money supply cannot be equated with M1. The actual money supply, M', should be considered as formed of M1 plus a portion, z, of the overnight deposits, B. The z coefficient, smaller than one, is determined by the rate of inflation and the corresponding nominal demand for money. The higher inflation, the higher will be z. This share, zB, of overnight deposits is the amount of money that economic agents indeed use as money. It is also the variable that, endogenously, equates the actual money supply with the demand for money. In this case, the actual income-velocity of money, V' is smaller than when we take the conventional or restricted definition of money, M1.

$$M'^d = Yp/V' = M1 + zB = M'$$

In this equation zB is used as money just as M1; it is as much a means of exchange as conventional money as currency. Economic agents habitually use part of their overnight deposits, zB, to make transactions. To do that they transform zB into M1 daily, increasing M1, but, as the recipients of the additional M1 invest it immediately in overnight Treasury bills, the M1 increase is automatically neutralized, disappearing from records – but not from the economic process.

Table 3.6 presents an estimation of the actual money supply as a proportion of GDP for Brazil at three points: 15 days before the stabilization plan, 15 days after and 45 days after. We have to admit that the estimation of the actual money supply is rather imprecise, but not arbitrary.

Before the plan this estimation was very difficult because the quasi-money stock, B, from which could be withdrawn the actual money supply, was very big. We estimate that the actual money supply should be around 14 per cent of GDP. To come to this estimation the parameters we have

Table 3.6 Money supply (% of GDP)

		28 Feb	31 March	14 May
1	M4 (potential money supply)	29.0	9.0	14.0
2	B overnight dep.	16.0	2.0	8.0
3	Savings accounts	9.0	3.0	1.0
4	Others	2.0	1.0	1.0
5	M1	2.0	3.0	4.0
6	zB	12.0	2.0	6.0
7	Actual money supply	14.0	5.0	10.0

Table 3.7 Financial assets (% GDP)

	Monet. base	M1	Treas. bills	Saving depos.	Time depos.	M4
1970/74*	4.65	15.04	5.08	1.68	3.28	25.08
1975/79*	3.75	11.70	6.85	5.62	4.44	28.60
1980/84*	2.50	6.30	5.80	8.01	4.57	24.69
1985	1.56	3.73	10.39	9.20	6.17	29.50
1986	3.22	8.20	9.33	8.09	6.05	31.67
1987	2.19	4.62	10.07	9.69	4.86	29.24
1988	1.39	2.76	12.22	10.75	4.11	29.85
1989	1.26	2.05	13.94	8.13	2.78	26.89

Annual average, adopting end of period positions.
*Average of these years.
Source: Central Bank.

are: M1 was around 17 per cent of GDP in the early 1970s, when inflation was moderate but not negligible (20 per cent a year) and it was reduced to 2 per cent of GDP at the beginning of 1990 (see Table 3.7).[16] In our concept of actual demand for money the demonetization caused by the acceleration of inflation is neutralized by the increase in zB that is considered as part of the actual money supply. But we admit that inflation and financial innovations allowed for some reduction of the demand for money from the 17 per cent of the early 1970s to 14 per cent of GDP in the 1980s. Of this 14 per cent, 2 per cent was represented by M1 and 12 per cent by zB. As B was 16 per cent of GDP, we are assuming a z of 0.75.

With the moratorium of the domestic debt, the supply of money was reduced drastically. M4, which we may understand as a potential money supply, was reduced from 29 to 9 per cent of GDP, overnight deposits, from 13 to 3 per cent of GDP, and our estimation is that the actual money supply decreased from 14 to 5 per cent of GDP. At this stage (31 March) we are assuming that z is equal to one; that is, that the total overnight deposits are part of the actual money supply.[17]

Such a reduction was not in the minds of the authors of the plan. They confused the amount of cruzeiros left in the economy (9 per cent of GDP) with the money supply. They said (in several interviews in the newspapers) that, in the second semester of 1986, after several months of price stability resulting from the Cruzado Plan, M1 was 9 per cent. Thus 9 per cent of 'money supply' would be enough. Actually the supply of money, even if we include the overnight deposits, was only 5 per cent. On the other hand, the demand for money was at least 14 per cent. In the Cruzado Plan period it was possible to live with a smaller M1 because there was an enormous amount of overnight deposits at the disposition of economic agents.

The effect of this reduction of the money supply on the business enterprises was dramatic. It disorganized production. The working capital of enterprises was blocked, causing an immediate termination of activities. The blockage was made without an economic criterion. Thus the disparities of situation among enterprises were considerable. The prospect was that banks would make the cruzeiros circulate, but, given the high interest rates, this role was only played by the banks to a limited extent.

According to a survey conducted by the FIESP (Federação das Indústrias do Estado de São Paulo), sales of the industrial firms in São Paulo, in the second half of March, were reduced by around 70 per cent. This fact was the result not only of lack of money (globally and sectorially) and of the disorganization of the economy, but also of psychological influences. The impact on expectation was very negative. Unemployment immediately began to rise. Many enterprises decided to send their employees on collective vacations while waiting for a clarification of the situation. Workers began to accept wage reductions coupled with a reduction of the working day.

In the next month the amount of cruzeiros was increased by various means, reaching 14 per cent of GDP in mid-May (in mid-June, 16 per cent). Part of this increase was under the control of government, part not. The government assumed that it would be able to control the increase of liquidity, but the market, taking advantage of the existence of two currencies, was able to increase its amount of cruzeiros, reducing correspondingly the stock of cruzados.

At this moment banks began to make it known that they were having difficulty in making loans, given a reduced demand for them. Several analysts and the economic authorities concluded that 'the liquidity problem' was solved – more than that, that there was now 'excess liquidity', which would provoke excess demand and/or bring back inflation.

It is easy to note in Table 3.6 that in mid-May the potential money supply (M1 plus overnight deposits) continued to be relatively small (10 per cent of GDP), and that the actual money supply, although increased, was still below the level previous to the plan (around 10 per cent in May, against 14 per cent of GDP in February).

Why, then, was the demand for loans weak? Why was the liquidity no longer tight but relatively loose? The increase in the money supply explains part of the change, but the real explanation is in the reduction of demand for loans. Given the pessimistic prospect about sales and the high interest rates (around 100 per cent a year in real terms), firms were not interested in taking loans.[18] They would rather reduce production. As a matter of fact, recession was most likely already installed in the economy. The demand for loans and the demand for money were reduced in accordance with the pessimistic expectations of economic agents.

VI THE DEMAND PROBLEM

Recession in this case was not demand-led but supply-originated. Its basic cause was not a reduction of aggregate demand, but the disorganization of production. Retail sales were the only indicator that initially did not point towards recession. They increased immediately after the freeze, as happened after the other three freezes. There are some general reasons to explain why this happens. First, although we have already said that this fact is often overemphasized, it is true that, with the end of money illusion, people tend to spend a little more for consumption. Second, either out of optimism or mistrust in the success of the stabilization, people tend to spend on consumption in anticipation of needs. Third, Helpman (1988) argued that a price freeze in an oligopolized economy has a similar effect to a reduction of real prices; thus demand will increase along the demand curve.

In the Collor Plan there were three additional explanations for the increase in consumption: first, the loss of credibility of financial assets led people to consume; second, the resumption of consumer credit, which had practically disappeared with hyperinflation, spurred sales of consumer durables; third, the plan implied a real wage increase in March of 23 per cent.

This 23 per cent real wage increase took place in March because the government decided that the 73 per cent February inflation should correct wages in March, according to existing wage indexation law. On the other hand, inflation in March, when calculated at end of the month against end of the previous month (instead of average of the month against average of previous month, as price indexes usually do) was only 41 per cent in March.[19]

Table 3.8 Indicators of economic activity in 1990 (% change in relation to previous year)*

	Level of activity	Level of employment	Average real wage (1)	Installed capacity utilization
Jan	6.2	3.8	−18.8	79.5
Feb	8.0	3.4	−22.7	79.0
Mar	−6.8	2.5	−10.5	72.5
Apr	−22.3	0.6	−22.4	62.5

*Except installed capacity utilization.
(1) Average nominal wage deflated by IPC/IBGE $t+1$.
Source: FIESP (data for São Paulo industry).

The 23 per cent increase could be interpreted as a basic contradiction of the stabilization plan (Sylvio Bresser Pereira, 1990). Usually to fight inflation means to reduce demand and, if possible, to increase supply. In the Collor Plan the opposite was done: supply was curtailed through the money supply squeeze, while wages were increased. The problem, however, is less serious because, differently from what happened under the Cruzado Plan, and similarly to the Bresser Plan, real wages were decreasing before the plan owing to the acceleration of inflation. Thus the 23 per cent wage increase only compensated the previous reduction.[20] It did not represent a distributive incompatibility. Firms did not *have* to increase prices compensatorily.

This increase in consumption was necessarily short-lived, given the rise in unemployment. In May retail sales, when compared with the corresponding month in the previous year, were already negative in Brazil. Given the reduction of production and of investments a depressed demand was now becoming a generalized fact.

VII RECESSION AND THE RESURGENCE OF INFLATION

Ninety days after the Collor Plan was launched recession continued to be the most likely outcome, while it was quite clear that inflation was back. Actually the slow-down of the economy had begun earlier. GDP growth was already slightly negative in the last quarter of 1989 (−0.3 per cent) and clearly negative in the first quarter of 1990 (−2.4 per cent). In April, as a result of the disorganization provoked by the Collor Plan, the FIESP index of economic activity showed a 22.3 per cent fall in relation to April 1989; for February and March the corresponding figures were an 8.0 increase and a 6.8 decrease (see Table 3.8). According to the Getúlio

Figure 3.1   Four weeks' inflation (%)

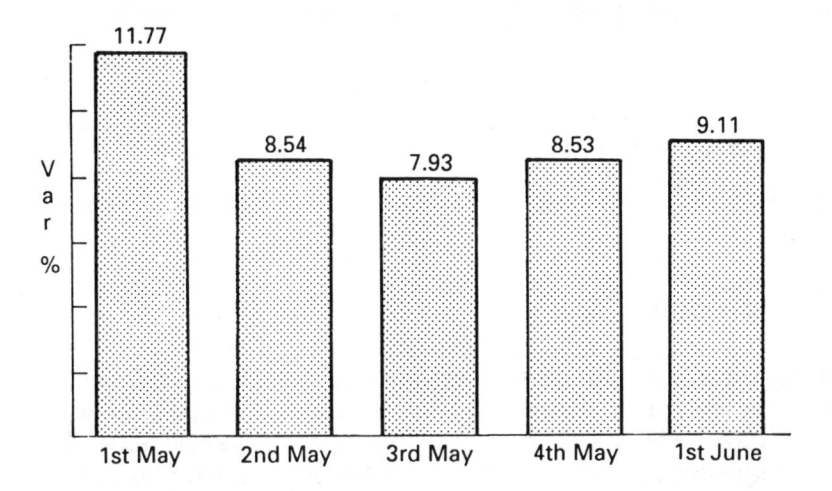

[Bar chart showing values: 1st May: 11.77, 2nd May: 8.54, 3rd May: 7.93, 4th May: 8.53, 1st June: 9.11; y-axis labeled "Var %"]

Source: FIPE/USP, cost of living index.

Vargas Foundation business survey the level of capacity utilization of the Brazilian industry in April was the lowest since this index began to be calculated in the mid-1960s (61 per cent); three months before, in January, it was 79 per cent. In May, as the economy started reorganizing after the shock, the level of production began to recover, as the first figures on electric power consumption indicated, but the May record increase of unemployment in São Paulo in relation to the previous month (2.4 per cent against 2.2 per cent) suggested that the recovery was limited. In this month, according to ABDIB (Associação Brasileira da Indústria de Base) the rate of idle capacity in the heavy capital goods industry reached a 48.6 peak against an average, for the 1980s, of 38 per cent. The recession trend seemed to be stronger than the recovery impulse. As to inflation, there is no doubt that it is back. Regular price indexes are inadequate to measure inflation after a freeze because they include a heavy inflation residuum, as they compare present month average prices against last month average prices. In consequence it takes some time for the index to show the halt to inflation. Up to May these average against average price indexes were still showing a fall (see Table 3.3). FIPE's four weeks' price index, however, was already beginning to indicate an increase (see Figure 3.1). Any doubts about the resurgence of inflation, however, were dismissed by FIPE's end to end price index. It was only calculated for two months, showing a clear increase from 3.3 per cent in April to 6.4 per cent in May (see Table 3.9).

Why did inflation reassert itself? There are three explanations for the

Table 3.9 Monthly inflation rate (1990) (end to end of the month)

Month	Var. %
February	84.3
March	41.0
April	3.29
May	6.36

Source: First two months: estimate of the authors based on IPC/IBGE; last two months, FIPE/USP.

fact: monetarist, Keynesian and neostructuralist or inertialist. The monetarist and the Keynesian reasoning depends on the increase of the money supply in the three months that followed the plan. The neostructuralist analysis is based on the relative price imbalances and on the corresponding distributive conflict. Government adopted a naive monetarism when it assumed that the drastic money supply reduction would eliminate inflation. In doing so they forgot that inflation is not a stock but a flow problem. In order to control inflation it is necessary to eliminate the budget deficit and to control the money supply, not the stock of money. When inflation has an inertial component, as is the case of Brazil, it is necessary, additionally, to freeze prices or, more broadly, to promote an incomes policy that supports (it does not replace) fiscal and monetary policy. For the authors of the Collor Plan the freeze was considered an accessory measure. The essential would be, in the first phase, the reduction of the money supply, and in the second phase, the elimination of the fiscal deficit. However inflation was back before the deficit could be controlled.

The true monetarist explanation for the resurgence of inflation is simple: prices increased again because in the two months following the plan high-powered money increased four times. The liquidity increase provoked expectations that inflation would return – and the 'rational expectation' is a self-fulfilling prophecy. Monetarists do not accept that the money supply has an essentially endogenous, passive character and forget that, after a hyperinflation, a sudden stabilization provokes a strong increase of the monetary base. For the neoclassic monetarist the belief that the increase in the money supply causes inflation has a quasi-religious character. The monetarist rhetoric – 'true' because part of mainstream economics – says that an increase in the money supply causes inflation; rational expectations theory adds that economic agents will form their expectations according to the 'true' theory and, again rationally, will behave according to their expectations, increasing prices. Thus the prophecy becomes self-fulfilling.

The monetarist explanation is implicit in most analysis. Pastore (1990) adopted it explicitly. Excess demand is not required for the resurgence of inflation. It is enough to have the increase of high-powered money. To be correct this explanation for the acceleration of inflation immediately after the Collor Plan would have been the result of the decisions of the business enterprises to increase their prices as they noticed that the monetary base was increasing. The textile industry, the suppliers of personal services, farmers, the home appliance industry – the first to increase their prices after the plan – would have taken this decision after an assessment of the increase of the monetary base.

The Keynesian explanation is more reasonable, but in the present case accounts only for part of the acceleration of inflation. According to this view, adopted among others by Toledo (1990), inflation returned because the money supply increase would have caused excess demand. The halt of inflation due to the liquidity shock would have been temporary. As liquidity was re-established, demand recovered and inflation returned. Actually we have already shown that the trend was rather to recession than to growth. There was an increase in retail sales in the first month after the plan, but soon sales slowed down. Some firms may have profited from this demand spurt to increase their prices, but only a few, since global demand was dwindling rather than expanding.

The neostructuralist or inertialist explanation for the resurgence of inflation is based rather on the nature of inflation in Brazil than on the errors related to the money supply. Inflation in Brazil is inertial, and was very high – actually hyperinflation already prevailed – when the stabilization plan was launched. The neostructuralist explanation emphasizes relative prices imbalances on the day of the freeze and the corresponding distributive conflict. In Brazil economic agents are used to inflation. They deeply believe that increasing price is the best way to protect themselves from the generalized distributive conflict. On 16 March, when prices were frozen, relative prices were necessarily unbalanced, since price adjustments were not synchronized. Thus there was an intertemporal relative prices imbalance. This imbalance, that may be measured by the dispersion of relative prices, tends to increase with the acceleration up to the moment that the economy is fully dollarized.

On the day that the freeze was implemented firms that had just increased their prices gained from the freeze, as their mark-up increased, while the ones that were on the point of doing so lost. When inflation is chronic, firms that lost – or that presume they have lost – from the freeze will increase their prices at the first opportunity. In the Collor Plan firms felt additionally injured by the retention of financial assets. This was a second reason to increase prices at the first opportunity.

Some factors favoured the price increase: (1) the increase in consumption expenditures just after the freeze; (2) the increase in the money supply that followed the recession; (3) the hasty liberalization of prices of clearly oligopolist industries. These were the opportunities business enterprises were waiting for. But the price increase would have taken place anyway, given the inertial character of the Brazilian inflation. The freeze and the blockage of financial assets induced a one-month truce. But immediately afterwards business enterprises began to increase prices. Nobody can lose with inflation or with a stabilization plan. Either profits or wages cannot be reduced for a while. It does not matter that it is impossible to stabilize the economy without some recession that will reduce profits and wages. A few days after the freeze firms, according to *Gazeta Mercantil*, the leading Brazilian business newspaper, 'were looking for an index for their prices'. Fearing unemployment workers halted their demands for a while, but two months after the plan they were already making huge demands and getting wage increases of 20 to 30 per cent.[21] Firms that agreed to these wage demands will almost certainly pass on the corresponding cost increase to prices.

It is important, however, to underline that since 1987 indexation in Brazil no longer means increasing prices according to past inflation. Economic agents are so worried about not losing with inflation that they either change indices to get a more favourable one, or they 'index' their prices according to their own prediction that inflation is accelerating. In other words, they tend to include a risk premium relating to the previous month's inflation in their price decisions. As all firms behave similarly, each firm individually does not need to worry that its price increase will not be followed by the competition. Thus inertial inflation will be also, and paradoxically, an accelerating inflation.

VIII ADDITIONAL ISSUES

The failure of the Collor Plan to control inflation may be related to some additional issues. Stabilization of chronic or inertial inflation requires a nominal anchor, besides some type of incomes policy (Kiguel and Liviatan, 1988). The end of hyperinflation usually took place when the exchange rate was stabilized. In Brazil, given its relatively closed economy, the exchange rate is not so important as in other countries. But a fixed exchange rate would certainly be an important reference for expectations formation. The Collor Plan, however, decided in favour of a floating exchange rate. It is true that market clearing for this floating exchange rate is very limited. The demand for foreign currency continues to be under the control of authorities: administrative import controls were maintained and payments of interest, dividends and all other capital movements continue under control of the Central Bank. Thus the possible advantages of a floating exchange rate are not present, whereas the disadvantages – the lack of a nominal anchor – are quite clear. The advantages are not present because the Brazilian economy really cannot afford a 'dirty' floating rate. It can live with a 'very dirty' floating rate (the Collor Plan option) but this is clearly a dangerous option. Government renounced a nominal anchor, and the exchange rate was exposed to unexpected and undesired fluctuations. If, for instance, international reserves are increasing because of a moratorium on foreign debt (the present situation of Brazil) the exchange rate will tend perversely to become overvalued. A safer alternative would be a competitive but administered exchange rate, that, after a radical stabilization plan such as the Collor Plan, should have been fixed.

The difficulties the Collor Plan is presently facing also have their origin in the problems that have not been directly faced. Three problems fall into this category: foreign debt, trade liberalization and a social and political pact. The preliminary information about the Collor policy in relation to the foreign debt is reassuring. The decision is first to make an agreement with the International Monetary Fund (IMF) and only after to negotiate with the banks. In the negotiation the basic ideas are to subordinate the payment of interest to the fiscal problem and to have as a parameter for the necessary debt reduction the secondary market price of the Brazilian debt. Actually there is not very much to negotiate with the banks. A reduction of 50 to 60 per cent in the foreign debt will allow a fiscal gain of 1.5 per cent of GDP. Following a burden sharing policy, this is the minimal contribution foreign banks can make to the Brazilian stabilization programme. The problem is to know if the Brazilian government will act firmly and quickly in this direction, deciding quasi-unilaterally the debt reduction and eliminating from the budget and from balance of payments accounts the reduced part of the debt. The alternative is arrears, which have very negative effects on expectations of economic agents.

The same reasoning applies to the trade liberalization issue. The government has already made clear its intention of liberalizing imports, but present prospects are for a gradual liberalization. Gradualism in this matter will not help the stabilization programme. It will not help to control oligopolies organized in cartels, which prevail in Brazil. Besides gradual policies in this matter seldom succeed. Interest groups will have time to react and stop the process. A World Bank-conducted survey of 37 successful experiences of trade liberalization showed that a condition for success was to begin the process with a radical move (Papageorgiou, Choksi and Michaely, 1990).

Finally we have the political problem. The Collor Plan was an authoritarian plan produced at a time when consultation and agreement were expected. Nobody was consulted. No previous negotiations took place. Up to the present moment the government has negotiated very little with Congress – where the plan was approved – and with workers. It is unrealistic to assume that workers will readily accept the plan for the simple reason that wages have been partially preserved. A basic cause of the acceleration of inflation in Brazil in recent years, besides the intertemporal distributive conflict among business firms, which originated in the asynchronous increase in prices, has been the distributive conflict between labour and capital. At the present time workers are making it quite clear that they are not convinced that their wages have been preserved. As with previous plans, they claim that the inflation of the month of the freeze (March, when official inflation was 84 per cent) was 'stolen' by the government. The claim makes no sense, the economic reasoning behind it is unsustainable, but, since no political or social agreement was tried, the probability of great labour and political disputes in the near future is very high.

To conclude: the Collor Plan was not able to control inflation. The Collor government failed in the first trial. But it will not be the last one. The times of chronic inflation are ending in Brazil. After the brief Brazilian experience with hyperinflation it seems clear that the control of inflation will have high priority in the Collor government. The first Collor Plan counted too much on the drastic reduction of the money supply. On the other hand, some mistakes related to the money supply and to wages, an incomplete fiscal adjustment, a wrong view of the exchange rate, the natural difficulties involved in getting out of a freeze in conditions of unbalanced relative prices, the delay in facing the foreign debt problem and in liberalizing trade, and finally the lack of a real social and political agreement worked against it. Once more the worst enemy of stabilization plans in Brazil – inertial inflation – was not defeated.

In mid-May, when it became clear that inflation was back, the government took the decision to control it by adopting a rigid monetary policy. A nominal anchor was defined. M1 is not supposed to increase by more than 9 per cent up to the end of the year, while wage indexation is barred. In the first month, at the time of writing, the Central Bank was able to control the money supply, but wages were being informally indexed, and inflation was continuing. Monetary authorities are once again underestimating the inertial and accelerating character of Brazilian inflation. Inflation is now nearing 10 per cent a month and most probably will continue to rise. Orthodox stabilization policies are costly and ineffective when inflation is high and has a strong inertial component, as is already the case of Brazilian inflation in June 1990.

A new stabilization plan will have to be started in the coming months.

The fight against inflation will be lengthy and hard. In order to succeed the new plan will have to be carefully prepared, it will have to be preceded by a social pact, and it will necessarily put together incomes policy and conventional fiscal and monetary policies.

NOTES

1. Transference of real resources is equal to current account minus factor payments (interest and dividends) or it is equal to real transaction surplus: surplus in the trade account plus the balance in real services account.
2. We exclude the Bresser Plan from these consequences because it was an emergency plan enacted in order to control the deep crisis of the failure of the Cruzado Plan. It did not intend to finish with inflation but only to put a halt to it for a moment. It did not include a monetary reform, the de-indexation of the economy and the freeze of the exchange rate, unlike the other plans. Launched in June 1987, it assumed that in December inflation would reach 10 per cent; actually it reached 14 per cent that month (Bresser Pereira, 1988b).
3. In this table we use the IGP/FGV because it is an index that has a consistent and long series, whereas the official consumer price index IPC/IBGE, that we often use in the text, was subjected to methodological changes (vectors) in the 1986, 1987 and 1989 freezes.
4. Actually this spread varied strongly during the year, as successive speculative attacks against the novo cruzado raised it. The government responded to these attacks with its only and self-defeating weapon: the increase of interest rates.
5. The difference between the public deficit (public sector borrowing requirements in operational terms) and the public sector interest burden is the primary or non-interest deficit. Only in 1987 and 1989 did Brazil present a primary deficit.
6. The IPC for a given month, m, is calculated taking the average prices between the sixteenth day of m-1 and the fifteenth of m, and comparing them with average prices collected between m-2 16 and m-1 15. Thus the IPC for month m is actually an approximation of the price increases taken place in the previous month, m-1.
7. This consensus was only broken by a few populist economists who either insisted that a budget deficit is acceptable when there is no full employment (actually Brazil was near full employment in 1989) or said that to reduce the stock of public debt was a more effective way to stabilize the economy than to cut the budget deficit, which was essentially a financial or structural deficit.
8. To quote only the first complete statements about the theory of inertial inflation in Brazil: Bresser Pereira and Nakano, 1983; Arida and Rezende, 1984; Lopes, 1984).
9. The real interest rate on Treasury bills was high between 1981 and 1984, and in 1988 and 1989, when monetarist policies prevailed. It was low or negative in 1985–86 for populist reasons. At the end of 1986, with the creation of a new system of Treasury bills, whose rate of interest was defined daily (the LBCs, Letras do Banco Central, and LFTs, Letras Financeiras do Tesouro, that replaced the OTNs, Obrigaçíes do Tesouro Nacional), it was possible to limit speculation and to reduce the rate of interest on the overnight market. In 1987 the government was able to pay low interest rates while maintaining a positive interest rate in the financial market. The trade-off was to make the money supply additionally endogenous.
10. The figures in Table 3.4 overestimate the interests on the internal debt and the public deficit. They were calculated by the Central Bank using as deflator the IPC of the month t. As the acceleration of inflation was very strong in 1989 this methodology is not acceptable. Since the IPC measures inflation with a lag of about one month, an alternative deflator ($t+1$ *IPC*) may be used. According to this more correct methodology the interest on the domestic debt will fall to 4.3 per cent of GDP in 1989; for the

other years it will probably turn negative. The public deficit in 1989 will fall to 7.2 per cent of GDP.
11. In the German monetary reform of June 1948, for instance, the conversion factor between Reich marks and Deutsche marks was 10 to 1. Thus 90 per cent of the old Reich marks were confiscated, whereas in Brazil the novos cruzados (the old money) have just been blocked.
12. M4 was NCz$ 4.2 trillions (US$ 100 billion, considering the official exchange rate on 16 March of 42.3 cruzeiros per dollar). Around US$ 33 billion were converted into cruzeiros, initially leaving US$ 77 billion blocked in novos cruzados.
13. There are no official figures about the operational deficit in 1989, but the estimates are around 7 per cent. Part of this increase can be explained by the extraordinary acceleration of inflation and the active interest policy adopted by the former government.
14. For financial asset holders who made their investment at the end of February this did not represent a loss, since the rate of inflation 'point to point', from 28 February to 31 March, was around 40 per cent. For investors who bought their financial assets before, however, there may have been a loss (that is, the government got a debt reduction) since there was some underestimation of inflation that would be compensated by the official rate of inflation of 84 per cent in March.
15. See Rangel, 1963, Kaldor, 1970; Merkin, 1982; Bresser Pereira and Nakano, 1983; Davidson, 1988. Merkin's paper includes a survey on the subject.
16. We are considering a GDP of US$ 365 billion dollars.
17. The stabilization plan did not change the rules of the financial market regarding the overnight deposits. It continued to be possible to transfer every afternoon (until 1 p.m.) part of the cash deposits to overnight deposits and have them automatically transformed into cash deposits next morning. Thus the increase of M1 and the reduction of the overnight deposits were smaller than if the government had established a minimum maturity of one week for Treasury bills. If something had been done in this direction the confusion about what is money and what is not would have been reduced, although not eliminated.
18. Real interest rates just after the plan were very high. They went down as nominal interest rate was lowered by the authorities (or by monetary policy). In early May they were still very high. In June, as inflation accelerated and the Central Bank did not acknowledge the fact, they became increasingly low and finally negative.
19. The consumer price index of March, utilizing the traditional methodology of comparing the average prices of the month against average prices of the previous month, was 84 per cent.
20. Average real wages decreased by 22·6 per cent from February 1989 to February 1990, according to the FIESP index of real wages (indexated by inflation of the next month ($t + 1$) because the consumer price index (IPC/IBGE) has a lag of one month). In March the real wage reduction had fallen to 10 per cent. In June, giving the pressure of unions, the great public issue relating to the plan was the 'compensation of losses' suffered by workers.
21. Workers, acting according to the previous wage law which indexed wages according to inflation (IPC/IBGE) of the previous month, demanded a wage increase of 84 per cent for April and 44 per cent for May (total of 166 per cent), whereas actual inflation, calculated according to the end of the month/end of the month methodology instead of the average of the month methodology, was 3·3 per cent in April and 6·2 in May.

REFERENCES

Arida, P. and A. L. Resende (1985), 'Inertial inflation and monetary reform', in J. Williamson (ed.) (1985), originally presented in a seminar, Washington, Institute of International Economics, November 1984.

Blejer, M. and N. Liviatan (1987), 'Fighting Hyperinflation: Stabilization Strategies in Argentina and Israel, 1985-86', Staff Working Papers, International Monetary Fund.
Bresser Pereira, Luiz Carlos (1988a), 'A Brazilian approach to external debt negotiation', *LASA Forum*, vol. XIX, no. 4, Winter 1989. Paper presented to the XIV LASA Congress, New Orleans, March 1988.
Bresser Pereira, Luiz Carlos (1988b), 'Two Brazilian price freezes'. Paper presented to the seminar *Run-away Inflation: Austerity at What Cost?: Argentina, Brazil and Israel*, School of International and Public Affairs, Columbia University, 25 March 1988, *Revista de Economia Política*, vol. 8, no. 4, October.
Bresser Pereira, Luiz Carlos (1990), 'The perverse logic of stagnation: debt, deficit and inflation in Brazil', *Journal of Post Keynesian Economics*, vol. 12, no. 4, Summer.
Bresser Pereira, L. and Y. Nakano (1983), 'Fatores aceleradores, mantenedores e sancionadores da inflação'. Proceedings of the *X Encontro Nacional de Economia da ANPEC*, Belém, December. Republished in Bresser Pereira and Nakano (1987, ch. 2).
Bresser Pereira, L. and Y. Nakano, (1987), *The Theory of Inertial Inflation*, Boulder: Lynne Riener Publisher.
Bresser Pereira, Sylvio (1990), 'O erro básico do Plano Collor', *Folha de S. Paulo*, 4 April.
Davidson, Paul (1988), 'Endogenous money supply, the production process and inflation analysis', *Economie Apliquée*, vol. 16, no. 1, 1988. Paper presented in Ottawa, October 1984.
Dornbusch, R. and S. Fischer (1986), 'Stopping hyperinflation: past and present', *Weltwirtschaftliches Archiv*, vol. 22, January.
Feldman, Gerald, C. Holtfreisch, G. Ritter and P. Witt (eds) (1982), *The German Inflation*, Berlin: Walter de Guyter.
Helpman, E. (1988), 'Macroeconomic effects of price controls: the role of market structure', *Economic Journal*, vol. 98, no. 391, June.
Kaldor, Nicholas (1970), 'The new monetarism', *Lloyds Bank Review*, July.
Kiguel, M and Liviatan, N. (1988), 'Inflationary Rigidities and Orthodox Stabilization Policies: Lessons from Latin America', *The World Bank Economic Review*, vol. 2, no. 3, September.
Lopes, Francisco L. (1984), 'Inflação inertial, hiperinflação e desinflacão', *Revista da ANPEC*, no. 7, December.
Merkin, Gerald (1982), 'Towards a Theory of the German Inflation', in Gerald Feldman *et al.* (1982).
Nakano, Yoshiaki (1989), 'Da Inércia Inflacionária à Hiperinflação', in J. M. Rego (ed.) (1989).
Papageorgiou, D., A. Choksi and M. Michaely (1990), 'Liberalizing foreign trade in developing countries: the lessons of forty years of experience', Washington: World Bank, working paper, May.
Pastore, Afonso Celso (1990), 'A reforma monetária do Plano Collor', in Clóvis de Faro (ed.), *Plano Collor: Avaliação e Perspectivas*, Rio de Janeiro: Livros Técnicos e Científicos.
Rangel, Ignácio (1963), *A Inflação Brasileira*, Rio de Janeiro: Tempo Brasileiro.
Rego, José Márcio (ed.) (1989) *A Aceleração Recente da Inflação*, São Paulo: Bienal.

Toledo, Joaquim Elói (1990), 'Plano Collor em zona de perigo', *Jornal do Economista*, no. 25, May.
Williamson, John (ed.) (1985), *Inflation and Indexation: Argentina, Brazil and Israel*, Cambridge: MIT Press.
Yeager, Leland B. and associates (1981) *Experiences with stopping inflation*, Washington, American Enterprise Institute for Public Policy Research.

4. A Post Keynesian Approach to Inflation, High Inflation and Hyperinflation

Fernando J. Cardim de Carvalho*

I A PERSPECTIVE ON INFLATION

Modern market economies are built on the assumption of stable prices. Time-related production and accumulation activities in a complex system of input/output interactions demand the development of forward contractual relations. The possibility of calculation which underlies decisions of firms to produce and to invest demands a unit of value that is recognized by all participants and that is expected to remain stable over time to serve efficiently as money-of-account to the acceptance of contractual obligations. Contracts denominated in a common unit are, then, a vital institution to connect agents in a market economy in a point in time and over time (Keynes, 1982, XXVIII, pp. 252, 255; Davidson, 1978).

Agents may have 'real' goals but money is their common language and the contract system serves to establish the code of this language. Price stability then means that the 'meaning' of a given money sum is intelligible to the agents entering into a contract, allowing them to judge whether or not to accept its terms.

Obviously, it is not thought to be required that prices should be absolutely stable. One could even doubt whether the notion of an absolute value of money makes any sense (Keynes, 1971, V, book II). What is important is the 'convention' of stable prices, the general belief that no systematic or irreversible general price level changes can take place that could invalidate monetary calculations. This convention sustained the inelasticity of price-expectations that characterized much of the history of modern capitalism, at least until recently.[1]

In the post-Second World War period, the situation changed. In contrast with cyclical movements around a zero (or quasi-zero) trend, one began to observe price movements around clearly ascending trendlines.

Periods of deflation became rare or non-existent. After a timid appearance in the 1950s, inflation grew steadily in the 1960s and early 1970s, and was put under relative control afterwards through policies that did not hesitate to sacrifice employment and income to obtain some measure of stability. In South America the changing environment was, if anything, much more visible. Much higher inflation rates were reached as early as the late 1950s and the evolution of prices was generally even worse in the following three decades.

Despite this worsened state of affairs, the performance of most of these economies was very satisfactory, at least until the early 1970s when stagflation ensued. This raises one important question: how much inflation could a country endure while still sustaining adequately its production activities?

A post Keynesian answer to it would focus on how and how far institutions are changed to deal with inflation. History has presented us with three kinds of experiences in relation to prices: (1) stable prices and transient moderate inflation, where no institutional change was introduced; (2) moderate to high long-term inflation, where innovations are introduced, notably indexation; (3) extremely high rates of inflation in explosive processes, called hyperinflations, where no institutional change is introduced in time to avoid disintegratory pressures on the economy. Of these three kinds of experiences, the second group is much less known. In fact, for a long time, countries like Brazil seemed to suggest that high rates of inflation could be neutralized by the device of indexation, allowing the coexistence of inflation with growth for an indefinite period of time.

In the 1980s, however, highly inflationary economies, with different degrees of contract-indexation, seemed to have met the limits of this institutional 'innovation', showing that tolerance of inflation is not increased indefinitely by indexation. As a matter of fact, indexation created a new contractual system with its own vulnerabilities. To characterize this new situation there was adopted the expression 'high inflation',[2] a notion to be explored below.

How do the new institutions affect the sources of uncertainty under which agents make decisions and, thus, both individual behaviour and social interaction? How is the coordination of productive and distributive activities affected? There is wide agreement around the proposition that inflation reduces the informational content of prices. As a consequence, it adds to the uncertainty under which agents have to make their decisions. It increases the possibility of making mistakes by misjudging the real 'meaning' of monetary values. High inflation rates, then, are a stronger factor of disorganization of economic life than low rates if the possibility and extent of misjudgements increase with the pace of inflation. To develop these points it is necessary to introduce a framework to treat decision making adequate to the specifically Keynesian notion of uncertainty. This is the subject of the next section.

II THE COORDINATION OF AN ENTREPRENEURIAL ECONOMY[3]

The Formation of Expectations

Real-world agents of entrepreneurial economies have to decide on 'policies' of prices and production (and investment) on the basis of whatever limited information they may possess. They have, to use Hahn's expression, to form 'theories' about their environment and to subject these theories to reality in tests that are not always entirely conclusive.

A 'theory' consists of the identification of a set of hypothetical outcomes of a given plan of action. To each outcome some degree of expected plausibility is attributed by the agent, varying from perfect possibility to impossibility.[4] One should note that the set of perfectly possible outcomes does not have to contain only one element. The decision-maker knows that he does not possess all the information necessary to identify a unique outcome of a given policy. Thus his 'theory' has to allow for different hypotheses about the nature of the missing pieces of information, such as, other agents' plans. As Shackle puts it:

> ... the knowledge which any person can possess of the present intentions and means of action of other people, and of what will be their reactions in the further future to each other's more immediately future acts, is so extremely slight and insecure that, in reality, the inner subset [that is, the set of perfectly possible outcomes] will always consist of a large number of hypotheses whose mutually most dissimilar members will differ from each other very widely. (Shackle, 1955, p. 14)

With a theory an agent can identify gains and losses that could plausibly follow a plan, choosing then the strategy that offers the preferred combination of possible losses and rewards (conceived *a priori*).

In the case of pricing policies, an agent's theory contains conjectures about size of markets, price and income elasticities, competitive policies, cost conditions and so on, but also hypotheses about relative prices that may influence customers, relative profitability of different activities, the expected evolution of input prices and other data that serve to orient the entrepreneur's decisions.

Coordination, Disappointments and Coordination Failures

We will say that decisions made by different agents are coordinated if the intersection between the inner subsets for a majority of them is non-empty.[5] In other words, coordination is achieved if policies are chosen that are consistent, so that they lead to results that do not falsify the theories of agents. As each agent accepts a given number of outcomes as perfectly possible, the space of coordination may have one, many or no elements, depending on how far there is a coincidence of individual inner subsets (Carvalho, 1990).

What would happen if agents were disappointed? A number of possibilities has to be examined. Let us see first the case of crucial decisions, that is, those that cannot be repeated. In this case, no relevant learning is possible, each experience is unique, so disappointment would just be an end to a given episode. This case is very important in Keynesian theory, especially in relation to investment decisions.

The choice of a pricing policy, in contrast, is in general a repeatable experiment. Pricing rules can be changed at short intervals in the light of actual observations. To decide on prices, therefore, agents are guided by what Keynes called short-term expectations.

Under normal or stable conditions these expectations may be believed to converge to consistent or 'equilibrium' values. Keynes himself assumed this convergence in *The General Theory* and made it explicit in a reply to a criticism by Hawtrey:

> Entrepreneurs have to endeavour to forecast demand. They do not, as a rule, make wildly wrong forecasts of the equilibrium position. But, as the matter is very complex, they do not get it just right; and they endeavour to approximate to the true position by a method of trial and error. Contracting where they find that they are overshooting their market, expanding where the opposite occurs. It corresponds precisely to the higgling of the market by means of which buyers and sellers endeavour to discover the true equilibrium position of supply and demand. (Keynes, 1973, XIV, p. 182)

Short-term expectations are continuously revised in the process of learning and adaptation. With a limited planning horizon, to create new theories on which to base radically new expectations 'would ... be a waste of time since a large part of the circumstances usually continue substantially unchanged from one day to the next' (Keynes, 1964, p. 51).

Thus, under stable conditions, one would be led to expect that disappointments of expectations, while unavoidable, could be part of a process of learning and adjustment of theories. The conditions for the convergence of individual theories are clear in Keynes's comments above: on the one hand, the mistakes must be limited to some neighbourhood of equilibrium (not to make 'wildly wrong forecasts') to allow clarification to become a process of increasingly precise focusing on the consistent values; on the other hand, the environment must be sufficiently stable to allow learning of the past to serve to focus decisions in the present.

If we are concerned with repetitive behaviour and the two conditions above are given, mistakes are not necessarily destabilizing in the sense that they are even expected by the decision-makers. As agents consider more than one outcome to be perfectly possible, observed data may differ from one period to the next without necessarily consisting in a disappointment. In contrast, if those conditions are absent, we may have a breakdown of theories. Agents are disoriented, adopting new theories built randomly and increasing the plausibility of non-coordination. Now disappointments do not tell the decision-maker how to correct them. Disequilibrium states confuse agents more and more.

In sum, unstable environments may lead agents to form 'wildly wrong forecasts'. In this case, coordination breakdown may take the place of clarification of expectations and the economy will suffer a crisis until new forms of coordination are recovered.

The larger the space of coincidence of theories, the greater the possibility of an outcome being seen as a confirmation of theories by a significant number of agents and, thus, the more stable this economy tends to be. Outcomes that fall into this 'corridor' (Leijonhufvud, 1981) will be absorbed by the economy without changes in the theories of agents. A narrow 'corridor' defines an unstable economy. In the following sections we will apply this approach to differentiate the notions of high inflation and hyperinflation and to evaluate the critical points of transition between one state and the other.

III INFLATION AS A COORDINATION FAILURE

Inflation and Relative Prices

Inflation is a problem because not all prices change at the same speed and therefore some change in relative prices results. Relative prices, however, change all the time for all kinds of reasons. The point, thus, is not the change in prices *per se* but changes that are caused by misinformation, sluggishness of reactions, contractual rigidities and so on.

In the *Treatise on Money*, Keynes criticized the efforts to separate real and monetary determinants of relative price changes. The idea that nominal variations, measured by a unique price index, can be isolated from 'real' changes is a fiction inadequate to entrepreneurial economies.[6] In any case, to some extent, relative price changes, as they happen all the time, must be part of the 'theories' decision-makers must entertain to decide on their pricing policies. These changes may be due to the traditionally 'real' arguments, like preferences or technical conditions of production, or to 'inflationary' pressures like wage demands, interest rate policies and so on. The occurrence of both kinds of change may be expected by the agent and thus be included in his theories. Low (even if persistent) inflation rates, thus, do not need to create special problems or induce institutional changes. This may lead to mistakes, but disappointments are part of the game and to some extent are allowed for. If the eventual losses or gains are contained in the acceptable interval (the inner subset) there is no reason to incur the costs of rethinking strategies. Evidence in favour of this hypothesis is given by the fact that low-inflation countries do not change their contractual institutions and, in particular, avoid introducing indexation.

Institutions, such as forward contracts, are crucial to monetary economies. They define a set of rules that are shared by agents, creating a stable environment in which to plan strategies, reducing the uncertainties of the future. Moreover, the longer an institution lasts, the more efficient it may become, since there is a strong component of 'learning by using' effect resulting from a continuous compliance with accepted rules. Of course, institutions cannot preclude losses with contingencies that are not explicitly allowed for. Institutional innovation occurs when these contingencies overcome the gains of sticking to the accepted rules. Strong shocks, that cannot be absorbed by the built-in defences, cause outcomes to emerge that are worse than the worst outcomes deemed *a priori* to be perfectly possible (and which the decision-maker had accepted to endure). New theories are then developed. Increased uncertainty surrounding the search for new forms of coordination leads to higher dispersion of theories and to a narrowing of the corridors of stability, intensifying thereby the overall systemic instability.

The relevant change therefore occurs if inflation accelerates. When prices rise much beyond what was expected by agents we may have a coordination problem. Now inflationary pressures differ from other sources of change by the intensity of the disturbance.[7] Persistence *per se* is not enough to lead to institutional change, but persistence of significantly high rates of inflation may lead agents to recalculate the costs of institutional innovation in the contractual system to take care of this new influence.

Indexation

When inflation accelerates agents begin to realize the costs of sticking to the assumptions of price stability on which the contract system is based.

An example of the way institutions are then changed is given by the Brazilian economy in the early 1960s. Agents had to form expectations about the behaviour of inflation and to translate them into the terms of money-denominated contracts. Long-term contracts, harder to adjust, were just eliminated. Labour and intersectoral conflicts to fix remunerations emerged, leading to strikes and supply shortages. The crisis that followed pointed to two alternative solutions: to fight inflation or to change the contract system. The notion that the first goal could only be achieved in the long run led to indexation.

This story is not exclusively Brazilian. Many countries flirted with the idea of indexation, seen as a way of drastically reducing the costs of conflicts for determining money payments. This is the main distinctive feature of what is now called 'high inflation'. A high inflation regime, therefore, is defined by the existence of one or more monies-of-account for forward contracts. These new units allow for *a posteriori* compensation for the depreciation suffered by the legal tender.

Indexed contracts have two elements: the choice of an adjustment index to correct for the loss of purchasing power of the legal tender and the choice of the period after which the correction will be paid.

The choice of an index, as Leijonhufvud (1981) pointed out, is not a trivial question. Different agents are concerned with different baskets of goods. The adoption of agent-specific baskets would mean the imposition of a barter economy, destroying the common measurement unit that allows economic calculus. In contrast, the adoption of one general price index will always penalize agents for whom that specific basket is inadequate.[8]

Even more important is the question of the extension of the adjustment period. Most of the mainstream models of indexation, in particular wage-indexation, suppose that it can make real wages rigid over time.[9] This assumption would only be valid if there were no delays between a rise in prices and its payment to wage-earners. As a matter of fact, real-world indexation systems contain two delays: (1) there is an interval of time necessary to collect and process price information; (2) payments are not made continuously, but at discrete points at the end of an established period (Frenkel, 1988). This means that payments are always adjusted by past, not current inflation. If inflation is increasing, integral compensation for past inflation cannot guarantee stable real incomes that depend on the current behaviour of prices.

Indexation, however, cannot be universal. Contractual incomes can be indexed, but flow supply prices cannot. Indexation means that periodically a given hierarchy of prices and incomes is restored. If the problem of inflation was to confuse relative price changes due to real and nominal causes, universal indexation would prevent all causes of relative price changes. Firms need to preserve the freedom of their pricing policy to adapt to market conditions. They are free to do so since most of them produce for the market instead of to order (see Davidson, 1978). Therefore flow supply prices may not be indexed.

This means that high inflation influences flow supply prices in a way that is different from the way it affects contractual incomes. As shown by Frenkel (1979), the firm knows that prices of inputs and labour in the future will be higher than they are now. For this reason, firms will increase their mark-ups on current production costs by as much as they judge necessary to allow them to buy inputs and labour in the future at the augmented prices. If the inflation rate is constant, we will see mark-ups that are higher than those in stable prices economies but that are also constant.

The Fragility of Indexed Systems

A high inflation regime is a very fragile arrangement. It constitutes a kind of knife-edge equilibrium in which agents compare their income losses (caused by lagged adjustment) with the saving in costs of conflict. Nobody can maintain their desired position, because peaks of real income reached when'corrected' payments are made begin immediately to be eroded by continuing inflation.On the other hand, firms have always to face the uncertainty of a dual system where production costs are at least partially indexed (labour costs, financial costs, taxes and so on) but their receipts are not. They have to engage in production processes without knowing how high some of their costs are really going to be. Firms that lose relative position, because they do not react as quickly as others to inflation, will see their costs increase with the average price level.

The root of fragility lies in the fact that contracts are indexed to the past while flow supply prices are 'indexed' to the (expectations of the) future. As long as the future repeats the past, the system works. However shocks can sever the past from the future, causing prices and contractual incomes to move in incoherent ways. With constant inflation rates income losses relative to their peak will also be constant and if they are lower than the estimated costs of conflict the system will last. Predictability will increase and production may then proceed as if prices were stable. If, on the other hand, the system receives a shock, which may be, for instance, a supply shock such as the oil price rises of the 1970s, or expectational shocks (when agents for some reason expect some acceleration of inflation), it can degenerate into a hyperinflation.

The fragility of the context is aggravated by the reduction in the field of action of economic policy resulting from institutional change. We cannot fully develop this point here but we may mention some of the constraints on policy. Monetary policy is doubly affected. To the extent that financial contracts are indexed, the supply of legal tender has to increase as the value of debts in terms of it increases. Indexed contracts are enforced by the State so the State has no choice but to supply as much legal tender as may be necessary to enforce them. In addition, interest rate policies are also made rigid. Money rates have to follow inflation to be competitive with indexed financial instruments. With high inflation, to do otherwise would cause a 'flight from money' to goods or to foreign assets that would intensify the disorganizing pressures already contained in the system.

Fiscal policy will also meet some important difficulties. Many government expenditures will be indexed. Certainly public debt will be subject to indexation. Government incomes, on the other hand, will suffer what is called the Tanzi effect: the lag between the tax-generating operation and the moment when the government actually receives the resources erodes the value of its receipts, causing deficits to emerge even in a budget that would otherwise be balanced. This imbalance will emerge even if taxes are indexed and will be worse the higher is the rate of inflation.[10]

In conclusion, a high inflation regime is an unstable system in which the possibility of coordination failures is institutionalized. Agents are always striving to recover their 'losses', only to see new ones appear. As long as these losses are contained in an acceptable interval, the system can work and, with a favourable environment, even prosper, as the Brazilian economy did in the late 1960s and early 1970s. However the system could not resist the crisis that came later. In countries like Argentina, which did not quite share the prosperity of those years, the crisis was permanent (see de Pablo and Dornbusch, 1988).

IV HYPERINFLATION AS A COORDINATION BREAKDOWN

The Transition to a Hyperinflation

Inflation reflects an inconsistency between the demands that are posed to the social product and is, therefore, a coordination failure. The high inflation regime does not solve or remove this inconsistency. Rather it organizes these demands, allowing each social group at a time to pose its demands.

We cannot say *a priori* how much acceleration inflation can suffer before indexation itself ceases to be seen as an efficient contractual instrument leading agents to search for other theories to orient their behaviour that eventually may cause a hyperinflation. Hyperinflations seem still to be too rare to allow stylization into a general model.

The European hyperinflations took place in economies that were not used to inflation and that were also going through some special kind of difficulties, such as, for instance, Germany's need to pay for war reparations in the 1920s. In modern times, hyperinflations are a threat to countries long used to inflation, like Argentina, Brazil or Bolivia.

A hyperinflation is taken to be a mode of forming prices where expectations of future inflation and defensive strategies against it are the main (and practically the only) determinants of current decisions by all agents. In a first stage, the breakdown of rules leads to wildly divergent expectations and to entirely inconsistent pricing policies. In a second stage, agents search for new units in terms of which they may recover the possibility of calculation. Some coordination is recovered and price stabilization can be successfully attained.

The existence of these two stages is clearly suggested in Bresciani-Turroni's classic 1937 study of the German hyperinflation. In it we can see that the period until August 1923 was characterized by a markedly divergent behaviour of prices (Bresciani-Turroni, 1989, ch. 1, graphs 5 and 6), followed by a strictly coincident path of relevant prices, pegged to the US dollar, revealing that the economy had found in the exchange rate a new source of information around which agents could form consistent 'theories' and coordination could be recovered (ibid., graph 7).

The passage to a hyperinflation can occur if excessive pressure is put on the institutions that define high inflation. External shocks, external debt servicing, sharpening of public sector disequilibria, attempts to anticipate stabilization policies – all these factors or expectations can influence current pricing rules because, as we saw, flow supply prices are not subjected to indexation. They are the open valve through which these pressures can be introduced into the contractual system, ultimately to destroy it.

Expectations of future acceleration of inflation lead firms to anticipate it by increasing their current mark-ups to cover for future cost increases (and to avoid being left behind in relative terms). As Frenkel (1979) has shown, with changing inflation rates the uncertainty of the pricing decisions increases. Now the firm has to choose between two risks. On the one hand, there is the income risk, which is the possibility of marking up too high prices and facing a lower than expected demand. On the other hand, there is a capital risk, which is the risk of fixing too low prices and being unable to buy inputs and labour. The experience of countries like Brazil suggests that with accelerating inflation capital risk becomes more important than income risk. If the firm overshoots the 'equilibrium' price it accumulates liquid capital which will not only surely increase in value with the continuance of inflation but also serve as collateral for short-term credit. Capital losses, in contrast, have nothing to attenuate their effect: they constitute a net wealth loss for the firm. In sum, facing the choice between too low or too high prices, the safest policy is to overshoot. It is interesting to note that this may become a self-fulfilling prophecy. If most firms overshoot, the price level will be higher and their strategy will be vindicated.

The Critical Stage of Hyperinflation

If pricing rules are altered in this manner the contractual institutions that define high inflation may collapse. The acceleration of price increases will depress real income between adjustments beyond what was expected and accepted by agents that saw indexation as a useful device. If the loss is meaningful agents will ultimately try to contain damages by reducing the duration of the period between adjustments.

The shorter this period, *ceteris paribus*, the lower is the loss. At the limit, if money incomes could be instantaneously adjusted to any price increase, no real loss would take place. Of course, the combination of this feature and mark-up pricing would lead to an explosion of prices. Long before this limit could be approached, however, the contractual institutions would already have been radically changed. On the one hand, shorter adjustment periods demand other kinds of indices than price indices. In most cases, the new adjustment index was the exchange rate to the dollar. Contracts cannot, however, in most cases, be enforced in dollars in countries with their own legal tender. This means that the uncertainties surrounding deals in dollars can only be accepted in the very short term. Besides, in countries where exchange markets are controlled the dollar may not reflect adequately price trends, inducing additional distortions in the pricing rules.[11]

The abandonment of accepted indexation practices feeds back into the pricing rules of firms that try to develop quicker means of reaction to the new pressures. The acceleration of the whole process makes it increasingly difficult to keep it ordered. Firms have to develop their own system of information and can no longer wait to see what others are doing. The disappearance of a common information source leads to widely divergent decisions. Drastic changes of pace take place and expectations become very elastic to current disappointments. Lagging behind competitors may be fatal: it is necessary to move all the time to try to stay put.

In this sense, a hyperinflation is not just a system where inflation rates are higher than before. Actually rates are higher than before because accepted coordination devices and sources of information collapse.[12] The breakdown of the indexation system destroys the last remnants of liquidity that the legal tender could still possess and the most visible hyperinflationary phenomenon, the flight from money, then takes place. Uncertainty overcomes all. Nothing but the shortest-term plans are actually implemented. Conflicts are intensified. This is the critical stage of a hyperinflation.

Dollarization and Recovery

The critical stage of a hyperinflation reflects the workings of an economy where firms and other agents lose every notion of normality. Heterogeneous expectations lead them to paths that are so entirely inconsistent that one cannot know with any degree of confidence what lessons to extract from disappointments. The only general rule is to avoid lagging behind others at any cost. The inflation rate jumps from one month to the next but the average price level conceals a high degree of dispersion, causing heavy windfall gains and losses to be distributed in an unpredictable fashion.

Keynes observed that paralysis in the face of uncertainty is not an acceptable choice for practical men. They try to

> behave exactly as we should if we had behind us a good Benthamite calculation of a series of prospective advantages and disadvantages, each multiplied by its appropriate probability, waiting to be summed. (Keynes, 1973, XIV, p. 114)

Calculation demands a unit of account. With the collapse of local alternatives agents sooner or later find in foreign monies a more efficient alternative unit. Historically, this foreign money has been the American dollar. Dollar prices of internationally tradable goods may serve as the anchor to the price system. The hierarchy of relative prices can be restored and a measure of normality is reintroduced. When these relativities are recovered, conditions are ripe for the recreation of a local money-of-account (Kaldor, 1982). Writing from Germany in June 1923, Keynes observed:

> The fresh collapse of the mark is a symptom of the progressive deterioration of Germany's economic position. Nevertheless, the adjustment between internal prices and external exchanges is now so rapid that the practical importance of the movement may be overestimated.... Debts expressed in mark have long ceased to be of any importance; wages and prices are adjusted rapidly; and people in Germany now hold such small quantities of cash in the form of marks that the injury inflicted on individuals, even by a big collapse, is not so

considerable as might be supposed. (Keynes, 1978, XVIII, pp. 161–2)[13]

The recuperation of a money-of-account is, then, the strategic factor in ending a hyperinflation. Hyperinflation creates an acute conscience of the need for a stable money and induces agents to search for that stable money themselves. In a high inflation regime, in contrast, the apparent normality of things sustained by indexation works as a powerful impediment to the adoption of more efficient stabilization policies. The discomfort and uncertainty of walking on a tightrope are concealed from agents as long as they do not move too much or too quickly. The risk of falling into the abyss of hyperinflation is, however, ever present.

The 1980s witnessed some attempts to achieve the stability that comes at the end of hyperinflations without suffering the coordination collapse of their beginning. Brazil, Argentina and Israel imposed stabilization plans which contained sophisticated price- and wage-freezing formulas conceived to obtain the zeroing of past inflationary losses and recoordinating agents around the new structure of relative prices. With the partial exception of Israel, where some special conditions applied (Bruno and Piterman, 1987), these policies did not work. After brief periods of stability, inflation returned stronger than before.

One important feature to be considered about the European experiences with hyperinflation was the 'memory' of stability. Their past history, as Keynes observed, was marked by a stable trend in prices. As a result,

> A sentiment of trust in the legal money of the State is so deeply implanted in the citizens of all countries that they cannot but believe that some day this money must recover a part at least of its former value. (Keynes, 1920, p. 224)

For these countries inflation was a temporary episode. Price stabilization was equivalent to going back to normal, secular habits and customs, to well-known rules. It is a very different situation for countries living with high inflation. For these, inflation was a mode of life implanted even in their material structure. Banks, for instance, have too many branches in order to gather interest-free deposits wherever possible. Entrepreneurs, accountants, brokers, unions – all of them have their views shaped by inflation. High inflation, lasting for so long, has accustomed people to think in terms of large numbers. To be aware of the rapid movement of prices is more vital than being aware of productivity gains, for instance.

Finally, while hyperinflation synchronizes price changes, in a high inflation regime price and incomes changes are scattered over time. This means that, if prices in the last stage of hyperinflation do achieve some measure of equilibrium (and then all move together, preserving that equilibrium), with high inflation at any point in time there are always those who are lagging behind in an arbitrary set of relative prices. A hyperinflation process may be suddenly stopped. High inflation processes demand some kind of 'correction' of relative prices and incomes.

V CONCLUSION

We began this chapter with the question of how much inflation is tolerable in an entrepreneurial economy. There is a critical range of rates that may take an economy from a stable-prices regime into a high inflation regime. A contract system is never entirely contingency-proof. If a contingency becomes systematic and strong enough to overcome compensating influences, contractual institutions are changed to deal with them. Annual inflation rates around 20 to 30 per cent have been sufficient to induce the introduction of institutional innovations in the contractual system that significantly changed the stability properties of these economies.

Indexation of contracts, however, does not eliminate the coordination failures reflected by inflation. It serves mainly to organize demands on the social product that remain inconsistent. The system is fragile and under sufficiently strong pressures or shocks it may degenerate into a hyperinflation. There is also a critical point beyond which a high inflation regime may pass into a hyperinflation. This will happen when the gains of having an organized system of claims to the social product, represented by indexation, are exceeded by the intensification of losses between periods of adjustment when inflation accelerates for any reason.

A hyperinflation is a state of coordination breakdown. But chaos is not a sustainable state. When the national money-of-account is completely destroyed, practical men search for substitutes. The adoption of the dollar as a surrogate money-of-account allowed the re-establishment of a common base of information allowing relative prices to be redefined around the dollar price of internationally tradable goods.

A hyperinflation, destructive as it is, allows an inflationary economy to erase its past. Stabilization should be accompanied by institutional reforms that could strengthen confidence in the newly-achieved stability.

A post Keynesian perspective allows the identification of behavioural and institutional changes, especially in the contractual system, as the relevant argument to understand the differences between plain, high and hyperinflation much beyond the usual approach, confined to an *ad hoc* classification of rates.

NOTES

* The author wishes to acknowledge the financial support of the National Research Council of Brazil (CNPq).

1. According to Keynes, the history of the nineteenth century confirmed these expectations: 'le caractère essentiel de cette periode fut la stabilité relative des prix. Les prix étaient approximativement les mêmes en 1826, 1841, 1855, 1862, 1867, 1871 et 1915. Ils étaient également semblables en 1844, en 1881 et en 1914' (Keynes, 1923, p. 29).
2. Term proposed by Frenkel (1979). Frenkel's perspective is actually (and explicitly) very close to the post-Keynesian approach to investigate behaviour under uncertainty and changes in contractual institutions as the way to approach fundamental aspects of capitalist dynamics.
3. Entrepreneurial economy is a term proposed by Keynes, when writing *The General Theory*, that defines the kind of economy he was studying in contrast to the neoclassical view of an economy dominated by independent consumers, aptly nicknamed by Minsky as the 'village fair' paradigm. The characteristics of entrepreneurial (or monetary production) economies are discussed by Keynes in Keynes, 1979, XXIX, and 1973, XIII.
4. The argument in this section is based on Shackle (1955). In Carvalho (1990) the present author discusses the compatibility between Shackle's scheme of potential surprise and Keynes's view of probability and uncertainty, the role of learning and adaptation, and the implications of this treatment for defining concepts of equilibrium and stability of equilibrium for entrepreneurial economies.
5. We are using the term coordination in the sense proposed by Leijonhufvud (1981), that is the global compatibilization of individual policies. General equilibrium is a form of compatibilization achieved through the determination of a price vector that induces consistent transactions. Without the auctioneer coordination may or may not be achieved. In any case, under uncertainty activities may be coordinated even if not perfectly compatible, as argued below.
6. There is a vast literature on the 'real' nature of money in entrepreneurial economies. A sample would include, besides Keynes's *General Theory*, Davidson, 1978; Chick, 1983; Kregel, 1988.
7. In this sense, the critical point for switching institutions would be reached when inflation exceeded, in a permanent and unambiguous way, other factors of change in the economy, such as productivity and growth in the availability of resources.
8. See Keynes, 1971, v book II, for an extensive discussion of the impossibility of finding one price index that could be generally satisfactory and of the illusion of finding an absolute measure of the value of money.
9. See, for instance, Gordon (1983) and Benassy (1984).
10. In fact other factors operate to reduce the efficiency of fiscal policies under high inflation. As Heymann and others (1988) have shown, budget calculations become very uncertain and programmed expenditures often exhaust assigned resources very early in the fiscal year. As a result the decision on additional provision of funds is taken outside the process of budget fixation, favouring special-interest political deals and reducing the macroeconomic efficiency of the State.
11. This is the case of Brazil. The monopoly of exchange operations detained by the government cannot avoid the existence of a black market for the dollar. The official market is controlled by the government. The relative small dimension of the free segment of the market on the other hand makes it very vulnerable to pressures from individual speculators, reducing drastically its 'informational content'.
12. The Brazilian government has tried in recent months to manipulate overnight interest rates to follow its expected rate of inflation. When inflation accelerated in the last quarter of 1989, these rates were kept even higher than expected inflation. Some firms in Brazil in the hyperinflationary months of January and February of 1990, as reported in the main financial newspaper of the country, *A Gazeta Mercantil*, increased their prices every week according to that rate plus some 'safety margins' that are set between 10 and 20 per cent more.
13. '... in Germany in September 1923, everything from newspapers to railway tickets and to daily wages was "indexed" to the daily market price of the US dollar ... so there was no accumulated backlog of wage and price adjustments left. If the dollar remained

unchanged for a day, prices and wages ... remained stable for the day ...' (Kaldor, 1982, p. 61). In contrast, as late as the end of 1922, there was still some heavy foreign bullish speculation with the mark on the expectation that it would recover its former value! See Bresciani-Turroni, 1989, pp. 53, 79.

REFERENCES

Benassy, J. P. (1984), *Macroéconomie et Théorie du Déséquilibre*, Paris: Dunod.
Bresciani-Turroni, C. (1989), *Economia da Inflacao*, Rio de Janeiro: Expressao e Cultura.
Bruno, M. and S. Piterman (1987), 'Israel's Stabilization: A Two-Year Review', mimeo.
Carvalho, Fernando (1990), 'Expectations and the Coordination of an Entrepreneurial Economy', discussion paper, Universidade Federal Fluminense.
Chick, Victoria, (1983), *Macroeconomics after Keynes*, Cambridge, Mass.: MIT Press.
Davidson, Paul (1978), *Money and the Real World*, London: MacMillan, 2nd ed.
de Pablo, J. and R. Dornbusch (1988), *Deuda Externa e Inestabilidad Macroeconomica en la Argentina*, Buenos Aires: Sudamericana.
Frenkel, Roberto, (1979), *Decisiones de Precio en Alta Inflacion*, Buenos Aires: Estudios CEDES.
Frenkel, Roberto, (1988), 'Extension de Contrato y Efectos Ingreso: Aspectos de la Dinamica Inflacionaria en Economia Indexada', Documentos CEDES, n. 6.
Gordon, R. J. (1983), 'A Century of Evidence on Wage and Price Stickiness in the US, the UK and Japan', in J. Tobin (ed.), *Macroeconomics, Prices and Quantities*, Washington: Brookings Institution.
Heymann, D. and others (1988), 'Conflicto Distributivo y Deficit Fiscal: Algunos Juegos Inflacionarios', *Anais do XVI Encontro Nacional de Economia*, Belo Horizonte: ANPEC.
Kaldor, Nicholas, (1982), *The Scourge of Monetarism*, Oxford: Oxford University Press.
Keynes, John Maynard (1920), *The Economic Consequences of Peace*, London: MacMillan.
Keynes, John Maynard, (1923), *La Réforme Monétaire*, Paris: Le Sagittaire.
Keynes, John Maynard (1964), *The General Theory of Employment, Interest and Money*, New York: Harcourt Brace Jovanovitch.
Keynes, John Maynard (1971–83) *The Collected Writings of John Maynard Keynes*, London: MacMillan and Cambridge: Cambridge University Press. Volumes are identified by number (roman) and date of publication.
Kregel, Jan (1988), 'Irving Fisher, Great-Grandparent of The General Theory', in P. Maurisson (ed.), *La 'Théorie Générale' de J. M. Keynes: Un Cinquantenaire*, Paris: L'Harmattan.
Leijonhufvud, Axel (1981), *Information and Coordination*, New York: Oxford University Press.
Shackle, George Lennox Sharman (1955), *Expectation in Economics*, Cambridge: Cambridge University Press.

5. What International Payments Scheme Would Keynes Have Suggested for the Twenty-first Century?

Paul Davidson

Except for perhaps a few all-too-brief years in the 1930s, the development of monetary and international trade theory on which many policy prescriptions are based has been dominated by a pre-Keynesian, that is neoclassical, logic which assumes away questions that Keynes thought of as fundamental to a market-oriented, money-using economy. These problems, which are extremely relevant for understanding current international economic relations, involve liquidity, persistent and growing debt obligations, and the importance of stable rather than flexible exchange rates.

An example of the sanguine neoclassical response to Post Keynesians raising these issues is Professor Milton Friedman's response to me in our 'debate' (1974) in the literature. Friedman stated: 'A price may be flexible ... yet be relatively stable, because demand and supply are relatively stable *over time*. ... [Of course] violent instability of prices in terms of a specific money would greatly reduce the usefulness of that money' (Friedman, 1974, p. 151). It is nice to know that as long as prices or exchange rates remain stable over time there is no harm in permitting them to be flexible. The problem arises when exchange rates display volatility. Should there be a deliberate policy which intervenes in the market to maintain relative stability or should we allow a completely free market to determine the price? Keynes helped design the Bretton Woods Agreement to foster action and intervention, Friedman has sold the public on the beneficence of inaction and the free market determination of exchange rates.

Since the breakdown of Bretton Woods, it has been popular to assume that freely fluctuating exchange rates in a *laissez-faire* market system are efficient. Every well trained neoclassical economist, who is logically consistent with a Walrasian, Arrow–Debreu microfoundation, 'knows' that the beneficial effects of a freely flexible exchange rate include:

1. the impossibility of any one country running a persistent balance of payments deficit;
2. permitting each nation to pursue monetary and fiscal policies for full employment without inflation independent of what is occurring in its trading partners;[1] and
3. encouraging the flow of capital from the rich creditor (that is, developed) nations to the poor debtor (that is, less developed) nations. This capital flow is the result of a neoclassical belief in the universality of the 'law of variable proportions' which determines the real return to the factors of production.[2] The effect of this normal neoclassical international capital flow is to encourage more rapid development of the LDCs and hence, in the long run, a more equitable distribution of the rapidly growing global income and wealth. Moreover, it is often implied that investment projects financed by this free market capital flow from rich to poor nations will generate sufficient sales and foreign earnings for the LDCs to repay the capital loans; that is, the international capital flows are temporary *and self-liquidating*.[3]

When we look at the facts since the break-up of Bretton Woods, however, the evidence does not appear to be consistent with these neoclassical Panglossian promises. Freedom of movement of 'flight capital' has only made it easier to hide income and wealth from tax collectors and profits from drug and other illegal transactions from law enforcement agencies, thereby encouraging uncivilized behaviour by self-interested economic agents – and thus imposing an important, if often neglected, real cost on society.[4] More importantly, flight capital has drained resources from the relatively poor nations towards the richer ones, resulting in a global inequitable redistribution of income and wealth, thereby increasing the immiseration of a majority of the people on this planet.

The floating exchange rate system has not permitted the panacea of full employment without inflation – despite the glowing promises made by monetarist economists in the 1960s and 1970s. Even London's *Financial Times* and *The Economist*, both previously strong advocates of floating exchange rates, have recognized that the system was a failure and was sold to the public and the politicians under false advertising claims.[5] The world-wide Great Recession of 1979–82, engineered by the Federal Reserve attempting to end double-digit inflation in the US, has made an obvious mockery of the monetarist's claim that nations will be able to practise independent monetary and fiscal policies. Indeed, in recent years, the major industrial nations have seen it as imperative to coordinate monetary and exchange rate policies. The last time that the US and Germany publicly clashed over incompatible monetary policies (in September 1987), the great October 1987 crash of world financial markets followed. This experience has reinforced the idea among the central bankers of the developed nations that if they do not all hang together they will all hang separately.

During our great neoclassical experiment of floating rates, the world has experienced more global stagnation plus periodic bouts of inflation dampened by increasing world-wide rates of unemployment, and a horrendous growth of international debt obligations accompanied by a growing inequitable international distribution of global income – as many of the rich nations got richer, while most of the poor nations got poorer on a per capita basis and suffered huge 'flight capital' losses to the wealthy. The resulting free market exchange rates have rarely reflected purchasing power parities. Moreover one nation, the US, seems to be able to take advantage of the existing system to obtain a 'free lunch', that is, to run massive perpetual trade deficits.

KEYNES'S VIEW

Keynes objected to the view that a free market determination of exchange rates would automatically produce economically desirable results. In 1941 he wrote, 'To suppose that there exists some smoothly functioning automatic mechanism of adjustment which preserves equilibrium if only we trust to methods of *laissez-faire* is a doctrinaire delusion which disregards the lessons of historical experience without having behind it the support of sound theory' (Keynes, 1980, pp. 21–2).

Keynes explained that the "main cause of failure" of traditional exchange rate systems

> can be traced to a single characteristic. I ask close attention to this, because I shall argue that this provides a clue to the nature of any alternative which is to be successful.
>
> It is characteristic of a freely convertible international standard that it throws the main burden of adjustment on the country which is the *debtor* position on the international balance of payments – that is, on the country which is (in this context) by hypothesis the *weaker* and above all the *smaller* in comparison with the other side of the scales which (for this purpose) is the rest of the world. (Keynes, 1980, p. 27)

If the global economy is to avoid persistent deflationary forces, then a system has to be developed to transfer 'the *onus* of adjustment from the debtor to the creditor position', and 'aim at the substitution of an expansionist, in place of a contractionist, pressure on world trade' (Keynes, 1980, p. 176).

WHAT ARE THE EXISTING, ALTERNATIVE INTERNATIONAL PAYMENTS SYSTEMS?

Those nations that are generally perceived in the media as the most economically successful in the period since Bretton Woods – Germany, Japan, and the NICS – have not permitted market-determined, freely flexible exchange rates. The EEC, led by Germany, has attempted to maintain a relatively fixed exchange rate among a subset of trading partners, while 'permitting' – within reason – market determined floating exchange rates with other trading partners.[6] There is, however, no real basis in neoclassical logic for this schizophrenic exchange rate policy consisting of fixed exchange rates within an arbitrarily determined regional 'common market' and floating rates between the market and its other major trading partners. Justification for fixity within a common market and flexibility between market trading partners must ultimately be a pragmatic one. For example, the fact that the US as the world's largest common market maintains a fixed exchange rate among the dollars issued by the 12 regional Federal Reserve Banks provides a role model for the EEC.[7] Since the US economy has been so successful, at least until the 1980s, then a fixed exchange rate between all regions of a common market is apparently a good thing. If, however, we envision the goal of a global common market in the twenty-first century, then does not this imply that a global set of fixed exchange rates is a good thing? And, if so, how can this be compatible with the neoclassical claim that flexible exchange rates between regions is the system which promotes economic efficiency without inflation or persistent regional debt creation?

THE KEYNES–POST KEYNESIAN ALTERNATIVE VIEW

In contradistinction to the neoclassical analysis, Keynes's *General Theory* developed an alternative *analytical* monetary approach. Keynes (1936, p. 16) argued that neoclassical theorists were like Euclidian Geometers in a non-Euclidian world who,

> discovering that in experience straight lines apparently parallel often meet, rebuke the lines for not keeping straight – as the only remedy for the unfortunate collisions which are occurring. Yet in truth there is no remedy except to

throw out the axiom of parallels and to work out a non-Euclidean geometry. Something similar is required to-day in economics.

The Keynesian Revolution in theory therefore requires economics to 'throw out' the fundamental neoclassical axioms of the neutrality of money and gross substitution in developing the equivalent of a non-Euclidean economic theory for a non-neoclassical real world.[8] (Cf. Davidson, 1984.) In Keynes's non-Euclidean world, (1) monetary and exchange rate policy has short-run and long-run real effects on output, employment and resource flows among nations; (2) the rate of inflation is neither directly nor solely related to the rate of growth in the money supply; and (3) in the absence of specific governmental or international cooperative policies to prevent creditors from amassing continuing surpluses, trade deficits resulting in unemployment and slow growth can persist without being cured by changes in the exchange rates while perpetuating a recessionary bias to both the debtor and creditor economies. In recent years, only the Post Keynesian school has attempted to revive Keynes's revolutionary insights on the role and relevance of Monetary Policy in a global economy without money neutrality and without the assumption of a ubiquitous gross substitution.

A Lesson from the Post-Second World War History

In the two decades following the Second World War, major central banks around the world followed, more or less, the role that Keynes had justified for them in his *General Theory* – namely to provide an endogenous (real bills) money supply at low interest rates to support expansion of aggregate demand. While exchange rates were fixed under the Bretton Woods Agreement, the major creditor nation, the US, holding the major creditor position, attempted to avoid amassing surplus international reserves via the Marshall Plan and other foreign grants and aid. Hence the US unwittingly accepted Keynes's 1941 suggestion of bearing the major burden of balance of payments adjustments with the rest of the world. As a result a post-war depression was avoided and, for a quarter of a century after the Second World War, the US and its major trading partners experienced unprecedented long-run rates of real economic growth.

When the US withdrew from the Bretton Woods Agreement, the last vestiges of Keynes's enlightened monetary approach was lost – apparently without regret or regard as to (1) why the system had been developed in the first place; and (2) how well it had served the free world to recover from a devastating war which had destroyed much of the stock of capital accumulated over many decades. In the almost two decades since the breakdown of Bretton Woods, the world's economy performance has been unable to match what had become almost routine economic success in terms of low (from hindsight) rates of global inflation accompanied by high rates of employment and real growth. Instead international economic problems have multiplied.

Except for the US, any nation that tried to lift its (and its trading partners) economic growth performance by pursuing Keynes's policies for increasing domestic effective demand and creating 'real bills', and thereby committing its economy to an 'engine of growth' role, was quickly saddled with increasing international deficits for its laudatory efforts. The early socialist Mitterrand Administration in France, for example, was forced by its balance of payments deficits to abandon its brand of Keynes-type expansionary programmes and adopt conservative neoclassical stances.

Luckily for the free world, the Reagan Administration did not put 'its money where its neoclassical mouth was'. Despite his rhetorical support for neoclassical policies of balanced budgets and free market interest and exchange rates, that great Keynesian in the White House, Ronald Reagan, benignly neglected the internal and external deficits created by his Keynesian deficit spending policies. This expansionary policy stimulated, via the US propensity to import, world economic growth. Simultaneously, the Federal Reserve has supported this expansionary fiscal programme with a loose monetary policy. In the US in the six years between December 1981 and December 1987, for example, M1 increased 71 per cent, M2 increased 62 per cent and M3 rose 61 per cent while interest rates on three-month Treasury Bills declined from 14.029 per cent to 5.82 per cent. The US current account balance went from an annual surplus of $7 billion in 1982 to an annual deficit of $160 billion in 1987. With the decline in the dollar and in dollar oil prices in 1988 and early 1989, the US trade deficit improved as US exports increased, while the market value of the largest commodity component of US imports (oil) dropped significantly, even though the physical quantity of oil imported rose. By the end of 1989, the US trade deficit bottomed out at approximately $110 billion. With imports of barrels of crude oil rising over the next few years, if the dollar price of oil remains stable or rises the US trade deficit is not likely to improve much further.

In sum, the history of unprecedented economic success for a quarter-century after the Second World War and the Reagan expansion of the 1980s demonstrate the appropriateness of Keynes's logic compared to the neoclassical view. In the last section a Keynes-type international payments system will be proposed which will continue the progress the capitalist system has shown *vis-à-vis* the planned economies of Eastern Europe and China.

INTERNATIONAL LIQUIDITY AND RESERVE RECYCLING – NECESSARY CONDITIONS FOR WORLD PROSPERITY

A necessary, but not a sufficient condition for a significant expansion of production to occur in any market-oriented, entrepreneurial economy is a monetary payments system which endogenously expands to meet the needs of trade. Whenever entrepreneurs are unable to obtain sufficient additional financial commitments from bankers today to undertake expanded activities tomorrow (no matter how profitable these future production activities are expected to be in the future when output is sold to the final buyer) firms will not hire additional resources and expand their working capital positions. This requirement of increasing liquidity provisions to entrepreneurs to permit expansion of productive activities has a long history in economics, known as the *real bills* doctrine.

If, in addition to this endogenous monetary system there is provision for one or more entities who can always spend (or absorb) the necessary liquid reserves to act as a 'balancing wheel' spender or liquidity sponge in order to maintain full employment effective demand,[9] then the resulting economic system has built-in necessary and sufficient conditions for economic prosperity.

In capitalist economic systems, the normal problem is a lack of effective demand owing to liquidity hoarding and/or inadequate endogenous monetary responses to entrepreneurial financial needs and/or insufficient private 'animal spirits'. There are two situations where monetary (liquidity) shortages, resulting from a payments system that does not adequately accommodate, can limit production flows before full employment:

1. *The recessionary case* occurs when income earners allocate current 'savings' into idle surplus liquid reserves and refuse either to spend these savings directly on the products of industry or to lend (or give) them to others who wish to spend these on current output.
2. *The inability to expand production case* occurs when the payments system is unable, or unwilling, to expand financial reserves as rapidly as profit maximizing entrepreneurs desire to expand output. Without financial facilities to meet increased payrolls and raw material costs, entrepreneurs cannot undertake increased production activities, no matter how profitable they expect the sales from these expanded activities to be.

Accordingly, any well-designed international payments mechanism should provide for an accommodating (endogenous) system which not only supports, but encourages, spending to approach global full employment levels. This means that the system must provide entrepreneurs with financial facilities *at favourable terms*. The system must be able to create and maintain an adequate volume *and* distribution of an asset of ultimate reserve as quickly as entrepreneurs are capable of expanding production flows for international trade. There should be a built-in bias towards increasing member reserves as global productive capacity grows, as well as recycling idle reserves, preferably at little or no cost to the user. The user of otherwise liquid idle reserves is providing a useful function for society by paying otherwise involuntarily unemployed resources to produce goods. By definition, spending these liquid reserves provides additional utility to society in excess of the disutility involved in these productive activities. From a global utilitarian standpoint, as long as there are people who prefer employment to leisure we should not permit those with surplus credit accounts either hoarding reserves or draining them from the system and therefore imposing leisure on willing workers in the global economy.

Recycling Liquidity at Less Than Full Employment

Given some initial level of global effective demand, the development of any trade imbalances between regions – even those in a common market with a unionized monetary system (UMS)[10] – can induce recessionary liquidity (payments) problems which ultimately reduce production and thereby lower the real income of inhabitants of both the trade deficit and trade surplus regions. Since the trade deficit region's spending (cash outflow) on production from the surplus region exceeds its cash inflow (earning on sales) from those who have deposits in the surplus region's banks, it quickly runs out of export earnings to maintain its import purchases. In the absence of deliberate offsetting action by the monetary authority or the central government, these cash flow imbalances will create a loss of reserves and hence liquidity from the deficit region's banks. The deficit region can continue to finance the trade imbalance of imports over exports only as long as it is able either to (1) sell pre-existing liquid reserve assets to residents or bankers in the trade surplus region; (2) borrow funds from the surplus region by selling foreigners new debt contracts (or pledging other liquid financial assets); or (3) sell the family jewels, that is, equity rights in the otherwise illiquid and unique assets of the deficit region to foreigners.[11]

Neoclassical economists presume that the trade deficit cannot be expected to continue indefinitely since the deficit region's holdings of family jewels, liquid assets, and its creditworthiness are all limited. The surplus region's inhabitants are 'rational' self-interested agents and, therefore, will not continuously give up currently produced real goods for an undetermined period in exchange for promises (to pay back real goods) which are never redeemable. In other words, there is a presumption that the deficit will not be financed indefinitely (or at least as long as necessary) via unilateral transfer payments or accepting promissory notes which are never called. (Yet, as suggested above, unilateral transfers via the Marshall Plan were in the self-interest of both the deficit and surplus regions.)

Of course, if both regions are encompassed within the same national boundaries, then domestic monetary and/or fiscal policy may be used to recycle and even create additional reserves to be used to finance continually the trade imbalance. The nation's central bank could rediscount the deficit nation's promissory notes, or engage in differential interest rate policies or impose lower reserve requirements on deficit region banks. In recent years, however, the burden for maintaining reserves in deficit regions of a nation have been accepted by the central government whose enlightened taxation and spending policy can act as a unilateral transfer mechanism – even perpetually if desired or necessary. The magnitude of trade deficit finance thus provided depends on the tax burdens of each region and the central government's propensity to spend in the deficit region *vis-à-vis* the surplus region. Experience has shown that such regional transfers can create economic benefits for both regions if used to promote economic expansion and hence real income for the deficit region and markets for the industries of the surplus region (as with, for example, the development of TVA (Tennessee Development Authority) during the Great Depression).[12]

National monetary and fiscal policy administered by *pro bono publico* officials can help to offset the deflationary pressures which interregional trade deficits can generate. Unfortunately no global supranational *pro bono* monetary and/or fiscal authority is likely to be created in the foreseeable future – although the US Marshall Plan and US government military and economic aid programmes to LDCs have often played that fiscal role since the Second World War. In the days of 'cold war' politics superpowers provided unilateral transfers to LDC client states. As long as the cold war did not escalate to actual hostilities, superpower politics played an important role in fostering economic growth in Europe and many LDCs. With the sudden end of the cold war in 1989, the political need of the superpowers to provide economic aid in client states will diminish and, *ceteris paribus*, the gap between the rich and poor nations will widen. (In Appendix A, we show, using the Post Keynesian tool of Thirlwall's Law, the potential dismal future awaiting the LDCs if the world's payment system continues to perpetuate a balance of payments constraint which forces the major adjustments to be made by the debtors.)

WHAT CAN BE ACHIEVED?

In an interdependent world economy, trading partners must cooperate economically.[13] The twenty-first century global economy cannot rely on the accident of conservative presidents becoming great 'Keynesians' in the White House[14] – any more than it should suffer when Liberal Democrats such as Jimmy Carter enter the White House and embark on fiscally conservative, neoclassical policies which push the global economy in a contractionary direction.[15]

Furthermore, an important, if often unstated, reason why most of the world other than the US has become disenchanted with the current system is that it seems to permit only one nation – the US – to obtain a 'free lunch' by running what appears to be a decades-long (perpetual?) trade deficit. But, under the current system, since the US is the *de facto* central banker for the world, the rapid growth of its outstanding liabilities financed the significant economic growth of the developed capitalist world in the 1980s (compared to the stagnation of the post-Bretton Woods 1973–80 period).

Although advocated for the wrong ideological and political reasons, the Reagan long-term expansionary deficit policy was the 'engine of growth' for the US and, via the US income elasticity of demand for imports, for the entire developed capitalist world. It made the economic performance of Eastern Europe and the Soviet Union look paltry by comparison.[16] The Mexican debt default in 1982 forced the Federal Reserve to abandon its monetarist stance, just as the Reagan expansionary deficit policy took hold. The Federal Reserve therefore provided additional major reserve assets for liquidity holdings for high-saving trading partners such as Japan, Germany, and the newly industrialized countries (NICs). These high savers were willing to adopt export-led growth as the only acceptable expansionary policy; fears of inflation and/or balance of payments constraints prevented them from adopting a path of expansion via domestic demand stimulation. Consequently world-wide expansion required the US to issue dollar liabilities – because the surplus trade nations, as part of a deliberate policy, would not live up to their means! The resulting visible prosperity, in a world of international TV pictures, helped bring down the Berlin Wall, but simultaneously provided the central banker with what appeared to be a 'free lunch'.

The latter effect does not sit well with the rest of the world, partly because it does not see the connection between successful export-led growth policies of large developed nations and the free lunch of the trading partner. Hence, from a political standpoint, one of the selling points of the proposal that follows is that this new system will provide a global expansionary bias similar to the Reagan engine of growth period without simultaneously providing a free lunch for any trading nation.

I propose the creation of an institution based on the payment principles embedded in the real bills doctrine plus the creation of conditions to encourage 'balance wheel' spending in the international sector. This does not necessarily require the establishment of a Supranational Central Bank to create a UMS – even if this is believed desirable on other grounds. At this stage of the evolution of world politics, a global UMS is not feasible.[17] The following proposal is aimed at obtaining an international agreement among those nations and existing regional UMS's who do not wish to surrender further control of their local banking systems and fiscal policies, but yet wish to cooperate in a global payments mechanism which fosters expansion and economic prosperity.

The minimum requirement is a *closed*, double-entry bookkeeping clearing institution to keep the payments score among the various trading regions – similar to the Interdistrict Settlement Fund of the Federal Reserve – plus some mutually agreed upon rules, which (1) prevents a lack of global effective international demand due to any member(s) holding excessive idle reserves or draining reserves from the system; (2) provides an automatic mechanism for placing a major burden of trade imbalance adjustments on the surplus nations; (3) provides each nation with the ability to monitor and, if it desires, to control significant movements of flight capital and, thereby, as an added bonus, making tax-avoidance and profits from illegal trade more difficult to conceal; and (4) expands the quantity of the asset of ultimate redemption as global capacity warrants.

Some elements of such a clearing system would include the following:[18]

1. The unit of account and ultimate reserve asset (that is, the ultimate asset of redemption amongst regions) for purposes of international liquidity is the International Money Clearing Unit or IMCU. All IMCUs are held *only* by central banks, not by the public.
2. Each nation's or UMS's central bank is committed to guarantee one-way convertibility (at a fixed bid and asked price) from the IMCU unit of account for deposits at the international clearing union to its domestic money. Each central bank will set its own rules regarding making available foreign monies (via IMCU clearing transactions) to its own bankers and private sector residents.[19]

   Since central banks agree to sell their own liabilities (one-way convertibility) against the ICMU only to other central bankers and the International Clearing Agency while they simultaneously hold only IMCUs (no foreign currencies) as liquid reserve assets for international financial transactions, there can be no draining of reserves from the system. The provision of foreign exchange to domestic residents will be concentrated in the hands of central bankers.[20] All significant private international transactions ultimately clear between central banks on their own account within the international clearing institution.[21] Each central bank will have the ability to monitor and control, if desired, all private international transactions, thereby making criminal payments and tax-avoidance activities much more difficult to hide from the legal authorities.

3. Contracts between private individuals will continue to be denominated into whatever domestic currency permitted by local laws and agreed upon by the contracting parties. Contracts to be settled in terms of a foreign currency will therefore require some announced commitment from the central bank (via their regular banker) of the availability of foreign funds to meet such private contractual obligations.

4. An overdraft system to make available short-term unused creditor balances at the clearing house to finance the productive international transactions of others who need short-term credit. The terms are determined by the *pro bono publico*, clearing managers.

5. A trigger mechanism to strongly encourage any creditor nation to spend what are deemed (in advance) by agreement of the international community to be 'excessive' credit balances at the clearing union. Such excessive credit balances could be spent in three ways: (i) on the products of any other member of the clearing union; (ii) on direct foreign investment; or (iii) to provide unilateral transfers (foreign aid) to deficit members. In the unlikely event that the surplus nation does not spend or give away these credit balances within a specified time period, then the clearing agency would confiscate (and redistribute to debtor members) the portion of credits deemed excessive.[22]

Under the current international payments system, nations may run trade deficits because other nations are not living up to their means – that is, because other nations are oversaving and hence there is a lack of global effective demand. Under provision 5, such deficit countries would no longer have to reduce their real income (to deflate the real economy) merely to adjust their payments imbalance. Instead the system would remedy the problem by increasing opportunities to sell abroad.

6. A system to prevent the purchasing power of the IMCU in terms of each member nation's domestically produced market basket of goods from being eroded whenever a nation experiences inflation in the prices of goods it produces. This requires a system of fixed exchange rates between the local currency and the IMCU which changes only to reflect permanent increases in efficiency wages.[23] Each central banks

can therefore hold IMCUs and assure its citizens that the nation's reserves will never lose purchasing power in terms of foreign-produced goods, even if a foreign government permits wage-price inflation to occur in its domestic industries.

Under this provision, the exchange rate between the local currency and the ICMU would vary with inflation in the local money price of the domestic commodity basket. If, on the other hand, increases in productivity led to declining domestic money production costs, then the member nation with this decline in efficiency wages (say of 5 per cent) would have the option of choosing either (i) to permit the IMCU to buy (up to 5 per cent) less units of domestic currency, thereby capturing all (or most of) the gains from productivity for its residents, or (ii) to keep the exchange rate constant. In the latter case, the gains in productivity would be shared with all trading partners in exchange for an increasing relative share in the world market of the industries who have shown gains in productivity.

By altering the exchange rate between local monies and the ICMU to offset the rate of inflation of a basket of goods in terms of each domestic money, the IMCU's purchasing power is stabilized. By restricting use of ICMUs to central banks, private speculation regarding ICMUs as a hedge against inflation is avoided. Each nation's rate of inflation in terms of its local currency would then be determined solely by the local government's policy towards the level of domestic money wages and profit margins *vis-à-vis* productivity gains; that is, the domestic incomes policy (or lack of one) for stabilizing domestic purchasing power in terms of a domestic commodity standard.

Although provision 5 prevents any one country from piling up a persistent excessive surplus, this does not mean that it is impossible for one or more nations to run persistent deficits. If a country is at full employment and still has a tendency towards persistent balance of payments deficits, then it does not possess the productive capacity to maintain its current average standard of living for its inhabitants. If the payments deficit is due to a trade imbalance and this fully employed nation is a poor one, then surely there is a case for the richer nations who are in surplus to transfer some of their excess credit balances to support the poor nation.[24] If it is a relatively rich nation – in a globally fully employed world – then the deficit nation should be required to alter its standard of living by reducing its relative terms of trade with its major trading partners.

If, on the other hand, the payments deficit persists despite a positive balance of trade, this is evidence that the deficit nation is carrying annual international debt servicing obligations that are too heavy for its economy. The *pro bono* officials of the clearing union should bring this debtor and its creditor nations into negotiations to reduce annual debt service payments via (1) lengthening the payments period, (2) reducing the interest charges, and/or (3) debt forgiveness.[25]

If any nation objects that the IMCU provisions provide governments with the ability to limit the free movement of funds, then this nation would still be free to join other nations of similar attitude in forming a regional currency union (UMS) and thereby ensuring as free a flow of funds as the nations within the UMS will permit amongst their own inhabitants.

These proposals are suggestions of possible actions which should be discussed at a new Bretton Woods-type international conference. These propositions should not be considered unalterable either in principle or for practical reasons. I would hope they would provide the basis for the beginning of a sound analytical discussion of how to prepare for a twenty-first century international monetary system.

The problems facing the international payments system are not easily resolved. If we start with the defeatist attitude that it is too difficult to change the awkward system we are enmeshed in no progress will be made. We must reject such defeatism at this exploratory stage and merely ask whether these particular proposals for improving the operations of the international payments system will create more difficulties than other proposed innovations. The health of the world economic system will not permit us to attempt to muddle through!

APPENDIX A: THIRLWALL'S LAW – AN EXTENSION OF THE HARROD TRADE MULTIPLIER

Professor A. P. Thirlwall has developed Harrod's initial trade multiplier mechanism into a demand-driven model of economic growth.[26] By demand-driven we mean that the model does not make the neoclassical presumption of continuous global full employment. Consequently it does not assume that long-run economic growth is exogenously determined by technological progress and labour force growth. Thirlwall develops a simple relationship which indicates the rate of growth which a nation can achieve without suffering any deterioration of the trade balance. Thirlwall's balance of payments constrained growth rate is developed from the following model:

$$X_a = (P_d/P_f)^z Y^e_{rw} \qquad (5A.1)$$
$$M_a = (P_d/P_f)^u Y^e_a \qquad (5A.2)$$

where X_a and M_a are exports from nation A and imports into A during a period, (P_d/P_f) is the ratio of domestic prices to foreign prices expressed in terms of the domestic currency of A, z is the price elasticity of demand for A's exports, u is A's price elasticity of demand for imports, e_a is A's income elasticity of demand for imports, and e_{rw} is the rest of the world's income elasticity of demand for A's exports. If either z and u are small and/or relative prices do not change significantly, then, as a first approximation, one can ignore substitution effects and concentrate on income effects. Taking the natural logs of equations (5A.1) and (5A.2) and ignoring substitution effects, one obtains Thirlwall's Law of the growth of income that is consistent with an unchanged trade balance as

$$y_a = x/e_a \qquad (5A.3)$$

where y_a is the rate of growth of nation A's GNP, x is the rate of growth of A's exports, and e_a is A's income elasticity of demand for imports. Since the growth of exports for A depends primarily on the rest of the world's growth in income (y_{rw}) and the world's income elasticity of demand for A's exports (e_{rw}), that is,

$$x = (e_{rw})(y_{rw}) \qquad (5A.4)$$

so that equation (5A.3) can be written as

$$y_a = [e_{rw}y_{rw}]/e_a \qquad (5A.5)$$

According to Thirlwall's law, if international payments balance is a constraint, then, starting from a position of international payments balance the rate of growth that a nation can maintain depends on the rest of the world's growth and the relevant income elasticities for imports and exports.

If the growth of imports is to exactly equal the growth in the value of exports,

$$e_{rw}y_{rw} = y_a e_a \qquad (5A.6)$$

then

$$[y_a/y_{rw}] = e_{rw}/e_a \qquad (5A.7)$$

The ratio of the growth of income in nation A compared to growth in income in the rest of the world is equal to the ratio of the income elasticity of demand for A's exports by the rest of the world to A's income elasticity of demand for imports. Thus, for example, if $e_{rw}/e_a < 1$, and if growth in A is constrained by the need to maintain balance of payments equilibrium, then nation A is condemned to grow at a slower rate than the rest of the world.

If, for example, less developed nations (LDCs) of the world have a comparative advantage in the exports of raw materials, and other basic commodities for which Engel's curves suggest that the developed world will have a low income elasticity of demand, while the LDCs have a high income elasticity of demand for the manufactured products of the developed world, then for most LDCs

$$[e_{rw}/e_{ldc}] < 1 \tag{5A.8}$$

Accordingly, if economic development and balance of payments equilibrium are left to the free market, the LDCs are condemned to relative poverty and the global inequality of income will become larger over time.

Moreover, if the rate of population growth in the LDCs (p_{ldc}) is greater than the rate of population growth in the developed world (p_{dw}), that is, if $p_{ldc} > p_{dw}$, then the rate of growth of GNP per capita of the LDCs will experience a greater relative decline to the standard of living of the developed world, that is,

$$[y_{ldc}/p_{ldc}] < < [y_{dw}/p_{dw}] \tag{5A.9}$$

In the absence of Keynesian policies to stimulate growth, the long-term growth rate of the developed world taken as a whole tends to be in the 1–2.5 per cent range. As long as the developed world's population growth is less than its long-term growth rate, however, these nations can still enjoy a rising living standard.

If, however, we accept the reasonable values for the parameters implied in inequality (5A.9), then, since $y_{ldc} < y_{dw}$, while $1 < y_{dw} < 2.5$, a dreary prognostication for the global economy emerges. As long as the world permits the free market to determine the balance of payments constraint on each nation, then a shrinking proportion of the world's population may continue to get richer (or at least hold their own), while a growing proportion of the earth's population is likely to become poorer. Moreover the slower the rate of growth in income of the rich, the more rapidly the poor are likely to sink into poverty.

Thus there is an obvious case for exploring whether there is some policy intervention that can be developed to prevent market-determined balance of payments constraints from condemning the majority of the world's population to increasing poverty. Only if the rich can achieve historically high real rates of growth experienced in the first 25 years since the Second World War, where Keynesian rather than free market policies were actively pursued domestically and internationally by the developed world, can we hope significantly to improve the economic lot of the poorer nations of the world.

Finally, since we have argued that the US has not been constrained by Thirlwall's Law, equation (5A.8) can be interpreted in a different light for the US. Given the US rate of growth under Reagan since 1982, if one assumes the import and export income elasticities of demand (e_{rw} and e_a) are fixed, then solving equation (5A.8) for y_{rw} yields the income growth that would have been required of the US's trading partners in order to eliminate the US trade deficit. Alternatively, if y_{rw} is presumed unchanged, then solving for e_{rw} would be the required income elasticity necessary to avoid a US trade deficit.

Thirlwall's analysis demonstrates that international financial payment imbalances can have severe real consequences; that is, money is not neutral in an open economy. Keynes's *General Theory* was explicitly an analysis of a demand-driven, non-neutral money, closed economy. Hence it should be obvious that, if one expands Keynes's monetary analysis which emphasizes the liquidity motives of firms and households in the operation of an entrepreneurial production economy to an open economy, it should be possible to develop Keynes-like policy proposals to avoid the potential dire outcomes of a free market model based on Thirlwall's Law.

NOTES

1. In 1968, Professor Harry Johnson wrote (in *The Times* of London, 12 Sept. 'the basic argument for floating exchange rates is so simple that most people have considerable difficulty in understanding it ... a floating exchange rate would save a country from having to reverse its full employment policies because they lead to inflation and deficit'.
2. It assumes that the poor LDCs are capital-short and labour-rich, while the rich nations are capital-rich and labour-short. Accordingly the 'real' marginal product of capital must be higher in the LDCs than in the developed nations, and the real return on capital higher in the LDCs.
3. Apparently, neoclassical economists do not conceive of 'flight capital' as an economic problem. Indeed naive neoclassicists claim that those with wealth have the self-interest right in any circumstance to choose when and where they move their reserves, independent of the damage such moves may inflict on the national and international economy. But all the rights of the individual are always constrained by their potential impacts on society. For example, no one would defend someone shouting 'Fire' in a crowded auditorium as indisputably protected under an individual's right of free speech. In some circumstances, flight capital can cause more damage than yelling fire in an auditorium!
4. Floating exchange rates permit individual currencies to be valuable objects of speculation. Nations with banking institutions which make it difficult for foreign authorities to

obtain information regarding bank accounts held by their residents are likely to encourage the influx of funds trying to escape national tax collectors, criminal investigators and the central banks of nations that try to limit capital outflows. Thus it is not surprising that, often, exchange rates reflect speculative and flight capital flows, rather than purchasing power parity.

5. *The Economist* magazine (6 January 1990) indicated that the decade of the 1980s will be noted as one in which 'the experiment with floating currencies failed'. Almost two years earlier (17 February 1987) the *Financial Times* admitted that 'floating exchange rates, it is now clear, were sold on a false prospectus ... they held out a quite illusory promise of greater national autonomy ... [but] when macropolicies are inconsistent and when capital is globally mobile, floating rates cannot be relied upon to keep the current accounts roughly in balance'.
6. Similarly the successful NICs such as South Korea, Hong Kong, Taiwan and Singapore attempted, through most of the 1980s, to peg their currency to that of their major trading partner – the US. More recently, under tremendous political pressure from the US, these nations have permitted some limited exchange rate changes *vis-à-vis* the US dollar.
7. Each District Federal Reserve Bank is the 'central bank' for its region. Each District Bank is capable of issuing its own currency, but the exchange rate between, say, a Boston Fed dollar and a St. Louis Fed dollar is maintained at 1:1 by the Interdistrict Settlement Fund.
8. In 1933, Keynes (1973, pp. 408–10) specifically wrote that the 'monetary theory of production' that he was developing was based on the non-neutrality of money. In the *General Theory* (1936, ch.17) Keynes specifically attributes a zero elasticity of substitution as an essential property of money and all liquid assets *vis-à-vis* producible goods, thereby rejecting the ubiquitous applicability of the axiom of gross substitution.
9. A balancing wheel spender offsets private sector liquidity hoarding or overspending sprees.
10. In my *International Money and the Real World* (1982) I developed the concept of a unionized monetary system (UMS) for regions that, in essence, share a common currency to settle all contractual obligations among residents of the regions. This can be done either by having the same currency as legal tender or having a fixed exchange rate between the local currencies.
11. If the two regions are members of a UMS, adjustments via exchange rate changes are not possible.
12. If, for example, the deficit region is either undeveloped or an area of relatively high unemployment, modern non-conservative central government taxing and spending patterns are likely to permit the financing of regional deficits as long as these economic discrepancies between regions persist. Often it is recognized that such regional redistribution may have to continue indefinitely – if there are not sufficient regional development opportunities to permit these government transfers to be the equivalent of self-liquidating loans.
13. In *International Money and the Real World*, I have argued that this will ultimately require an international coordination of monetary, fiscal and income policies within any regime attempting to maintain a UMS among the regions in its community.

   Practical observation requires me to admit that politically it has become ever easier during the decade of the 1980s for governments to force an 'incomes policy' via deflationary monetary and fiscal policies than to operate under a direct incomes policy (and as a Tax-Based Incomes Policy) which would permit expansionary fiscal and monetary policies during a period of adjustment. Until such times as nations prefer to rely on domestic incomes policies which are compatible with *full employment* monetary and fiscal policies, it is unlikely that a coordinated, full employment expansionary international monetary system will be developed (except by accident at certain historical times).
14. It should be remembered that, since 1984, the US deficit on current account has greatly exceeded $100 billion in each year. Since Brazil, the second largest international debtor

has 'only' something slightly over $100 billion in total international debt, the US debt is equivalent to creating another Brazil each and every year for the last five years!
15. No one said that Keynes's revolutionary economic theory which was designed to save 'capitalism' was the sole domain of left-of-centre politicians.
16. Simultaneously it forced the Eastern block to waste precious resources on unproductive military expenditures.
17. This does not deny that some groups of trading partners may wish to integrate their central banks and banking systems into a regional UMS common market. If some nations were willing to develop an interregional UMS they would be free to develop their own UMS clearing mechanism which would operate as a single unit in the larger global clearing union proposed below.
18. As Keynes (1980, p. 168) indicated almost a half century ago,

> We need an instrument of international currency having general acceptability between nations . . . We need an orderly and agreed upon method of determining the relative exchange values of national currency units . . . We need a quantum of international currency . . . [which] is governed by the actual current [liquidity] requirements of world commerce, and is capable of deliberate expansion and contraction . . . We need a system possessed of an internal stabilizing mechanism by which pressure is exercised on any country whose balance of payment is departing from equilibrium *in either direction* . . . We need a method by which the surplus credit balances arising from international trade, which the recipient does not wish to employ, can be set to work . . . without detriment to the liquidity of these balances.

19. Correspondent banking will have to operate through the International Clearing Agency, with each central bank regulating the international relations and operations of its domestic banking firms.
20. Small-scale smuggling of currency across borders, etc., can never be completely eliminated. But such movements are merely a flea on a dog's back – a minor, but not debilitating, irritation. If, however, most of the residents of a nation hold and use (in violation of legal tender laws) a foreign currency for transactions and as a store of value (for example, it is estimated that Argentinians hold close to $5 billion US dollars) this is evidence of a lack of confidence in the government and its monetary authority. Unless confidence is restored, all attempts to restore economic prosperity will fail.
21. This is equivalent to requiring all transactions between Federal Reserve Districts to be cleared via the District Federal Reserve Bank through the Interdistrict Settlement Fund. Moreover each central bank may – but is not required to – provide its own currency to its domestic banking system in exchange for foreign currency accepted for deposit by bankers from their clients. It would then exchange this currency to the foreign issuer for credit in its clearing house account (provided that the issuing bank has agreed to exchange its currency for ICMUs at the clearing union). Thus is similar to the agreement that was in force in the Federal Reserve System until the mid-1970s. Until that time currency from one Federal District which showed up in the banking system of another district was returned, via the Interdistrict Settlement Fund.
22. Whatever 'excessive' credit balances are credited shall be apportioned among the debtor nations, perhaps according to a formula which is inversely related to each debtor's per capita income and directly related to the size of its international debt, to be used to reduce debit balances at the clearing union.
23. The efficiency wage is related to the money wage divided by the average product of labour; it is the unit labour cost modified by the profit mark-up in domestic money terms of domestically produced GNP.
24. This is equivalent to a negative income tax for poor fully employed families within a nation. (See Davidson, 1987–8 for further development of this argument.)
25. The actual programme adopted for debt service reduction will depend on many parameters, including the relative income and wealth of the debtor *vis-à-vis* the creditor, the ability of the debtor to increase its per capita real income, and so on.
26. A. P. Thirlwall, 'The Balance of Payments Constraint As An Explanation of Interna-

tional Growth Rate Differences', *Banca Nazionale del Lavoro Quarterly Review*, 1979, *128*, pp.45–53.

REFERENCES

P. Davidson (1982), *International Money and the Real World*, London: Macmillan.
P. Davidson (1982–3), 'Rational Expectations: A Fallacious Foundation for Studying Crucial Decision-Making Processes', *Journal of Post Keynesian Economics*, 5, Winter.
P. Davidson (1984), 'Revising Keynes' Revolution', *Journal of Post Keynesian Economics*, 4.
P. Davidson (1987–8), 'A Modest Set of Proposals For Solving The International Debt Problem', *Journal of Post Keynesian Economics*, x, Winter.
M. Friedman (1974), 'Comments on the Critics', in *Milton Friedman's Monetary Framework: A Debate with His Critics*, R. J. Gordon (ed.), Chicago. University of Chicago Press.
J. M. Keynes (1936), *The General Theory of Employment Interest and Money*, New York: Harcourt, Brace.
J. M. Keynes (1973), *The Collected Writings of John Maynard Keynes*, XIII, London: Macmillan.
J. M. Keynes (1980), *The Collected Writings of John Maynard Keynes*, XXV, London: Macmillan.
A. P. Thirlwall (1979), 'The Balance of Payments Constraint as an Explanation of International Growth Rate Differences', *Banca Nazionale del Tavoro Quarterly Review*, 168.

PART II

East and West European Reconstruction

6. A German Perspective of a European Single Market and EMU

Stephen F. Frowen*

In our time, if we compare the different nations of Europe, we find that the richest are also the most powerful, the most humane and the most happy.
 – Henry Thomas Buckle, *History of Civilization* (1857)

By the end of 1992 the European Community with Germany as its strongest member, will create a single market with all internal frontiers for goods, services, labour and capital removed. According to the original Treaty of Rome this degree of integration should have been achieved by 1970, but the partial realization of this aim did not include such essentials as the integration of markets for services and a complete liberalization of capital markets. And, despite the EC customs union that was achieved, the movement of goods was often hampered by such drawbacks as differential rates and structures of indirect taxes, the multitudes of technical standards and differences in licensing laws and regulations.

The world-wide structural breaks during the 1970s did nothing to further the process of integration. However it was the undoubted success of the European Monetary System (EMS) – coming into operation in March 1979, following planning and discussion initiated by the then President of the EC Commission, Roy (now Lord) Jenkins, in his Jean Monnet Lecture[1] delivered at the European University Institute in Florence on 27 October 1977 – and in particular the stabilizing effect of the European Exchange Rate Mechanism, which led to renewed attempts during the 1980s finally to achieve a single European market through the creation and acceptance by all member states of the Single European Act of February 1986. The objective of the latter is to ensure integration in the fields of monetary and fiscal policy, regional policy, technology, the freedom of establishment and mutual recognition of professional qualifications and socio-political issues. The Act was supplemented in the agricultural field by the Agricultural Reform of 1988.

To achieve the single European market, there has to be a complete liberalization in the four key markets; that is (1) the market for goods, (2) the market for labour and the professions, (3) the market for services, and (4) the capital market. For a single market to be complete and to function smoothly, the freedom in these markets has to be supported by a common monetary policy, far-reaching economic coordination, a common technology programme and integration in the sphere of social policy. A common fiscal policy is not generally regarded as a pre-condition for a single market, although a point at issue may be its necessity for a successful economic and monetary union. Attempts have been made to quantify the possible effect of liberalizing the markets themselves (see the optimistic Cecchini Report, 1988, and the more pessimistic view taken by Franzmeyer, 1989). A more difficult problem is to arrive at even rough estimates of the possible effect these supporting policies may have because of considerable divergencies in the view of member states with regard to these issues.

Largely responsible for the creation of the Single European Act, which sets out the conditions for the single European market, was the problem of what has been termed 'Eurosclerosis'. In addition, the financial innovations starting in the 1970s, first in the US and the UK, but not followed to the same extent in West Germany and Japan, played their part. Financial innovations ultimately led to a large-scale European integration of financial markets during the 1980s, and it was only natural for all other internal frontiers to be removed in due course.

The Single European Act changes the Treaty of Rome through Article 8a, which in fact places the freedom of capital movements as a vital prerequisite next in importance to the freedom in the goods, services and labour markets. The liberalization of capital markets is therefore no longer subordinated to the realization of the single European market but is an essential part of it. At the same time the framework for capital market liberalization has been greatly improved by placing the EMS (through adopting Article 102a) into the Treaty of Rome.

A set of macroeconomic objectives should be achieved through Article 104, which aims at the so-called magic pentagon, consisting of price stability, balanced growth, a maximum level of employment, converging living standards and the external equilibrium of the European Community. These aims are to be achieved largely through a European Monetary Union (EMU) aiming at totally fixed exchange rates, ideally a single European currency and an independent European System of Central Banks (ESCB) which would be entrusted with the conduct of monetary policy.

This chapter will be restricted to looking at the effect the single market is likely to have on some of the major aspects of the German economy and Germany's part in the establishment and running of the European Monetary Union.

THE SINGLE MARKET AND THE STRUCTURE OF WEST GERMAN INDUSTRY

Looking first at the possible effect of the single market on the structure of German industry, the indication is that the economic effect will probably reveal itself as an expansion and restructuring of trade flows. To be considered here is the fact that the unified Germany is likely to become not only the Common Market's but also the world's most important cross-border trading nation. So far just under one-third of the West German economy as a whole has depended directly or indirectly on exports. For the most important West German industries the degree of export dependence has amounted to nearly 60 per cent. In 1989, 55 per cent of total West German exports went to other EC countries (a rise from just over 50 per cent in 1986).

West Germany's specialization lies in the production of goods intensive in human capital, such as electrical and mechanical machinery and transport equipment, chemicals, pharmaceuticals and medical equipment, and is in these areas heavily engaged in research and development. Answers to questionnaires revealed that most German companies, regardless of the branch of industry and the size of the company, expect positive effects from the removal of non-tariff barriers, enabling a greater exploitation of comparative advantage. Expectations of considerable cost reductions resulting from the single market appear to be particularly strong in the Federal Republic of Germany (FRG). However there appears to be some apprehension regarding the adverse effect of a possible increase in company mobility which the single market may bring about.

Some studies, among them that by Franzmeyer (1988), have looked more closely at the possible and differing effect the single market may have on the main branches of German industry. Let us first take mechanical machinery – by far the largest German export sector, accounting for almost half of total investment goods exports. Here the impact of the single market could be expected to be positive. Intensified competition throughout the Common Market will require increased investment expenditure to raise efficiency. Secondly, higher growth rates throughout the Common Market will make the expansion of productive capacity desirable. Germany is likely to benefit from both trends and developments as she is the most important European producer of investment goods. No less than 56 per cent of total West German exports in 1989 consisted of investment goods. The mechanical engineering industry is likely to benefit most strongly from this. The pattern of the first German economic miracle following the currency reform of 1948 could repeat itself. Then, too, it was the ability of Germany to meet the upsurge in the demand for investment goods which led to a considerable and extended boom. The process now may be somewhat less dynamic but could still be quite considerable.

In contrast to mechanical machinery, the outlook for electrical machinery looks less promising. A significant number of German industrial companies still consist of small and medium-sized firms. They often specialize in supplying larger domestic industrial concerns. If the latter are subjected to stronger international competition, they in turn will try to reduce costs by putting pressure on their suppliers to reduce prices. In this sector the larger companies often supply nationalized industries in Germany, such as the electricity industry, railways and the telecommunication part of the postal services; so far they have faced little competition from abroad. In a single market and with the liberalization of the procurement of public works, a far sharper competition is likely to develop and could cause some problems for the electrical machinery industry. However electronics giants such as Siemens – already planning to invest more than one billion DM in East Germany, providing jobs for an estimated 30 000 workers – are likely to survive quite comfortably. Any negative effects for Germany in this industry could be compensated by the expected rise in the demand for investment goods. But this process will have consequences for the structure of industry.

For transport equipment – the third major export industry with an EC market share approaching 40% – the single market might well turn out to be favourable as a result of reduced protectionism in norms and standards within the EC. This might lead to cost reductions and an improvement in competitiveness, especially *vis-à-vis* Japanese exporters. The German passenger car industry, too, could show improved results if certain EC countries – especially the UK, France and Italy – should insist on retaining their present import protectionism *vis-à-vis* Japan and other third countries. So far German car manufacturers have had to cope with fairly unrestricted imports from third countries. If under the single market rules Germany had to follow the restrictive practices of some of the other EC countries, the market share of Japan and other third countries in EC car imports would fall, with the benefit going primarily to German car manufacturers.

Other factors favouring German car manufacturers lie in their concentration on the production of larger cars for which market trends in most EC countries point towards an increased demand. Here Germany has expert knowledge and experience, enjoying a certain superiority over car manufacturers in other EC countries who have so far specialized more in the production of smaller cars. Furthermore the benefits of a VAT reduction on the part of EC countries with, at present, high VAT rates would be more than proportionate for larger cars, again favouring German car exporters. There is also the possibility of stricter environmental laws pushing up the cost of car production. In Germany high standards in this respect have always been maintained. If other EC producers now have to raise their standards to those already existing in Germany, they will lose some of their relative cost advantage, giving further impetus to the German car industry. The demand for lorries is expected to rise throughout the EC following an increased intra-European division of labour and the liberalization of intra-European trade. A liberalized transport market leading to increased competition and price reductions is likely to favour road transport. Considering the environmental problems involved here, German producers of lorries, with their product quality, research input and financial strength, would appear to be strong competitors.

However, a word of caution may be justified to qualify the optimistic view taken above of the prospects for the German automobile industry after 1992. Some experts accept the view that the abolition of trade restrictions within the EC offers certain possibilities for cost reduction, but disagree with the *Ludvigsen Report* (1989) which maintains that the Single Market will benefit the European automobile industry only. They feel instead that Japanese competitors will profit from the removal of technical and fiscal barriers just as much. Furthermore, even after 1992 there will be no import restrictions on Japanese cars entering Germany. Trade measures will therefore not reduce Japan's market share. Although the EC Commission and the Council of Ministers have agreed to extend for a transition period the special rules applying to protected car manufacturers in France, Italy, Great Britain and Spain, competition on the hitherto free markets should not be influenced thereby. But an 'open' Europe has always been favoured by the German automobile industry.

The fourth among the German key export sectors comprises chemicals, pharmaceuticals and medical equipment. Here the prospects look less favourable. The production centres are situated mainly in the Rhine valley, where strict environmental protection has been enforced, substantially raising production costs. The chemical industries in the UK, France and Italy have so far been much freer and are therefore enjoying a cost advantage. Stricter control, for medical and safety reasons, also characterizes the German pharmaceutical industry. The way the German health service is currently organized provides the industry with high profit margins, which act as a part compensation for the strict regulation. As the EC market segmentation breaks down, these margins are bound to suffer from increased competition.

In addition, as part of the West German government's attempt to reduce public expenditure, the German health service, too, is likely to come under increasing pressure to induce the medical profession to prescribe cheaper medicines in lesser quantity. Thus the prospect for German pharmaceuticals – in contrast to their counterparts in, for example, the UK – does not look too good. However, as in the case of electronics, the giants in this field are actively reviewing their position and will no doubt cope. The larger multinational groups and some of the medium-sized companies have been operating in the EC through subsidiaries for a number of years, a process which is likely to intensify to avert any negative impact of the Single Market. The smaller companies' survival rate is far less secure.

COMPANY MOBILITY

Estimates as to the effect of the single market on the four key sectors of the German export industry are of course based on the assumption of no structural change in the location of industry. However company mobility might well become a more crucial issue once the single market is completed. The degree of mobility would depend firstly on the degree of restrictions on the movement of capital and services, secondly on regional differences in production costs, thirdly on the extent to which growth centres are regionally dislocated, and fourthly on the importance to companies of a direct presence in any new growth centres.

A vital question concerns the advantages and disadvantages of Germany as a location for production and investment. The FRG falls into a special category among other EC countries in the sense that it not only has a high wage level, but also high standards in the field of social security, consumer protection, technical security and the protection of the environment. It also has the most advanced system of worker participation in management and the most far-reaching control of mergers. In addition to all this, there is a relatively high corporation tax and a stiff top rate for income tax. All this is aimed at maximizing the quality of life and the effectiveness of the economic system as a whole. But the costs involved are high for industry. For example, the highest wages worldwide are now being paid by the German automobile industry. In an open economy, as the FRG economy will continue to be in the single market, either costs in excess of those in other EC countries will have to be offset by a rise in productivity exceeding productivity increases in competing countries, or the FRG will have to reduce costs by lowering the standard of living and/or social security if a move of companies to lower-cost EC countries is to be prevented. But German labour mobility is not high and firms depending on highly-skilled workers may have difficulties in recruiting suitable staff elsewhere. A continued compensation through a correspondingly high level of productivity increases – to be achieved mainly through further technological advances and sufficient investment – is therefore vital.

German authorities could also consider a reform of company taxation and a lowering of the very high level of ancillary wage costs; they could further ease rules and regulations, restrict worker participation and introduce a more generous merger control system. A deregulation of road transport and telecommunications would also be necessary to make Germany again attractive as a location of industry – not least to foreign investors.

An indication that the process of dislocation of German industry has been going on for some time may be the increasing amount of German direct foreign investment, which rose from a mere DM 6 billion in 1982 to over DM 25 billion in 1989 if long-term credits and reinvested profits are included. But even direct foreign investment in the form of the acquisition of equity and other types of capital participation alone rose from DM 6 billion in 1982 to DM 19 billion in 1989. This may simply be the counterpart of the rapidly rising current account surpluses in Germany, but could also be an indication that Germany's position as a location for industry is weakening. The Deutsche Bundesbank itself sees the rise in German direct foreign investment more as a sign of German companies making special efforts to gain a share, or to expand their share, in selected foreign markets through a personal presence close to their prospective customers. That the four key export sectors as the chief generators of current account surpluses, are also those with the highest level of net direct foreign investment is natural and does not seem to strengthen the Bundesbank's view.

What Germany has to offer as a location for industrial investment, apart from its central geographical position, is a high degree of skill among workers, a favourable economic, social and politically stable climate, a good infrastructure and a highly-skilled and -motivated management (see Breit, 1988). But despite these qualitative advantages (favouring in particular the production of high quality goods), it is not excluded that some German investors might in fact prefer other locations within the EC with lower social and other costs arising from regulations of various kinds, once the single market is completed. The fundamental question here seems to be whether the prospect of a rise in incomes and lower consumer prices with some doubt as to the certainty of a higher level of employment is a price worth paying for a reduction in social security and a lowering of the quality of life. At this price some might find the single market less acceptable.

An alternative which many German experts hope for is an upward adjustment in standards of the average EC level – if possible an adjustment to the German standards. Such a policy would probably also be more in accordance with the spirit of the Single European Act and would help to keep the dislocation of German industry within acceptable bounds. With regard to worker participation it is felt that the more progressive German regulations should not be overruled simply by German companies switching their head offices to other EC countries, or through mergers with foreign companies. As far as environmental and health protection is concerned, there is little doubt that the Federal Government will if necessary make full use of its right under the new Article 100a, Section 4, of the Treaty of Rome to extend to imports the stricter regulations of Germany.

However, having considered the above points, the German authorities and many German observers quite realize, and accept, the desirability of some growth centres moving to more backward regions of the EC in order to raise living standards there, which will of course ultimately benefit not only Germany but the rest of the single market countries and the world economy. However one has to remember that German industry is dominated by small and medium-sized companies employing no less than 75 per cent of the working population. Neither these companies nor their staff have so far shown a high degree of mobility.

How German reunification will affect these issues is difficult to predict. For the territory of the former German Democratic Republic (GDR) the transition period will no doubt be difficult and may be prolonged. However the long-term prospects for the two parts of Germany in the economic sense look promising, provided the economic turmoil does not undermine political stability. Overall the additional economic impulses expected from the inherent dynamism of the Eastern part of Germany will in all probability soon make themselves felt, not only in the Western part of Germany but also in other parts of the EC and, it is hoped, the rest of the world. For the German industrial empire itself, the prospect for further rapid trade expansion may well lie more in Eastern Europe than in the rest of the EC.

THE SINGLE FINANCIAL SERVICES MARKET AND GERMANY

Plans for European financial integration prepared by the EC Commission are based on three major components: a free flow of capital, free trade in financial services and financial service companies, and standardization of banking technology across Europe. In practice, one may well have either free capital movements but laws prohibiting local banks from intermediating in other states (as in the US) or cross-border banking operations without permitting free capital movements. While the freedom of capital movements within the EC is the priority, the key initiative taken by the EC is no doubt the removal of trade barriers within the market for European financial services. This is firmly anchored in the *Second Banking Directive*, which was initially agreed by the Council of Ministers in January 1988, supported by the *Solvency Ratio Directive* and *Own Funds Directive*.

The principal objective of the *Second Banking Directive* is to ensure that through increased competition the most efficient operator within the EC will be providing specified services in any location of the EC. Thus no government regulations should be allowed to obstruct a strictly observed neutrality between purchasing financial services from a domestic financial institution, purchasing them domestically from a local branch of any other EC financial institution, or importing them from other parts of the EC. The proposed change is to merge the 12 independent markets for financial services into one market. This implies that, once a financial services company has been sanctioned to operate in one part of the EC, it will automatically acquire the right to operate throughout the EC.

For Germany, in particular, this development will have far-reaching consequences. It endangers, for example, cartel profits arising from high profit margins and artificial market conditions which West German insurance companies have enjoyed so far. Their monopoly position is likely to be severely undermined through, for example, British insurers with their better priced insurance products expanding their share of the German insurance market. Mergers and takeovers will lead to further concentration in the industry and the disappearance of smaller companies. From the economic welfare point of view, such an outcome would tend to be beneficial, of course.

The West German banking sector, too, is currently still more regulated than in other EC countries – certainly the UK. Once entry barriers are removed, German banks will be faced by sharply increased competition. However national differences between domestic markets are often the outcome of national preferences and developments which are likely to prove persistent even after 1992. This applies especially to the German banking sector; German companies are fairly conservative and have always maintained close links with their 'house' bank, which is often represented on their board of directors. So far foreign banks in Frankfurt have not done too well in a market as traditional and reserved towards financial innovations as the German market has proved to be (see Ambrosi, 1990). The Chase Manhattan Bank is not the only foreign bank in Frankfurt to have recently greatly reduced their staff and operations.

THE PROBLEM OF NATIONAL SOVEREIGNTY

The realisation of the single market and the European Monetary Union will require a far-reaching abolition of national sovereignty. In Britain, the issue of sovereignty still plays a major part. This is only too clear from repeated recent statements by the British Prime Minister – not necessarily shared by all. In Germany national sovereignty does not appear to play the same dominant role. The majority, especially among the younger generation, are too internationally minded. However hidden issues of sovereignty do seem to be of some importance in Germany. These are often concealed as technical or other reasons, such as the status and independence of the Deutsche Bundesbank. Also, according to the German view, German efficiency and high standards in areas such as environmental protection, economic competitiveness, technology research and monetary policy should, in the view of some, not be sacrificed on the altar of EC integration. In fact it is often difficult to differentiate between objective quality standards being put forward and the desire to retain autonomy or sovereignty.

Even the European reforms carried out so far strengthen the power of the EC Commission in Brussels and reduce the power to take decisions at national level. Towards the final stage of completion of the single market, member states will also have to give up a great deal of their fiscal sovereignty; they will have to tolerate products which do not conform to standards previously adhered to and laid down by authorized domestic institutions. Control over mergers in the case of European-wide operating companies can then no longer be controlled at national level. Entrepreneurs, labour and capital will be able to escape domestic restrictions simply by moving to other EC regions. The procurement of public works can no longer be pursued in order to support domestic industrial or regional policies. Furthermore member states will cease to be sovereign in their anti-cyclical economic policies, especially in the area of monetary policy; in future the exchange rate can no longer be used as a regulator by individual EC states, although restrictions of capital movements will continue to be possible under the protective clauses of the EC Treaty.

In contrast to Germany, France and the Benelux countries, successive British prime ministers violently objected to these developments, although they did reluctantly consent to the convening of two vital conferences that will irrevocably bind the European Community into a closer political and economic Federation. These were two inter-governmental conferences on economic and political union held in December 1990. However at the same time the British Government firmly attacked all proposals and plans for a single European currency and an independent European system of central banks on the ground that Britain was not prepared to hand over monetary control to a group of 12 central bank governors, among whom would of course be the Governor of the Bank of England (see Frowen, 1990); that, it was felt, would be the bitter end of British Parliament.[2] Thus a decision by Britain's 11 EC partners to begin Stage 2 of economic and monetary union on 1 January 1994, without the UK, was made at the EC summit in Rome on 28 October, 1990. Not surprisingly, Germany, together with France and a selection of other hard currency EC states, appears to have every intention of going ahead with the completion of the European Monetary Union, that is Stage 3 of the Delors Plan – with or without British participation.[3]

GERMANY AND THE EUROPEAN MONETARY UNION

To realize the European Monetary Union there is a price to be paid. Mr Pöhl, the President of the Deutsche Bundesbank, made quite clear once more in a recent interview that the West German government and the Bundesbank favour a single European currency only on the condition that a European system of central banks would enjoy independence in the day-to-day conduct of its monetary policy. In other words, monetary union yes, but only by fully accepting the German monetary policy model. According to this model the principal objective of the central bank is to maintain the stability of its currency. Such a mandate, in the German view, can only be fulfilled in the EC if the European system of central banks is independent in its monetary policy decisions of the EC Commission and national governments, as well as any prospective Federal European Government, although it may be accountable to the European Parliament.

In many of its functions the Deutsche Bundesbank is no different from most other central banks, except in one crucial respect: the Bundesbank Act provides in Article 12 that in its relationship to the Federal Government the Deutsche Bundesbank shall be obliged, in so far as is consistent with its principal functions, to support the general economic policy of the Federal Government. But in the exercise of the powers conferred on it under this Act, it shall be independent of instruction from the Federal Government. In the event of a conflict between the Federal Government and the Deutsche Bundesbank, the Federal Government's power is limited to claiming a postponement of any decision by the Bank for up to two weeks. If agreement has then still not been reached, the Bundesbank can pursue its chosen course of action. In the final analysis, therefore, the

Bundesbank's decisions and actions are based on its own interpretations of the duties imposed on it by the Bundesbank Act. Neither before nor after the enactment of the Stability and Growth Law in Germany in 1967 have the policy objectives of the Central Bank Council been understood in the sense of a policy embracing all economic aims. Nevertheless safeguarding of currency was interpreted by the Bundesbank system as safeguarding not only the stability of the domestic price level but also equilibrium in the balance of payments and, whenever possible without creating inflationary pressures, promotion of employment and growth.

The decision-making power actually lies with the West German Central Bank Council. The integral constituents of the Bundesbank system are the Directorate of the Bundesbank itself and the State Central Banks. The Central Bank Council therefore consists of the President, Vice President and Executive Directors of the Bundesbank as well as the presidents of the state central banks. The Bundesbank President is *ex officio* also the chairman of the Central Bank Council. Among the presidents of the state central banks there are some powerful monetary experts, such as Norbert Kloten, whose influence equals that of the Bundesbank contingent and must not be underestimated. The Central Bank Council is not accountable to the Federal Parliament. The Federal Government's only influence is over the appointment of the President, Vice President and Executive Directors of the Bundesbank, the presidents of the state central banks being selected and appointed by the governments of the state concerned.

The Central Bank Council bears sole responsibility for monetary policy. The Federal Government cannot restrict its responsibilities – not even through a decision of the European Council – unless the Lower House of Parliament were to find a majority beforehand to amend the Bundesbank Act. Although the Central Bank Council is obliged to support the general economic policy of the Federal Government, as stated above, its monetary policy mandate always takes precedence. Thus it would *de jure* be at the dutiful discretion of the Central Bank Council to decide whether and to what extent it should take the objectives and objections of the Committee of EC Governors into account in its decisions. However the Central Bank Council will *de facto* not be able (and is unlikely to wish) to avoid taking into consideration the new environment of European policy making. It already does this with respect to events within the European Monetary System. Thus conflicts, both within the Central Bank Council and between it and other EC bodies, are likely to arise. The President of the Bundesbank, who has no more than a seat and a vote, like every other member, on the Central Bank Council, is supposed to be both at the service of European economic and monetary issues within the Committee of EC Governors and totally committed by the mandate laid down in the

Bundesbank Act of 1957 (see Kloten, 1989). It will be interesting to see how all this will affect monetary policy in Germany and the rest of the EC. The importance of having the reunited Germany firmly anchored economically in the EC and politically in NATO cannot be stressed enough and fortunately this has been fully recognized by the German authorities. The conflicts set out above may be exacerbated by the adoption of a single European currency.

The position of the Bundesbank, one from which it will not budge, is that the European System of Central Banks (ESCB) must have as its priority the stability of any single European currency probably to be introduced by the year 2000. For EC member states with a stable currency, giving up national sovereignty in the monetary field will be possible only if this condition is fulfilled. Germany therefore emphasizes that the guiding principle of monetary policy for the entire EC must, clearly and bindingly, be the overriding aim of price stability. The responsibility for monetary policy of the EC in the final phase is to be exclusively the responsibility of the European Central Bank Council, to be established. This Council, as well as the European Central Bank, must be quite independent in its monetary policy decisions of other bodies responsible for economic policy, including the various bodies of the EC itself. Neither the Council of Ministers nor the EC Commission nor the government of any individual member state of the EC should have the right to give instructions to the ESCB (see Pöhl, 1990a[4] and 1990b). Despite the legal and institutional independence of the ESCB, democratic control is meant to be maintained through the ESCB creation by means of a legal Act – similar to the Bundesbank Act – which would itself be subject to parliamentary approval. The bodies to be created under the Act would have legally binding duties and the members of all ESCB bodies would be appointed by democratically legitimate EC organs, the European Parliament or eventually a Federal European Government. The ESCB should, according to the Bundesbank and the *Delors Report* view, be refused the right to grant credits for financing budget deficits of any EC member state. It should, further, be free of any obligation to take up new issues of governments' securities or to acquire them on the secondary market (see Deutsche Bundesbank, 1990). All this makes an anti-cyclical monetary policy in the Keynesian or post-Keynesian sense virtually impossible.

The ESCB should also – following the Bundesbank model – be a federal system, but with due regard to the unity of monetary decision making. The instruments of monetary policy applied by individual member states would then have to be unified so that at the European level the monetary targets fixed within the framework of a monetary policy oriented on the potential of the European economy can be realized on financial markets without conflict. A coordinated minimum reserve system in all member states is regarded as commendable, to be used as a quasi-automatic brake upon money creation in addition to classical discount policy and a flexible open market policy. Direct interference in the market mechanism through quantitative credit controls or administered interest rates should then be able to be dispensed with (as has been the case in the UK since 1971).

These recommendations by the Bundesbank and the German Central Bank Council are of course in complete contrast to the view of the former British Prime Minister, Margaret Thatcher[5] (and incidentally to the view of her successor, John Major). In a 1990 House of Commons debate, she said:

> If you cede sovereignty over all monetary and economic matters, you have ceded the fundamental core of the things we are here [the House of Commons] to decide. We have not gone into discussing EMU yet in the inter-governmental conference. I hope they will listen to the view of this House and of this Government, and may perhaps be influenced by it. (*Weekly Hansard*, House of Commons Parliamentary Debates, 1990).

Time will tell.

NOTES

*The author wishes to thank Victoria Chick, H.-P. Kassai and Norbert Kloten for their helpful comments and suggestions. However, he alone is responsible for any remaining errors or shortcomings.

1. For details of the role played by the former German Chancellor Helmut Schmidt and the then French President Giscard d'Estaing in the creation of the EMS, see R. Jenkins (1989), pp.197–9.
2. On this point a large part of the British population might well share the view expressed by Michael Ignatieff that 'If the British economy needs the protection and the discipline of full membership in a European Monetary Union, it is because we've made such a mess of our sovereignty in the economic domain' (Ignatieff, 1990).
3. Nevertheless in a speech to the Mont Pelerin Society in Munich on 3 September 1990 President Pöhl expressed 'substantial doubts as to whether all or any governments would really be willing to relinquish the monetary policy sovereignty of their countries and transfer it to a Community institution'. He also said that in his view, 'It will certainly be some time yet before we come to a common currency in Europe'. To achieve this final goal cohesion between national economies and their currencies would have to be strengthened (Pöhl, 1990c).
4. For an outline of the framework of the European system of central banks, see Pöhl (1990a).
5. Margaret Thatcher is now the honorary president of the Bruges Group, founded to support the view of the European Community which she outlined in her Bruges speech 'Britain and Europe' on 20 September 1988 rejecting federalism.

REFERENCES

Ambrosi, G.M. (1990), 'Finanzinnovationen und der europäische Binnenmarkt 1992. Geldpolitische Perspektiven für die Bundesrepublik Deutschland', in H.

Riese and H.-P. Spahn (eds), *Geldpolitik und ökonomische Entwicklung – Ein Symposium*, Regensburg: Transfer Verlag, pp.183–200.

Breit, E. (1988), 'Europäischer Binnenmarkt kein Selbstzweck: Für ein soziales Europa', *Hamburger Beiträge zur Wirtschafts- und Währungspolitik in Europa*, no. 4, October, edited by Wilhelm Nölling.

Cecchini, P. (with Catinat, M. and Jacquemin, A., written by Robinson, J.) (1988), *The European Challenge 1992: The Benefits of a Single Market* (The Cecchini Report), Aldershot, Hants (UK): Wildwood House Limited.

Delors, Jacques (1989), *Report on Economic and Monetary Union in the European Community* (The Delors Report).

Deutsche Bundesbank (1990), 'Statement by the Deutsche Bundesbank on the Establishment of an Economic and Monetary Union in Europe', *Monthly Report of the Deutsche Bundesbank*, vol. 42, no. 10, October, pp. 40–44.

Franzmeyer, F. (1988), 'EG-Binnenmarkt – Integrationskonsequenzen für die Bundesrepublik', mimeo, September.

Franzmeyer, F. (1989), 'Zur Kehrseite des Binnenmarktkonzepts', *Konjunkturpolitik*, vol. 35, no. 6, pp. 311–28.

Frowen, S. F. (1990), 'Die Rolle Grossbritanniens im Europäischen Währungssystem', in H. Riese and H.-P. Spahn (eds.) *Geldpolitik und ökonomische Entwicklung – Ein Symposium*, Regensburg: Transfer Verlag, pp. 156–62.

Ignatieff, M. (1990), 'Last Stand of the Little Englanders', *Observer*, 4 November, p. 19.

Jenkins, R. (1979), *Jean Monnet Lecture*, Florence: European University Institute.

Jenkins, R. (1989), *European Diary 1977–1981*, London: Collins.

Kloten, N. (1989), 'Der "Delors-Bericht" ', *Europa Archiv*, vol. 44, no. 9, 10 May, pp. 251–60.

Ludvigsen Report (1989), Vol. 11 of the EC Research Programme on 'The Costs of Non-Europe', Brussels: EC Commission.

Pöhl, K. O. (1990a), 'Basic Features of a European Monetary Order', Paris Lecture, January 16.

Pöhl, K. O. (1990b), 'Two Monetary Unions – the Bundesbank's View', *Central Banking*, no. 1, Summer, pp. 64–71.

Pöhl, K.O. (1990c), 'Doubts on EMU', *Central Banking*, no. 2, Autumn, pp. 53–7.

7. Alternative Economic Analyses of German Monetary and Economic Unification: Monetarist and Post Keynesian[1]

J. A. Kregel

INTRODUCTION

Until a short time ago it was generally believed that the most pressing economic problems of the 1990s would be linked to the persistent international trade and budget imbalances between the US on the one hand and Europe and the Pacific Basin on the other, and to the failure of the Latin American economies to reduce their debt burden. The fall of the Berlin Wall made an uncertain future international environment even more complicated as the already indebted Eastern European economies sought the ways and means to economic progress that would match the rapidity of their political liberalization. Yet the prospect of reunification of East and West Germany was initially greeted by an outbreak of optimism and euphoria in German and international capital markets. However, after this early optimism, German bond markets began to weaken at the beginning of 1990, and led to a stock market reversal which created a mood of widespread pessimism over the economic implications of German unification.

This chapter identifies the basis of such a rapid change in market opinion concerning the impact of German economic and monetary unification in the mistaken application of monetarist analysis grounded in a fundamental misunderstanding of the reasons which led the Bundesbank to oppose the West German government's proposal to achieve monetary unification by converting the East German mark (EM) at parity with the West German Deutsche Mark (DM). The first part of the chapter will present the monetarist analysis, which led to the belief that the Bundesbank opposed the government programme because it would be excessively inflationary, and suggests reasons why the analysis itself is questionable. The second part of the chapter will suggest that the source of the differences between the West German government and the central bank may be found in their divergent analyses of the basic problem to be solved by unification. The government was primarily concerned to stem the inflow of immigrants from East Germany by assuring East Germans that they would share the same rights and economic future if they remained in their homes, while the Bundesbank was concerned to safeguard the stability of the financial system by ensuring the quality of the loans to East German enterprises held as assets by East German banks. This difference may be simplified as a difference concerning the correct prices of banks' liabilities, represented by the savings deposits of the East German public, on the one hand, and the correct prices of banks' assets, representing loans to East German firms, on the other. This difference could also be presented as similar to the current debate between 'fundamental uncertainty–liquidity preference' advocates and 'endogenous money' theorists within the post Keynesian approach to economic analysis. From this point of view the German government emerges as being more concerned to use monetary policy to influence the expectations and liquidity preference of the public, while the Bundesbank is motivated by an endogenous money analysis of the factors of stability in the banking system.

I MONETARY UNIFICATION AND THE PROBLEM OF INFLATION

The primary cause of the change in financial markets' assessment of monetary unification between the two Germanies seems to have been the result of suggestions made during the East German election campaign that East German marks would be converted to Deutsche Marks at a rate of 1:1. The world's financial press appears to have assessed the implications of this promise by applying a crude version of the 'equation of exchange', complete with images of Friedmanesque helicopters dropping bundles of Deutsche Marks on East Germans ready, and now able, to rush to West German shops to deplete supplies of consumption goods and drive up prices.[2] What had first been considered as a unique opportunity for supply-side stimulus for the sluggish German economy and the ultimate confirmation of the superiority of free market capitalism suddenly became a devious communist plot to weaken the monetary control of the Bundesbank and destroy the roots of German prosperity in price stability.

The Bundesbank's public criticism of the government's unification programme, and its counterproposal of a 2:1 conversion rate, were widely interpreted as representing the Bundesbank's fear of sharply higher inflation resulting from parity conversion. To counter the resulting increase in inflation the Bundesbank would be forced to apply monetary stringency, leading to expectations of sharply higher interest rates and the subsequent reign of pessimism in capital markets. The implications of unification based on currency conversion at par were thus forecast as higher inflation, higher interest rates, falling bond and stock prices and a slow-down in demand and growth.

A reconstruction of the formal reasoning behind the monetarist forecast of the inflationary implications of monetary unification might be as follows. Estimates made by the DIW Research Institute in Berlin (Wochenbericht, 26 April 1990) on the basis of the 1989 report of the East German Staatsbank place savings deposits held by the East German public at EM 162 billion, and currency in circulation at EM 17 billion for year-end 1989. For purposes of calculation a figure of around 180 billion may thus be used as the creation of new DM resulting from the 1:1 conversion promised by the government. This would have meant an increase in West German M3 of around 14 per cent, more than double the Bundesbank's current target of 4–6 per cent. Straightforward application of the 'equation of exchange' to a DM 180 billion expansion in M3, using the 1989 West German velocity of circulation of around 1·8, implies an increase of about 14 per cent in nominal GNP. The real component of this 14 per cent increase could be broken down into the domestic growth in real output, expected to be around 4 per cent, and the trade balance, which might provide an additional 4 per cent in real output available for domestic consumption. The difference between the maximum increase in real output for the year of 8 per cent and the change in nominal GNP of 14 per cent leaves 6 per cent as the implied initial year rise in prices resulting from the government's conversion plan. When added to the rate of inflation of 3 per cent prevailing at the beginning of 1990, the impact of monetary unification could thus be interpreted to imply a three-fold increase in the rate of inflation and the certain intervention of the Bundesbank to tighten credit and increase interest rates. Bondholders reacted to this argument, which was repeated as a litany in nearly every story on unification in both the financial and popular press – a sort of financial terrorism – by quickly exiting from DM fixed interest assets and German shares, causing the rapid turnaround in market performance.

But simply setting out the formal monetarist analysis in this way suggests that it is based on some questionable assumptions. First, it assumes that East Germany will contribute no net output to the German union and that East Germans will only buy West German goods with their new DM.[3] Second, it assumes that all accumulated East German savings, once converted into DM, will be spent, down to the last mark.[4]

It is extremely difficult to evaluate the net material product accounts of socialist countries because they cannot be easily translated into western-style national income and product accounts. The socialist accounts generally exclude services unrelated to material production; that is, government services, financial services, personal services and full capital consumption allowances included in the national accounts. Indeed services will probably be one of the most important contributions to German output after unification.

Rough, optimistic, estimates of East Germany's pre-unification productive potential suggest a figure of 10–12 per cent of West German GDP.[5] On this basis East Germany's contribution to unified German output would be only slightly below the increased purchasing power created by full parity conversion of outstanding EM assets. It may be true that East Germans will prefer western goods, but the monetarist argument given above requires that no one else will. In 1987 East Germany exported goods worth $2.4 billion (between 4 and 5 billion DM) to the industrialized countries, excluding West Germany to which it exported an estimated $7 billion. This suggests that, even if East Germans shun domestic goods, there is no justification for placing a zero value on the East German contribution to real output. A pessimistic, but perhaps more realistic, estimate made with reference to the export figures would be to reduce the optimistic estimate by 50 per cent to around 5–6 per cent of West German production.

With respect to the second assumption, all proposals for monetary unification included as basic prerequisites both the removal of price subsidies for consumption goods (estimated at around EM 50 billion) and the eventual privatization of all East German state property. Thus, while the parity conversion would mean an increase in East German residents' purchasing power over West German goods as their prices fall, there will be a concomitant decrease in purchasing power over East German goods as their prices rise. This will obviously lead to some substitution, but for some domestically produced food and other basic goods and housing and rents this will be difficult. Goods, which are of necessity produced in the East, even though they will become absolutely more costly, should remain relatively cheaper than western goods. This increase in the price level of East German goods should increase the transactions demand for money and decrease the potential increase in expenditure over West German goods.

Given that privatization should also apply to the housing stock, there would now also seem to be long-term incentives to save, which did not exist in the past. Whereas East Germany had a large consumption overhang because of the absence of goods of acceptable quality, this surplus may now be converted into a large household savings surplus to acquire private property and consumer durables which were not previously available. In addition, with the opening of the financial system, new financial assets paying positive real rates of return will be available for the placement of accumulated savings.

Finally, the reconstruction of East German industry will clearly increase the risk of unemployment and introduce for the first time to the East German population the risk of loss of employment and income. All of these arguments suggest that there are a number of reasons – rising prices of East German necessaries, the possibility of purchasing and owning housing, positive real rates of return to financial assets and the risk of unemployment – which lead to the conclusion that it is extremely likely that East Germans will treat DM assets in exactly the same way that foreigners have treated them since the 1960s, as extremely good long-term stores of value and choose to hold them, rather than spend them in a one-time splurge which reduces their net wealth position to zero.

The official treaty of unification did not fully incorporate parity conversion. Instead adults between the ages of 15 and 60 were allowed parity conversion on EM 4 000 and 2:1 on deposits above this amount. The initial parity allowance given to the young was 2 000 lower, and to the old 2 000 higher. Taking an average of 4 000 EM per man, woman and child (an overestimate, given that the age distribution of the population) yields around DM 66 billion. Converting the remaining 114 billion at 2:1 yields 57 billion for a total of DM 123 billion. This is less than half the optimistic estimate of East Germany's addition to output, but roughly equal to the pessimistic estimate. Thus a full reckoning of the factors involved at the conversion rate included in the final treaty gives no reason to believe that there should be anything more than a marginal impact on prices. Indeed it appears that this was also the Bundesbank's internal estimate of the situation.

Of course there are other reasons that have been suggested to explain the expected rise in the inflation rate and the necessity of higher interest rates. The most common is that the reconstruction of East German industry will require capital goods produced in West Germany; since capacity utilization is already near 90 per cent of normal for the manufacturing sector as a whole any additional demand would cause increased pressure on prices. Apart from Keynes's *Treatise on Money* argument that 'capital inflation' has no direct effect on the cost of living and thus does not have a direct impact on wage rates, it is unclear that even capital goods prices would rise initially. The German economy has a large export surplus in capital goods and exports could be redirected to East Germany without any necessary impact on prices.

Even more important, it is not obvious that the initial impact of industrial reconstruction will be felt in the capital goods sectors. The first priority of reconstruction will be to replace social overhead capital and infrastructure, such as roads, railways and communications, all of which are essential preconditions for the profitable production and distribution of industrial goods for the European market. None of these investments should require substantial additional machine tools, while many depend on computer technology in which costs are falling rapidly and many, such as road building, are relatively labour-intensive.

Only after these basic facilities are in place will the second impact of expansion of investment in plant and equipment be possible. But plant must be constructed before equipment can be installed. And the housing stock must be improved and enlarged. Thus on both counts it is likely that it will be the construction industry which will feel the initial increase in demand over the first two or three years. With November equipment utilization in the construction industry proper reported at 64.4 per cent of normal, there appears to be excess capacity available and there will certainly be East German labour available. All this suggests that capital goods producers should have some leeway to adjust capacity to meet the needs of reconstruction, either by redirecting exports or by expanding domestic capacity, as well as the time necessary to train the required labour force.

The most sophisticated argument that has been made in support of increased inflationary pressure causing a rise in interest rates has nothing to do with the inflationary impact of the conversion rate of EM to DM, but argues that the financial needs of reconstruction will put such a burden on the given supply of world savings that real interest rates will have to rise to attract the necessary capital. East Germany will thus enter the increasingly intense world competition with the US government, the LDCs, the Italian government and other East European countries for the decreasing quantity of private savings provided by West German and Japanese families. The world shortage of savings relative to demand for capital should then drive up interest rates, just as a shortage of footwear would drive up the price of shoes. Apart from the dubious theoretical basis of this argument, in the case of East German reconstruction this will be an internal problem for a unified Germany. The German capital account balance is now in the range of 110 to 120 billion marks (nearly 50 per cent of the optimistic estimates of East German GNP), while the current acount is nearly DM 100 billion, or around 5 per cent of GDP. The current government expenditure deficit is around 1 per cent, leaving a net savings surplus of around 4 per cent of GDP. Half of this surplus would give East Germany a 25 per cent share of investment in GNP without taking into account any internally generated savings.

Thus, while it is true that reconstruction will require capital, it is by no means evident that higher real interest rates will be required to attract it. Internal sources should be more than adequate to satisfy even the most rapid recovery. On the other hand, there will be other financial burdens, such as responsibility for maintenance of pensions (which in the East are roughly a third of West German levels), unemployment benefits and other social expenditures which have been guaranteed conversion at par. But, again, these cannot be assessed against a zero contribution of the East German economy, nor should the contribution of approximately a 1 per cent increase in the West German growth rate be overlooked; this amounts to the tax yield on an extra DM 20 billion in 1990.

While the supply of capital does not seem to be the really binding constraint, ensuring adequate incentives to investment in East Germany will be crucial. In addition to the essential social overhead investments already mentioned, this is a question of contract law and property rights and expected profitability. This concerns another part of the unification treaty which has been postponed to a later date, when a formal political unification treaty is agreed. This is perhaps the most damaging part of the existing plan for monetary unification, for it places substantial legal impediments in the way of the required flow of investment funds to the East. This separation of political and monetary unification has other disturbing implications for the way monetary unification is to take place, which will be dealt with more fully below.

Another aspect of the problem of investment incentives concerns the likely behaviour of wages. When Chancellor Kohl announced the final agreement on monetary unification it was interpreted as a complete victory for his earlier announced position of one-to-one conversion. But, on closer inspection, complete one-to-one conversion is applied only to wages and salaries, pensions and scholarships. The economic implications of setting a conversion rate for wages are not clear (although it is clearly necessary for legal purposes such as labour contracts and calculation of pensions), since conversion is only relevant to liquid monetary assets which have fixed prices in EM. Conversion of the unit of account has no impact on the value of other assets or services whose prices will be determined by local market and labour union conditions. Wages may be converted at any rate; as long as money wages are subject to negotiation and bargaining the conversion rate is meaningless. Thus one of the most important aspects, perhaps the most important aspect, of generating the appropriate incentives to investment in the East will be the new trade union structure and the bargaining goals for wages and conditions that will be adopted.

If wages were to remain 'at parity', that is, at their current levels in EM converted to DM, then average East German wages after conversion to DM at 1:1 would be between a third and a half of equivalent West German levels. Given that generally accepted estimates place East German labour productivity at around 50 per cent of that in the West, this means that wage differentials will more than offset productivity differences between the two countries.[6] It does not seem likely that East German workers are to be 'priced out of jobs'[7] or that wage costs would be an impediment to attracting adequate investment.

HORIZONTALISTS VERSUS LIQUIDITY PREFERENCE

The aspect of the conversion plan which is completely overlooked in the monetarist analysis is the rate at which bank assets are converted. But this is where the crux of the difference of opinion separating the Kohl government and the Bundesbank would appear to be found. The Bundesbank started its analysis of unification by trying to calculate the conversion rate for firms' debt required to keep the East German banking system solvent. The answer was not the same as the conversion rate for households' deposits that the government thought necessary to stem the flow of labour from East to West. Indeed we may contrast the two approaches to conversion adopted by the German government and the Bundesbank as representing an initial concern with different sides of the financial sector balance sheet. The government, concerned to stem the flow of East German immigrants, believed that the most rapid way to do this was to try to quell East German uncertainty over future economic conditions by guaranteeing integration into the successful West German economy. This they felt could best be symbolized by guaranteeing that East German marks would be accepted at a par with Deutsche Marks. This was an action that the government thought could be done instantly, without waiting for the slow process of political negotiation between East and West Germany and between Germany and the occupying powers. East Germans could thus be instantly guaranteed 'equal' economic and political status, inducing them to wait for full integration, rather than seeking instant integration by emigrating to the West. This implied 1:1 conversion of the savings deposits recorded on the liability side of the balance sheet of the East German financial system. The government sought to use monetary policy to diminish the uncertainty over the economic prospects of the East German population.

On the other hand, the primary concern of the Bundesbank was the asset side of the financial sector balance sheet. Like post Keynesian endogenous money advocates, the West German central bank recognized the basic fact that loans create deposits – deposits which would be denominated in DM, and thus part of the Bundesbank's legal responsibility, after the conversion. These deposits could only be supported if borrowers were capable of earning a sufficient amount of DM to service and repay their loans. Given that the East German Staatsbank was (correctly) presumed to have little or no equity, the only support for the liabilities of the banking system was the quality of the outstanding loans. It was clear that most firms would be unable to compete in western markets, much less meet interest charges, now in DM, on their outstanding loans, which would also be denominated in DM. Indeed the market value of their debts relative to historic book value is probably not very different from that of the least developed countries; that is, about 20–30 per cent. On the basis of the 50 per cent productivity differential between West and East Germany, and given the one-to-one conversion of wages which, as seen above, places wages at less than half West German levels, it must have seemed reasonable to suppose that East German firms might be able to meet between 30 and 50 per cent of their debt obligations. This suggests a maximum 2:1 conversion rate for firms' debt. From the perspective of the survival of East German industry, and of minimizing unemployment, the lower the conversion rate the better. This was the general reasoning behind the Bundesbank proposal for a 2:1 conversion rate for financial assets. But, as every student of money and banking knows, the asset and the liability sides of a balance sheet must be equal. If firms' debts were to be written down by one-half, then the liabilities of the financial system, represented by household savings deposits, had to be converted at the same rate of 2:1. This explains the Bundesbank's resistance to the government's 'unrealistic' proposal; it had little, if anything, to do with the fear of rampant inflation. The greater fear of the Bundesbank was that, in the event of a breakdown of East German industry or, more directly, of the banking system, the West German government would have no choice but to intervene directly in support of East German firms or banks. A West German government takeover, providing direct subsidies to East German banks or industry, would also require an increase in government debt which the Bundesbank was keen to avoid because of the difficulties this would create in implementing monetary policy and as being contrary to the German economic philosophy of the social market economy. In this argument the Bundesbank prevailed and a conversion rate of 2:1 was included in the unification treaty as the major and clear exception to 1:1 conversion.

It would thus appear that the government had as its main concern the rate of conversion of households' assets which would stop the flow of emigrants and create sufficient confidence in improvement in future economic conditions to keep East German workers and production in place, while the Bundesbank was more concerned by the rate of conversion of firms' liabilities which would allow them to be able to meet their interest obligations and to remain solvent after their liabilities were converted to DM. The government was concerned to stabilize expectations of future economic conditions, while the Bundesbank recognized that a conversion rate that was too high would provide an endogenous creation of the money supply that would produce fragile financial conditions in the East German economy.

From a banker's point of view, the plan eventually adopted for unification is possibly the worst of all possible solutions, for it violates the equality of the two sides of the balance sheet by converting assets and liabilities at different rates. It will thus be necessary to provide the banks with compensating asset balances for the difference.[8] These will be provided by 'ausgleichsforderungen' or 'equalization accounts' which will offset the loss due to the writing down of their existing credits at the 2:1 conversion rate. In addition, a special West German institute will be set up, funded by the issue of government debt, which will provide East German firms with equalization assets paying interest sufficient to service their debts in DM in the event that they are unable to meet their financial commitment, even at the reduced 2:1 rate. This system will be necessary until the political treaty is signed and full political integration takes place. In the absence of the full political treaty, specifying private property and ownership laws, it will be impossible to recapitalize firms (or even for banks to lend to firms who have no clear title to assets which might serve as collateral) so that granting additional equalization assets against any shortfall in interest and principal payments by firms will be necessary to keep the economic system operational. It is clear that many of these problems could have been avoided or resolved in a more expeditious fashion had monetary and political union been simultaneous: thus the explanation of the Bundesbank's insistence on delaying monetary and economic union until the question of political unity, and in particular property laws, could be resolved. However, given the cross-border immigrant flows registered at the beginning of the year, it is also clear that the government had little choice but to act as rapidly as possible.[9]

This suggests that the monetarist analysis was not only inappropriate, but misinterpreted the concerns of the Bundesbank concerning the risks of the government's parity proposal for unification. It was not the fear of inflation that motivated the opposition of the Bundesbank, but rather its concern to minimize the debt financing of unification and the technical problems concerned with guaranteeing the solvency of East German firms and the fledgling East German banking system in the absence of political unification and clear legislation concerning property rights. The arguments presented earlier suggest that it is not the potential increase in the West German deficit necessary to support unification that is the most pressing danger, but rather the impending collapse of the economy as firms find it impossible to borrow additional working capital until the resolution of the problem of property rights is worked out.

III CONCLUSIONS

In summary, it does not appear that any of the widely feared inflationary consequences of monetary unification predicted by monetarist analysis are likely to result from the announced unification plan. The conversion of the existing stock of savings should not lead to any appreciable impact on prices; the increase in the demand for capital should not put undue pressure on available capital resources; nor is it likely that East German labour will price itself out of the market or that widespread unemployment will result. If anything the greatest risk is that the agreement is not sufficiently attractive to stem the flow of immigrants from East to West and produces the collapse of those parts of the East German economy which might have made a contribution to national income under free market conditions. However the longer political unification is delayed the more costly and the more difficult will be the successful integration of the two economies.

NOTES

1. This chapter is drawn from material first presented in February 1990 as the Laws Lecture, 'Some Implications of European Economic Integration for the United States Economy', while I was Alcoa Visiting Scholar in the College of Business Administration of the University of Tennessee and subsequently published as 'Zum Verhältnis von deutscher, westeuropäischer und gesamteuropäischer Integration', in *Die Zukunft der DDR-Wirtschaft*, Reinbek: Rowohlt, 1990 and from a seminar presented at the Wissenschaftszentrum Berlin für Sozialforschung, 14 May 1990 and subsequently published as 'German Monetary and Economic Unification: Are Financial Markets Asking the Right Questions?' in the *Banca Nazionale del Lavoro Quarterly Review*, September, 1990. It was presented to the Workshop on 1 July 1990, and has only been able to take into account information available up to the middle of June. I am indebted to Dr Doris Cornelsen, Dr Dieter Hiss, Professor Dr Lutz Hoffmann and Professor Dr Egon Matzner for discussion clarifying a number of inaccuracies and errors in the original analysis.
2. This imagery is actually employed in the Economist of 17 February 1990, p. 85 to explain how monetary unification would stoke inflation by distributing increased money balances without any change in available output.

3. The London Economist of 3 March 1990, pp. 15–6 provides an analysis based on such an argument.
4. Such an assumption is implicit in *The Economist*'s (3 March 1990) calculations of the consumption 'overhang' which would be created by 1:1 conversion.
5. Estimates of per capita GDP for East Germany range from a low of $4 000 to a high of $13 000. With a population of around 16.7 million, this produces figures of $66.8 billion to $217.1 billion. $9 000 is considered to be a fair estimate and yields around $150 billion or about DM 265 billion, roughly 12 per cent of West German GDP.
6. DIW (Berlin) gives estimates for 1988 for gross monthly wages in West Germany of 3 855 and 1 190 for East Germany (2 070 and 935 net, respectively). An earlier study (1982) concluded that the real purchasing power of wages in the East was 53 per cent of that in the West.
7. When *The Economist* (17 March 1990, p. 17) finally gave up their 'helicopter' terrorism of the financial markets they substituted a similar argument concerning East German labour being 'priced out of jobs', because it would be 'overpaid at Ostmark 1 equals D-mark 1'.
8. The conversion plan of 1948 also made use of 'ausgleichsforderungen' to bring banks' accounts into balance after the writing down of their existing credits. The present case is perhaps even more difficult, for the East German banks will have to be insured against any default by East German firms until the political treaty is signed and full integration of the banking system takes place.
9. The East Germany economy has virtually been put on hold until X-day, the conversion day set for 1 July, owing to the complete uncertainty over conditions likely to prevail thereafter. In particular, the internal distribution system for East German goods has virtually ceased to function as it seeks western suppliers thought to produce better prospects.

8. Should there be a Marshall Plan for Eastern Europe?*

Irma Adelman†

The case for massive economic assistance by the US to Eastern European countries in support of their political liberalization rests on the following propositions: (1) it is in the self-interest of the US to support the political liberalization sweeping Eastern Europe, both in order to win the ideological contest between the two political and economic systems and to reap the dividends of peace through changes in the level and structure of US government expenditures; (2) political liberalization without better economic performance will invite a political backlash in Eastern Europe; and (3) economic assistance is necessary to enable the restructuring to take place. I shall take the first proposition for granted and concentrate on what the experience of economic development in developing countries has to teach us about the other two propositions.

In this chapter, I shall use the term 'Marshall Plan' generically, as a symbol for the extension of substantial low-interest loans and grants, and the term 'Eastern Europe' to include Bulgaria, Czechoslovakia, East Germany, Hungary, Poland, Rumania and Yugoslavia.

I THE COMPLEX RELATIONSHIPS BETWEEN ECONOMIC AND POLITICAL DEVELOPMENT

Two very different definitions of political development are found in the political science literature. One definition focuses on the degree of responsiveness and accountability of political systems to individuals, classes, ethnic and religious groups, and to economic interest-group pressures. This definition of political development equates political development with the development of western-style parliamentarian systems. It accords with popular notions concerning political development in the West, as well as with the history of political development in developed capitalist countries of the last 150 years or so.

The second meaning of political development equates political development with the efficacy of a political system, in the sense of the ability of the state apparatus to carry out effectively the programmes it wishes to carry out. This notion has become equated in the literature with the concept of 'the degree of autonomy of the state'. Some development economists (Ranis and Fei, 1988) have argued that political development in the second sense is essential to economic development. In practice, these two notions of political development have not gone hand in hand, even in market-oriented developing countries. The systematic relationships between economic and political development have differed, depending on which notion of political development is used. More importantly for the subject at hand, recent political developments in Eastern Europe are increasing the political development of Eastern Europe in the first sense and reducing its political development in the second sense, at least in the short run. This, in part, is the economic and political dilemma posed by recent political events in Eastern Europe.

What can we learn from the experience of developing countries about the prospects for continued political liberalization of Eastern Europe and about the way economic development and economic performance impinge on these prospects?

Economic Development and Political Participation in Developing Countries

Every political system represents a specific relationship between two kinds of elements: political and social norms, on the one hand, and political and economic institutions, on the other. Political norms translate the sociocultural and ideological attitudes of various groups into political views concerning legitimate methods and outputs of government. Satisfaction of these norms constitutes the basis for the government's legitimacy. Political norms relate to such matters as equity, participation and due process. Since the 1950s, political norms in developing countries have come to include economic development as an ideology as well. At the normative level, economic development as an ideology has changed the nature of what the citizenry of a country expects of its government. Once development becomes an explicit goal of government, the normative bases of government are implicitly transmuted into those of a welfare state. Governments are expected to deliver not only national security, a modicum of personal and group-security and a modicum of group-justice but also national prosperity and growth in personal and group living standards for the different strata of society. The developmental ideology has been particularly strong in developing countries and, somewhat paradoxically, in communist countries. Marxism has a developmental ideology as its foundation.

Political and economic institutions represent a patterning of roles and structures in society. 'Political institutions' describe characteristics of political systems such as the structure of authority, the nature and distribution of access to power, the nature and distribution of access to influence over the outcomes of the political process, and the degree of autonomy of the state. 'Economic institutions' describe characteristics of economies such as the significance and scope of the economic marketplace, the role and scope for economic calculus at the micro and macro level, the system of incentives, the conditions for access to factor markets, the distribution of income and assets, and the extent of economic and social stratification and its transmission across generations.

Stable government by consent is based upon a measure of correspondence between political norms, including developmental ones, on the one hand, and political and economic institutions and their outcomes, on the other. Such correspondence confers legitimacy upon the government and enables non-coercive maintenance of order and of a structure of authority. By contrast, political change which is not imposed from the outside is the consequence of large and continuing non-correspondences among normative and structural elements. Non-correspondences generate political tensions whose resolution requires political, economic and social adaptations. These adaptations can be postponed for a while either by appeal to unifying symbols (for example, external threat, such as the cold war, or nationalist or religious values) or by the use of force (as with Iran under the Shah, and the Philippines under Marcos). But eventually adaptations must take place, either because otherwise further economic development is blocked or because the extent of force required to suppress the political tensions becomes unacceptable to the political and military elites themselves.

By its very essence, the process of economic development changes not only the economy and its institutions but also both the normative and the structural bases of the polity. At the normative level, economic development as an ideology expands the nature of expectations from government to include economic performance. At the structural level, economic development increases the degree of differentiation of the economy and the complexity and diversity of society. (Parsons, 1951; Smelser, 1963; Adelman and Morris, 1967). In addition, at least initially, different groups and sectors benefit unevenly from development (Kuznets, 1955; Adelman and Morris, 1973). The national and political elites, the middle-income groups, the bureaucracies and import-substitute-producing manufacturers and workers benefit at the expense of the rest. The groups that benefit have a direct stake in the stability of the government, its structure and in the continuation of its policies. They therefore come into overt political conflict with the groups that lose, to the extent that the latter succeed in articulating their demands upon the government.

Thus economic development gives rise to a complex process in which the normative changes that accompany development greatly increase the demands for system deliveries placed upon the polity and in which both the normative changes and the process of economic development make the management task of the government more complex. Integrative mechanisms do develop in the course of economic development, but only with a lag, and only in response to perceived failures in the existing structures. The effects of these integrative mechanisms are also unevenly distributed, with some 'modern' integrative mechanisms which are primarily growth-oriented replacing traditional mechanisms which are often more safety-net-oriented (North, 1973; Adelman, 1972). Initially the institutions for integration of individuals and groups themselves serve to increase overt tensions by permitting overt articulation of group demands and therefore making tensions more explicit. In mid-level developing countries, political conflicts, political tensions and political instability are generally higher (Adelman and Morris, 1967). Mass communication and literacy make these tensions more visible, raise individual and group expectations, and increase awareness of inter-group inequities. In addition, the unevenness of economic change and the dissolving of traditional social safety nets generate increased uncertainty and greater perceived insecurity, even when mean per capita incomes are rising. The more rapid the change, the higher the potential for tensions (Adelman and Morris, 1967). The process of economic development can be represented by a dome-shaped curve depicting the systematic variations of both economic inequality and political tensions with levels of economic development. At middle levels of development, the share of income accruing to the poor is least and therefore inequality and political tensions are greatest. As long as these political tensions and insecurities are not resolved, they need to be managed and contained. Thus, the combination of economic development with political development of the first type increases the need for political development of the second kind.

Political systems must perform the tension-management function, both in the actual delivery sphere and in the value/symbol sphere. They can do so either by consent or by decree, and can operate either on the actual outputs of the system or in the symbolic sphere. All governments employ mixtures of these methods. Some governments, such as those of post-Shah Iran and of the communist countries, have operated primarily in the symbolic/ideological spheres. Others, such as those of South Korea and Taiwan, have used their authority to increase actual deliveries and widen economic participation, while suppressing political participation. The particular mix of techniques of tension-management chosen has depended not only on the political culture but also on the perceived options for change. But in developing countries at middle levels of economic development, political development of the second type has generally been achieved at the expense of increased political participation, that is, at the expense of political development of the first kind.

There exists in popular perceptions a theory that economic development and democratization tend to go hand in hand and that, as one increases, so does the other. Unfortunately this 'democratization' theory is not anchored in fact. Only once quite high levels of economic and social modernization have been reached in developing countries is a harmonic evolution of political development of the first type (democracy) and economic development possible; and, even at high levels of economic development, the harmonious marriage of increases in economic development with increases in democracy requires perceived 'good' economic and political performance by governments leading to reductions in discrepancies between 'just aspirations' and the 'actual deliveries' of the system.

The political science theories (Apter, 1965 and 1973; Huntington and Nelson, 1976) and the empirical studies of the seventies (Adelman and Morris 1973) have concluded that there is no unique relationship between democratization and economic development. The process of economic development typically expands some channels and types of participation while contracting others. But the very lack of uniqueness in the relationship between economic development and political participation provides an opportunity for choice. The wise exercise of that choice poses the major challenge for the design of development in developing countries and for Eastern Europe currently.

Adelman and Morris (1973) and Huntington and Nelson (1976) see the major choices as consisting of the trade-offs between expanding two dimensions of equity: economic participation, as reflected in the equity of distribution of income, assets and opportunities, versus political participation, as reflected in enlarging the base of political participation, increasing the channels of participation and developing methods of participation at lower levels of government. Empirically the scope for trade-offs among the two types of equity has tended to vary with the levels of socioeconomic development. In the early stages of development, typical of sub-Saharan Africa, the system is low in political development of the second kind. There a political elite that is strongly committed to radical egalitarian ideology and nation building tends to oppose increases in political participation by all groups in order to reduce probabilities of effective opposition to its modernization, nation building and reform agenda. At subsequent, but still early, stages of development, expansion of political participation to a nascent economic and bureaucratic middle class tends to actually delay expansion of both economic and political participation by the lower class. Also increases in middle-class political participation (embourgeoisement) at early stages of economic development tend to lead to the subsequent establishment of technocratic states that (as in South Korea and Taiwan) suppress working-class political participation in the interest of rapid, labour-intensive, export-oriented economic growth. A similar process occurred in East European socialist countries. There expansion of participation took the form of sharing power within the party by moving from the Leninist concept of 'cadre party' to a broad-based communist party membership.

At later stages of socioeconomic development, typical of many contemporary Latin American countries, elites have tended to expand political participation to peasants and workers in order to quell revolts (Central America) or put pressure on the middle class (Argentina under Peron, Brazil after 1964) and continue import-substitution policies. Briefly, economic and political participation tend to go hand in hand. However, since increases in both forms of participation occur at least partly at the expense of the middle class, the alienation of the middle class and the polarization of society are the likely consequences (Adelman and Hihn, 1984). Upper and middle class-sponsored military coups, right-wing backlash, government death squads, centralization and oppression become likely. If they take place, both economic and political participation decrease drastically and the focus is shifted to increasing the rate of economic growth. This was the phase of the political–economic cycle in Latin America of the 1970s and in Central America today. The trade-off became one between economic growth, on the one hand, and greater economic and political participation, on the other. If the suppression of greater economic and political participation does not deliver improvements in living standards, then there is a return to civilian regimes with greater political participation but not necessarily with either greater economic participation or higher rates of economic growth. This has been the phase of the political-participation–economic-development cycle in most Latin American countries since the beginning of the 1980s.

The parallel political process in East European socialist countries consists of the decentralization–recentralization waves. Expansion of participation to the socialist establishment (bureaucrats, military, police, upper echelons of management and 'honest' intellectuals) gives rise to struggles within the elite to capture the state apparatus. The socialist establishment then, in effect, opposes broader popular economic and political participation by workers, peasants and dissident intellectuals.

In the 1980s the pressures of debt repayment, mounting inflation, escalating unemployment and fiscal stringency have lowered the real standards of living of urban workers and of the urban middle class very substantially and increased the economic uncertainty of all groups. The prospects for near-term improvements in standards of living in all heavily indebted countries are low. The gap between 'just aspirations' and 'actual deliveries' is again increasing, with a lowering of both economic and political participation being the most likely outcome.

The experience of developing countries suggests that the path to democratization is oscillatory, alternating between various degrees of participation and oppression, even at relatively high levels of development for developing countries. The ability of the polity to deliver on the 'just economic aspirations' of the politically articulate and mobilized members of society is a critical element in determining whether political participation in the first sense survives or is replaced by increases in political development in the second sense, at the expense of both economic and political participation. The experience of developing countries, especially those at higher levels of development, thus validates the proposition that quick improvements in living standards in Eastern Europe are necessary if democracy and political liberalization in Eastern Europe are to survive.

Economic Development and the Autonomy of the State

Greater autonomy of the state, that is, political development of the second type, is needed to manage the development process. Economic development consists of a combination of changes in the structure of production with institutional change (Kuznets, 1955). Both types of change require government action to initiate, even when the institutional change is in the direction of greater reliance on markets, greater liberalization of international and domestic trade, and privatization. It is a mistake to think that liberalization and privatization can take place autonomously. Indeed World Bank and IMF reports urging privatization and liberalization are littered with recommendations for government actions to achieve these goals. The instances of successful shifts from import-substitution development to export-led growth have entailed strong government guidance, in at least three of the four 'little Tigers' (South Korea, Singapore and Taiwan). More fundamentally, change requires ignoring the desires of those who would benefit from the *status quo* and of those who would be injured by change. It therefore requires greater autonomy of the state. Greater autonomy of the state entails both more effective public administration and greater authority of the state. More effective administration increases monotonically with economic development, (Adelman and Morris, 1967) since it requires greater education, more literacy, better communication and so on. On the other hand, greater authority by the state does not increase automatically with development. It necessitates better tension management and can be achieved in three major ways. First, better tension management can be achieved by gaining legitimacy through performance which lessens the gap between 'just aspirations' and system deliveries for the majority of the population that participates in some manner in the political process. Since development increases inter-group tensions, proceeds unevenly and is unequalizing, this route to greater state authority is quite hard to follow, especially at middle levels of development. Second, legitimacy can also be increased through symbol manipulation; this is an especially effective approach in newly independent (or newly reformed?) countries relying on a nationalist ideology; theocratic governments (Apter, 1973), like Iran and the communist countries until very recently, derive their primary legitimacy from this source and depend on the integrative force of a system of widely shared ethical beliefs, secular or religious, to lower tensions. But this route to government authority does not produce lasting effects unless accompanied by either increased system deliveries or by suppression of opposition and suppression of information. Neither will 'free market symbols' in Eastern Europe, USSR and China, unless accompanied by genuine improvements in standards of living. Finally, greater authority can be achieved by reducing participation, through outlawing or intimidating opposition parties, individuals and groups, and by centralizing decision making. Often this is achieved through a technocratic/military alliance, as in bureaucratic authoritarianism (Brazil under the generals and East European countries while the communist party was consolidating its position).

Multi-party political systems, labelled 'reconciliation systems' in Apter's terminology, that are based on high participation (Chile under Frei, and India), are generally characterized by at best moderate degrees of government authority. Central control in reconciliation systems tends to be weak and bureaucratic and is characterized by corruption and uneven access to power. Developing countries with reconciliation systems usually have shifting developmental priorities that are specified mainly by politicians, with technocrats playing marginal roles. The polity consists of competing coalitions based on caste–ethnic interests and on differentiated class relationships. Political development of the first type is acquired at the expense of political development of the second kind.

Liberalization in Eastern Europe consists of a shift from a theocratic political system, with high government authority, towards a reconciliation system, with low to moderate government efficacy. It occurs at a time in which economic restructuring to achieve higher standards of living (that is, developmental priorities) is a high priority for the survival of the newly adopted reconciliation systems. But the experience of developing countries suggests that reconciliation systems, with their changing economic priorities and shifting coalitions, are ill-suited to the tasks of economic modernization and institutional change.

Economic Development, Political Development and Welfare

Both real incomes and political participation in the first sense are arguments in the individual's utility function (Adelman, 1975; Dasgupta, 1989). Individual political freedoms from arbitrary exercise of state power, and the provision of lawful channels for exerting a measure of control over one's own destiny through participation in decision making are important to individuals. Individuals care not only about their economic well-being but also about their personal security and personal freedoms. Furthermore political restrictions have their counterpart in economic restrictions upon the use of income (availability of goods, freedom of movement and travel, security of property rights). The extent to which these are important to individuals is made clear by events in Eastern Europe during the last few months.

But this review of the relationships between economic and political participation indicates that, up to reasonably advanced levels of development, individuals must, unfortunately, trade off among economic and political elements of their welfare function. Traditionally, in non-communist countries participation expresses itself through either 'voice' or 'exit' (Hirschman, 1974). In Eastern Europe, where 'voice' has been blocked and official 'exit' has been denied, the trade-off between economic growth and political and economic participation has taken a different form: 'exit on the job', in the form of downward adjustment of individual productivity and shift of resources towards black market and moonlighting activities; or 'exit as a consumer' through the accumulation of liquidity as a form of economic non-participation; or 'voice' through informal channels ('samizdat' – self-publication, political jokes, rumours, dissident movements) the exercise of which is subject to state reprisals. The trade-off occurs not only between economic and political participation, but also between the two forms of political development. The latter trade-off is all the more pronounced when, as in Eastern Europe, institutional reforms are required in order for the system to be able to deliver higher standards of consumption. These trade-offs constitute one of the basic dilemmas of the process of development.

Political Events in Eastern Europe

The winds of political change in Eastern Europe have been occasioned by the coincidence of several different processes: (1) pervasive dissatisfaction with the limited ability of the planned Eastern economies to deliver consumer goods and economic lifestyle prospects equivalent to those in Western Europe and the US, despite growth rates of gross material product that, up to the late 1970s exceeded those of market-oriented economies; (2) pervasive dissatisfaction with the suppression of individual freedoms, and suppression of nationalist, ethnic and religious aspirations; (3) a loss of legitimacy of the political leadership through the transition from a generation of Second World War communist leaders to a generation of communist party and government 'apparatchiks' with no charisma, no historical achievement, and of limited competence; (4) political 'perestroika' and 'glasnost' in the Soviet Union, which have lessened fears of Soviet military suppression of popular participation and nationalist movements; and (5) the lessened ability of local communist parties to suppress domestic popular-participation explosions by using the military and the not-so-secret police following the increased political liberalization of the Soviet Union.

The economic consequences of these political events, however, have been to lessen the economic efficacy of the governments of Eastern Europe in exercising control over the direction and pace of economic development. This loss of government authority has not yet been accompanied by the substitution of the mechanisms required for indirect guidance of the economy by market signals. The institutional reforms undertaken to date in most East European countries (Hungary may be a partial exception) have been insufficient to enable enterprises and individuals to be responsive to economic calculus based on correct economic signals. Currently the economies of Eastern Europe have the worst of all possible worlds: central planning as a guidance mechanism has been discredited, while still in force in varying degrees, but the structures and policies to place the economies of Eastern Europe on automatic pilot via the invisible hand are not in place. Political development in the first sense has led to a retrogression in political development in the second sense. At the same time, political liberalization is enabling overt expression of heightened economic aspirations, while generating greater impatience with the inability of the economic and institutional system to deliver improvements in standards of living. In the absence of quick improvements in living levels, there is a genuine possibility of economic and political chaos followed by political backlash and large-scale violations of human rights. As indicated above, this is a process familiar to observers of Latin American development.

Herein lies the case for economic assistance to Eastern Europe by the West, in view of the West's vested interest in the establishment and survival of multi-party systems in Eastern Europe.

II THE HISTORY OF ECONOMIC REFORMS IN EASTERN EUROPE

The interplay between economic and political development is well illustrated by the history of economic reforms in Eastern Europe. Eastern Europe has not been a stranger to economic reform. Indeed most East European countries have gone through three waves of reform, the most recent of which started in the early 1980s. The actual reforms introduced varied country by country, but they shared common goals and timing (Nyers, 1983).

The early industrialization programmes of all East European countries were modelled on Soviet industrialization: stress on heavy industry; on production characterized by high resource–output coefficients and leading to resource-and-consumption constrained growth; centralization and planning; administered prices coupled with both input and output target allocations; large-scale vertically-integrated enterprises; and inward trade-orientation.

The period between 1954 and 1960 was marked by a wave of institutional reforms aimed at correcting some of the adverse effects of Stalinist economic policies. Comprehensive institutional reforms were introduced in Yugoslavia, shifting its institutional structure from the standard Soviet model to the worker-management model with a substantial decentralization of decision making. Partial reforms, aimed at better satisfaction of consumer demand and at increasing total-factor productivity (that is, shifting the economy from resource-extensive to resource-intensive growth, in the Ricardian sense), were adopted in the Soviet Union, Hungary, Poland and East Germany. In the Soviet Union, emphasis was placed on agricultural production and a system of partial decentralization through regionalized economic controls. In Hungary, the reforms started in 1957 introduced free trade in agricultural products, amalgamated small technologically obsolete farms into producer cooperatives, and introduced incentive pricing and decentralization measures into agriculture. Concentration of industrial and commercial enterprises was increased in the early 1960s, with a (mistaken) view that this would increase the efficiency of resource use. The Hungarian agricultural reforms were successful, while the industrial reforms undertaken in the early 1960s were largely unsuccessful.

The second wave of reform in Eastern Europe occurred during 1964–70. The emphasis was on raising living standards, accelerating economic growth and increasing the efficiency and flexibility of enterprises. In all East European countries this period was marked by a shift in industrial policy aimed at increasing technology-based industries (Brada and Montias, 1984). In some East European countries (Hungary and Poland, but not Czechoslovakia) there was an intent to shift from inward orientation to export orientation and greater trade with the West by fostering industrial exports as mechanisms for increasing economic efficiency. The extent to which this shift occurred and the degree to which it was accompanied by institutional reforms varied among East European countries.

East Germany was the first to propose fostering technology-intensive industries (electronics, precision instruments and optical industries) so as to diffuse technical change in industry more generally. Czechoslovakia identified about 60 technology-intensive sectors and subsectors for priority development (Brada and Montias, 1984). But, as a result of the death of the Prague Spring movement, it aborted earlier reform attempts and recentralized decision making. Targets applying to the gross value of output rather than profits were reintroduced as measures of enterprise performance and investment autonomy was curbed.

In Poland, Gomulka stated in 1968 that planning should aim at 'the maximum growth of the most profitable export' – that is, growth should become export-led. But the food riots that took place in December of 1970 forced the resignation of Gomulka. Gierek, who followed him, continued the outward orientation, viewing it as an instrument to enable a simultaneous increase in wages and investment, both of which were to act as mechanisms for raising labour productivity. The outward orientation was implemented by increasing investment, credit and input access and accompanied by partial reforms in the price system and in the legislation governing joint ventures with foreign enterprises. Reforms to tie domestic prices in raw materials and semi-finished products more closely to world prices were introduced. Incentives to export were introduced, tying wage increases and foreign-exchange retention for imports by firms to their enterprise's value-added in exports. But there was no decentralization of either price setting or investment. The Gierek reforms met with initial success (1972–4) but then led to a spectacular build-up of foreign debt and economic crisis. In 1968–9, Rumania extended some material incentives to enterprises, granted some measures of enterprise independence, introduced greater flexibility in banking and credit, and decentralized foreign trade. Bulgaria undertook comprehensive price reforms in 1968. Yugoslavia embarked on a very comprehensive programme of economic reforms as early as 1965, aimed at more enterprise autonomy in investment financing from commercial sources, production and marketing decisions, income distribution and price setting.

The most far-reaching institutional reforms were contained in the New Economic Mechanism (NEM) introduced in Hungary in 1968. The NEM introduced decentralized decision making in industry by permitting market relations among firms, limiting the scope of administered prices through linking the prices of tradables to world prices, and decentralizing about half of investment (Balassa, 1983).

In most East European countries, the reforms of the 1960s were either partially or completely reversed in the 1970s. The reasons were mixed: some of the reforms were abandoned for sociopolitical reasons; others because the expected benefits in productivity-increase did not materialize; others for administrative reasons relating to management and coordination problems; and still others because, in the absence of binding constraints and obvious benefits, conservative and ideological pressures could prevail. The particular mix of reasons was country-specific but the general retreat from reforms was also influenced by common political considerations. The relevant political considerations for Eastern Europe were the student movements of 1968 opposing the government and, with it, the government-sponsored reforms of the late 1960s; the start of the Brezhnev era that accorded greater influence to a stronger state; and the coincidence of the wars in Vietnam and the Middle East that gave an impetus to growing military spending and stronger states. All these strands led to partial recentralization of enterprises and of decision making.

The counter-reforms were facilitated by the ample availability of foreign finance as a result of the recycling of the petro-dollars through Western banks and financial markets. The 1970s were marked by import-intensive, debt-led growth in Hungary, Poland, Yugoslavia and East Germany, especially after 1974. Some East European specialists call this process 'import-led growth'. The imports served to mask the failure of the domestic producers to supply goods at competitive prices and the systemic failures of the partially reformed economic systems. In Hungary, the dollar value of imports tripled between 1970 and 1975, and again doubled between 1975 and 1980. In Yugoslavia imports quadrupled between 1970 and 1975, and more than doubled between 1975 and 1980. Investment continued to increase, and so did total absorption. As in developing countries, the 1970s were marked by adverse external shocks. The terms of trade of East European countries deteriorated, owing first, to world inflation and drought and, then, to OPEC. After 1975, East European countries also experienced a reduction in their export volume, owing to a world-wide recession. Of these the decline in export volume was the more significant, though its relative role varied from country to country

(Bekker, 1987). Even though some East European countries narrowed their trade deficits towards the end of the 1970s, foreign debt mounted very rapidly because of debt servicing. By 1980, the combined net convertible currency debt of Eastern Europe (excluding Yugoslavia, the USSR and debt to the two Council for Mutual Economic Assistance (CMEA) banks) stood at $68 billion. This debt amounted to almost $500 per capita and the debt service excluding amortization stood at 30 per cent of export earnings for Bulgaria and Poland, 10–25 per cent for East Germany and Hungary and at 11–14 per cent in Czechoslovakia and Rumania (United Nations, 1981).

The debt crisis in Eastern Europe started with the inability of Poland to meet its foreign obligations and a rescheduling of Polish debt in 1981. As a result there was less willingness to lend to East European countries. During the 1980s, all Eastern European economies experienced sharp drops in their rates of growth of real output as compared to the 1970s. After 1981, Eastern Europe achieved a current account surplus, but, except for Rumania, Eastern Europe continued to borrow on international credit markets for debt servicing, increasing its hard currency international debt by 24 billion between 1980 and 1988. At the end of 1988, the total indebtedness of Eastern Europe (excluding the USSR and Yugoslavia) to market economies stood at 85 billion, of which Poland accounted for 45 per cent, East Germany for 23 per cent and Hungary for about 20 per cent. Polish debt was about 450 per cent of its convertible currency exports and Hungarian debt was almost 350 per cent. In 1988, both Poland's and Hungary's net resource transfer to market economies was about 3 per cent of their GDP. In 1987, Hungary's net resource transfer was 6 per cent of GNP!

The debt-adjustment problem and popular dissatisfaction with the supply of consumer goods ushered in a new wave of economic reforms during the 1980s in all Eastern European countries other than East Germany and Rumania. The Soviet Union introduced 'perestroika', with the aim of improving the quality of products, the mechanisms for accomplishing this being decentralization of decision making by firms, including investment autonomy, and a realignment of trade relations both with the West and CMEA countries. Hungary introduced a set of comprehensive price reforms in 1980–1 aimed at linking most industrial prices to world prices and at reducing the average size of industrial enterprises. But the path of Hungarian reform in the 1980s has not been a smooth one, with 1983 marking the introduction of some administrative controls aimed at curbing enterprise autonomy. In 1983, Poland increased the role of prices in the management of enterprises and is currently introducing new, far-reaching legislation intended to transform it into a market economy.

Several points emerge from this abbreviated economic history of East European reforms. First, there are vast differences among East European countries, in development levels, industrial and agricultural policies, degrees of decentralization and use of market prices. Rumania is both the least developed and the most Stalinist in structure. Yugoslavia and Hungary have undertaken the most extensive institutional reforms, but are at middle levels of industrial development. East Germany and Czechoslovakia have the most developed industrial sectors. The economies of Rumania and Poland are both in a shambles.

Second, crises are favourable to reforms. The debt crisis of the 1980s and the food riots in Poland in 1970 led to significant institutional reforms. The current political-cum-economic crises are similarly favourable.

Third, success of reforms is necessary to ensure their survival. The recentralization wave of the 1970s in Eastern Europe suggests that disappointment with the economic outcome of reforms leads to retreat from reform.

Fourth, while the state has had a great deal of autonomy in Eastern European countries, it has not been immune to pressures from the bureaucracy and from enterprise managers, nor is it invulnerable to popular revolt. The waves of decentralization and recentralization evident in the history of East European reform reflect the interplay of these pressures. Policy makers have difficulty in prevailing over those administrative layers in the bureaucracy, ministries and enterprise management that have a vested interest in the preservation of the *status quo*. The result is the socialist equivalent of populist policies: a lavish use of resources, a generous allocation of investment funds and soft budget constraints leading to 'extensive growth', X-inefficiency at the enterprise level, over-ambitious investment plans, substantial consumption subsidies, and open and hidden budget deficits. Pressures from those echelons of the central administration who lose power as a result of reform lead to a cyclical character in the reform process. When decisions are decentralized and incentives to shift production patterns (for example, towards exports) are granted, specialization strategies are difficult to carry out because of pressures from enterprise managers and ministries to be included among the priority sectors. For example, the priority sectors identified in Poland in 1968 included over 60 per cent of the output of heavy industry and machinery and encompassed over 70 per cent of all industrial enterprises (Brada and Montias, 1984). On the other hand, when decisions are centralized, there is conflict between bureaucrats and managers over norms concerning gross output, material inputs, the wage fund, the distribution of profit, exports and prices. These conflicts tend to be resolved at the cost of enterprise productivity. The cyclical character of institutional reform processes is, incidentally, familiar to students of land reform in Latin America.

Fifth, the planned economy is not without some advantages. It offers a great deal of security to managers and workers. Both the bureaucracy and enterprise managers have evolved styles of behaviour which result in less uncertainty than is prevalent in market economies. Central planners base their norms on small changes from the previous year. Enterprises are guaranteed survival through soft budget constraints that absorb their losses. Workers are guaranteed employment through the same soft budget constraints and through the tight labour market that low worker productivity and lavish investment generate. Prices of basic consumption goods are subsidized and therefore below world market prices, and prices of services such as housing, education and health are extremely low. Under non-crisis circumstances, real wages are sufficient to guarantee a basic standard of living which is well below the European average but extends to the overwhelming majority of the population. Inequalities are small. By contrast, reform towards market socialism promises higher average standards of living at the cost of increased uncertainty, unemployment, inequality and, at least during the transition, even higher inflation. Eastern Europe appears to want the advantages of market socialism. But is it willing to pay the price?

Sixth, decentralization does not necessarily increase efficiency in resource use when enterprises operate under targets and allocations, have employment constraints and face administered prices which bear little relationship to underlying scarcities and opportunity costs. At a minimum, for administrative decentralization to lead to greater efficiency in resource use, it needs to be accompanied by price reform, investment-decision and investment-financing decentralization, and changes in norms for enterprise performance from quantitative norms to profit norms. More substantial incentives must also be granted to managers, tying their remuneration to the profitability of their enterprises, with profitability valued at world market prices. In short, the economic success of decentralization in socialist countries depends on their being able to simulate the behaviour of a market economy within the socialist framework of ownership. In all Eastern European economies reforms to date have been partial and have not successfully simulated the operations of a market economy. Disappointment with their success has therefore been inevitable.

Seventh, the cyclical character of reform patterns in Eastern Europe is inherent in the economic character of the partial reforms and in the political–bureaucratic interplay of reform-minded and reform-resistant interests. Partial reforms have not yielded hoped-for benefits. Exposure to foreign competition and imports of foreign technology have not generated the increases in total factor productivity that had been anticipated. And, despite deflationary measures with a large cost in lost economic growth undertaken in some East European countries, efforts to tie domestic prices to world prices have led to rapidly escalating inflation. This situation gives fuel to both conservative and reform-minded elements. The argument that 'a return to the old ways of doing business is preferable' and that 'reform has not gone far enough' can both be supported by appeal to past performance under partial reforms. At the moment, because of popular identification of political participation with market-oriented economies, the reformers appear to be in the ascendancy. But how long will the honeymoon last? Can greater political participation survive disappointment with yet another set of reforms? It is the doubts implicit in these nagging questions which make the affirmative case for a Marshall Plan aimed at Eastern Europe.

III SHOULD THERE BE A MARSHALL PLAN FOR EASTERN EUROPE?

There are two different economic problems faced by most Eastern European countries. The first, and most urgent, is the problem of transition between two different guidance and management systems; the second is the longer-run problem of structural change in the economy to achieve more efficient use of resources. The aim of structural change is to provide a sufficient supply of wage-goods at competitive prices, particularly non-tradables. Both types of reforms are necessary for the success of the current political reforms in Eastern Europe.

The Transition Problems

In economies characterized by substantial rigidities, any change in system, even a change from an inherently lower-productivity system to an inherently higher-productivity system, creates severe adjustment problems in the short run. These manifest themselves in bottlenecks, inflationary pressures, slow-down in gross production, and balance of trade problems. Foreign capital inflows can, in part, substitute for the short-run lack of flexibility of the economy and facilitate adjustment. But the temptation to use foreign capital inflows to postpone adjustment, rather than facilitate it, is great.

These phenomena are familiar to development economists who have watched attempts to switch from import substitution to export orientation in economies with prolonged histories of import substitution and without institutional change. Indeed the literature on bureaucratic authoritarianism, which argued that political development in the second sense at the cost of political development in the first sense was necessary to support a switch to export orientation in Latin America, was spawned in partial recognition of these phenomena. (The other strand of support for bureaucratic authoritarianism was that the political influence of entrenched import-substitute interests needed to be curbed to effect the necessary changes.)

These phenomena are also familiar to students of the adjustment history of Latin America, which highlights the dual role of foreign assistance in this regard. During the 1970s, Latin American countries used foreign debt to postpone structural adjustment, maintaining their rates of growth of absorption and imports through increases in debt. This led to more severe adjustment problems in the 1980s.

The same sort of postponement of adjustment through foreign debt was also evident in Eastern Europe during the latter part of the 1970s. Eastern European countries other than Hungary reacted to the external shock mostly by increasing their foreign borrowing. But the specific adjustment patterns varied: Poland increased both imports and exports, borrowed massively and experienced a very substantial decrease in growth rate (the growth rate of the net material product during 1975–80 fell to one-eighth of that during 1970–5). Bulgaria's growth dropped very little, and the increase in exports accounted for almost 45 per cent of its total adjustment (Bekker, 1987). Hungary adjusted by cutting the rate of growth in its real GNP in half, increased exports and imports equally, and decreased its reliance on additional foreign debt, in part by using up foreign reserves.

This postponement of adjustment through debt-led growth in the 1970s led to severe debt problems in the 1980s in both Latin America and Eastern Europe. The debt problem of Eastern European countries, like that of heavily indebted developed countries, became critical in the 1980s. All heavily indebted countries are now facing a similar adjustment problem – the need to restructure their economies to achieve positive trade balances while confronting very stringent foreign exchange constraints arising from debt service problems. In principle this can be achieved either by cutting imports, in a new round of import substitution, or by increasing exports. As in LDCs, the responses varied, with some countries turning more inward (Rumania and Czechoslovakia) and others (Yugoslavia and Hungary) becoming more outward-oriented in their policies. As in LDCs, adjustment was easier in economies that adopted an outward-oriented approach (Balassa, 1984), though painful even in those countries (Adelman, Vujovic, Berck and Labus, 1989).

In the early 1980s, Eastern European countries other than Bulgaria adjusted to the debt crisis primarily by cutting the rate of growth of hard currency imports. By 1982, all except Bulgaria and Czechoslovakia had achieved a balance of trade surplus in convertible currency trade. Deflationary measures were adopted in Hungary, Poland and Yugoslavia under the impetus of the IMF, leading to sharp declines in domestic absorption. Fixed investment fell sharply between 1980 and 1985. In Yugoslavia real household incomes fell by almost 40 per cent between 1980 and 1987. Hungary and Yugoslavia cushioned real private consumption, but Poland experienced a 6 per cent real decline over the period, most of it in 1982. In an effort to service their debts, all East European countries transferred part of their growth abroad. As indicated by the difference in the growth of GNP and domestic absorption, the fraction of growth transferred abroad between 1981 and 1985 averaged 109 per cent,[1] and ranged from 170 per cent in Hungary to 3 per cent in Bulgaria.

The current system-restructuring problems in Eastern Europe are even more severe than their debt-adjustment problems were up to now. The system reforms must be undertaken starting with a heavy debt overhang;[2] in economies that are import-starved; whose standards of living have declined to varying degrees;[3] and that are plagued by rigidities, lack of experience with production under market institutions, and are experiencing galloping inflation rates.[4] They also have very substantial excess liquidity in the hands of consumers (reputed to be 80 per cent of GDP in Poland)[5] ready to fuel increases in inflation once subsidies to basic goods are removed, domestic market prices are freed, and domestic prices are brought in line with world prices. At the same time, delivering improvements in living standards is a political imperative for democracy to survive. But the control of inflation requires reductions in government subsidies to both consumers and producers and tighter credit conditions for enterprises. Enterprise bankruptcy will then become a genuine possibility. Unemployment can then mushroom, leading to severe sociopolitical problems in economies whose expectations and institutions are adjusted to full employment.

Experience with developing country adjustment programmes of the 1980s suggests that they rarely succeed without additional external resources. There were numerous instances of postponed adjustment programmes in less developed countries in the 1980s owing to foreign resource unavailability, often resulting from disagreements with the IMF. But how does one follow IMF-conditionality and, at the same time, succeed in delivering immediate improvements in living standards? Will countries that have already undergone about 40 years of austerity, with the promise of improvements in living standards around the corner, agree to further austerity under similar promises? Will the ideology of market economies be more credible to Eastern Europe than the ideology of communism?

Clearly some stabilization and restructuring loans are needed. But how much, of what kind and under what conditions should vary country by country. On the whole the response should be timely but modest, so as not to obviate the need for domestic restructuring. Countries whose economies are in a shambles, such as Poland and Rumania, will require Western support of substantial commodity-import programmes to enable them rapidly to deliver wage-goods. These commodity-import programmes should be limited to food, especially perishables, in order to reduce possibilities for speculation, hoarding and abuse. A Polish programme of this nature is already under way.

Support of Restructuring

There are two important points that we have learned from the experience of developing and Eastern European countries in the last two decades. The first is that the productivity of borrowed-resource use is critical in determining whether foreign loans generate or do not generate a 'debt problem'. If the productivity of borrowed resources exceeds the rate of interest on borrowed funds, as it did in South Korea, then borrowing now and repaying out of growth later is a rational economic policy. (The analyses undertaken in the early 1960s, under the auspices of the Agency of International Development, to explore the period of transition to self-supporting economic growth, which indicated that between 20 and 25 years of foreign assistance would be required in most middle-income developing countries, were all based on this assumption.) If the productivity of investment of borrowed resources in developing countries is lower than the rate of interest, as has been the case in the majority of heavy borrowers in Latin America, then a 'debt problem' will surely arise.

Past experience with international loans to Eastern European economies indicates that they have low productivity of borrowed resources and therefore are more like Latin American than East Asian economies in this regard. The economic growth of communist countries has been more resource- and capital-intensive than that of market-oriented developing countries (Chenery *et al.*, 1986). This indicates not only low average productivity of material input use in East European economies but also low marginal productivity of resource use. Indeed, as we saw above, the desire to increase total factor productivity has been a major motivating force in virtually all waves of Eastern European system reforms. High growth rates in Eastern European countries up to 1980 were supported by very high rates of savings and investment, enforced by shortages of consumer goods and either suppressed or open inflations. This is precisely the type of economic growth that has led to the current disillusionment with the communist countries' economic performance. But this growth pattern also bodes ill for the probability of Eastern European economies being able to handle the 'debt problem'.

Foreign borrowing also gives rise to 'transfer problems', so that not only must the productivity of investment exceed the rate of interest; the investment must also enable the economy to generate, either directly or indirectly, sufficient foreign exchange for debt servicing and debt repayment. If foreign exchange earnings are not sufficient and the economies cannot grow their way out of debt (as is the case when the productivity of resource use is lower than the rate of interest) then achieving the transfer of resources into foreign currency requires reductions in domestic absorption and expenditure switching between domestic consumption and tradables and gives rise to high rates of domestic inflation. Declines in domestic absorption imply declines in household incomes and, in less developed countries, have usually led to even larger relative declines in the incomes of the poor.

The second lesson we have learned from the experience of both types of countries is that reforms tend to be slowed down when increases in debt allow for ample increased imports. This is what happened during the 1970s in the overwhelming majority of countries. It was only under the impetus of the debt crisis of 1981–2, which led to a sharply reduced willingness by banks to lend to both developing and socialist countries, that a new wave of reforms was introduced in Eastern Europe.

In Eastern Europe debt-supported restructuring is a two-edged sword. Expansion of output and investment in Eastern Europe has not been liquidity-constrained: on the contrary, enterprises have tended to operate with soft budget constraints (Kornai, 1980). The availability of state credit has enabled enterprises to produce to inventory, rather than to satisfy final demands, and thus enabled them to be less responsive to consumer demand. To generate incentives for restructuring at the enterprise level, one wants a tauter rather than a more lavish credit regime. This tautness is compatible with aid-financed restructuring only if foreign aid is accompanied by IMF-type constraints on credit expansion. Also, while economic expansion in East European countries is resource-constrained, it is less foreign exchange-constrained than in the typical developing country. In the more developed East European economies (such as East Germany and Czechoslovakia) import-substitute industrialization has produced machinery and technology-intensive intermediates which need to be imported in the typical Latin American less developed country. Finally, while increased imports make restructuring easier, state debt offers a disincentive to restructuring. Divestiture of state assets is inherently incompatible with increased state foreign liabilities.

These considerations, which have been validated by the experience with debt-led growth in Eastern Europe, all suggest the need for great caution on the side of both borrower and lender in using further foreign debt to support economic restructuring.

Trade versus Aid

Experience with aid to developing countries has indicated that trade is considerably more potent than aid in supporting growth and structural adjustment. The total foreign assistance budget of the World Bank is about the same size as the welfare budget in New York city. This consideration alone suggests that the inflow of resources by itself cannot make a perceptible difference when spread over 3 billion people and over 100 countries. What matters is the leverage which the aid flows can confer on the lender for negotiating the restructuring of domestic institutional arrangements and policies within LDCs.

Trade, on the other hand, has been found to be potent in the following areas: raising the growth rates of export-oriented, open economies; increasing the efficiency of resource use in the economy; generating international competitiveness; restructuring production patterns towards higher value-added goods in the product cycle; facilitating adjustment to external shocks; and increasing the market responsiveness of domestic institutions. All of these effects have been documented by Balassa (for example, 1989).

Foreign Investment

Foreign investment in the form of joint ventures is also an attractive alternative to debt for restructuring. To the foreign investor, joint ventures offer low wages, a work force that is better educated than that in the US, and a large domestic market that is starved for goods. In Eastern Europe, wage rates including fringe benefits are between 10 and 15 per cent of the US. Taken together, East Germany, Hungary and Czechoslovakia offer a market with a combined GNP that exceeds that of China. To East European countries, joint ventures provide access to risk-bearing foreign exchange without borrowing, to foreign markets and marketing services, and to more advanced technologies, know-how and management skills without paying for them. Foreign ventures thus look attractive to both parties. There are, however, potential conflicts of interest between the host country and the foreign investors which could affect the way the foreign ventures are managed. Also, to date, the transfer of technology from joint ventures with foreign investors to other domestic enterprises has been disappointing. Nevertheless increased trade and foreign investment offer superior alternatives to foreign aid.

IV CONCLUSION

My gut reaction to recent developments in Eastern Europe was to urge the initiation of a Marshall plan by the OECD (Organization for Economic Cooperation and Development) countries in support of the economic restructuring of East European countries. However, once I started thinking about the subject, I talked myself out of this. It became clear to me that, if the aim is economic restructuring, lavish foreign assistance was likely to be counterproductive for Eastern European economies. Instead the short-run response should consist of substantial commodity assistance programmes where needed, along with modest adjustment loans, and some debt forgiveness structured on a case-by-case basis. The longer-run response should be aimed at providing the proper international environment for reform. This would entail opening up trade possibilities for Eastern European countries, providing insurance of foreign investment, and technical assistance with technology, training and management. Thus the long-run response should consist mostly of measures to facilitate trade and investment (including technology transfer). The current programmes structured for Poland and Hungary appear about right, as does the approach of the EEC to Eastern European restructuring.

Ultimately, in all countries, it is internal policies and institutions that matter. The international environment can either facilitate or hamper the adoption of appropriate domestic development strategies. Foreign aid is, at best, the tail that can be used to generate incentives for wagging the dog. Attempts to do much more than provide a receptive international environment for East European restructuring are likely to do more harm to the cause of restructuring and generate more problems for Eastern European countries in the medium run than they would solve in the immediate run.

NOTES

* Published by permission of Transaction Publishers, from the *Review of Black Political Economy*, **19** (2). Copyright © 1990 by the National Economic Association and the Southern Center for Studies in Public Policy of Clark–Atlanta University.
† I am indebted to Peter Berck, Edward Taylor, Dusan Vujovic and Pinhas Zusman for their

insightful comments.
1. Excludes Rumania.
2. Rumania is an exception.
3. Bulgaria is an exception.
4. In some East European countries the inflation is suppressed.
5. Excess liquidity is defined as the ratio of nominal financial assets held by households to GDP at current prices.

REFERENCES

Adelman, Irma (1972), 'Social and Economic Development at the Micro Level – A Tentative Hypothesis', in Eliezer B. Ayal (ed.), *Micro Aspects of Economic Development*, New York: Frederick Praeger.

Adelman, Irma (1975), 'Development Economics – a Reassessment of Goals', *American Economic Review*, **65** (2), p. 302–9.

Adelman, Irma and Cynthia Taft Morris (1967), *Society, Politics and Economic Development: A Quantitative Approach*, Baltimore: Johns Hopkins Press.

Adelman, Irma and Cynthia Taft Morris (1973), *Social Equity and Economic Growth in Developing Countries*, Stanford: Stanford University Press.

Adelman, Irma and Jairus M. Hihn (1984), 'The Dynamics of Political Change', *Economic Development and Cultural Change*, **33** (1) pp. 1–23.

Adelman, I., D. Vujovic, P. Berck and M. Labus (1990), 'Adjustment Under Different Trade Strategies: A Mean–Variance Analysis with a GCE Model of the Yugoslav Economy' in Jaime de Melo and Andre Sapir (eds), *Trade Theory and Economic Reform: North, South and East – Essays in Honor of Bela Balassa*, Cambridge: Basil Blackwell.

Apter, David E. (1965), *The Politics of Modernization*, Chicago: University of Chicago Press.

Apter, David E. (1973), *Political Change*, New York: Frank Cass.

Balassa, Bela (1983), 'The Hungarian Economic Reform, 1968–82', *Banca Nazionale del Lavoro Quarterly Review*, **141** (1) pp. 163–84.

Balassa, Bela (1984), 'Adjustment Policies in Developing Countries: A Reassessment', *World Development*, **12** (9) pp. 955–72.

Balassa, Bela (1989), *Comparative Advantage, Trade Policy, and Economic Development*, New York: Harvester Wheatsheaf.

Bekker, Zsuzsa (1987), 'Adjustment Patterns and Problems in East European Countries: An International Comparison', International Labor Organization, International Employment Policies Working Paper 12.

Brada, Josef C. and John M. Montias (1984), 'Industrial Policy in Eastern Europe: A Three-Country Comparison', *Journal of Comparative Economics*, **8** (4) pp. 377–419.

Chenery, Hollis B., Sherman Robinson and Moshe Syrquin (1986), *Industrialization and Growth: A Comparative Study*, London: Oxford University Press.

Dasgupta, Partha (1989), 'Well-being and the Extent of its Realisation in Poor Countries', Development Economics Research Programme, London School of Economics No.19.

Hirschman, Albert O. (1974), 'Exit, Voice, and Loyalty: Further Reflections and a Survey of Recent Contributions', in *Essays in Trespassing*, Princeton: Princeton University Press.

Huntington, Samuel P. and Joan M. Nelson (1976), *No Easy Choice: Political*

Participation in Developing Countries, Cambridge, Mass.: Harvard Press.
Kuznets, Simon S. (1955), 'Economic Growth and Income Inequality', *American Economic Review*, **45** (2) pp. 1–28.
Kornai, Janos (1980), *Economics of Shortage*, Amsterdam: North Holland.
North, Douglass C. (1973), *The Rise of the Western World: A New Economic History*, Cambridge: Cambridge University Press.
Nyers, Rezso (1983), 'Interrelations between policy and the economic reform in Hungary', *Journal of Comparative Economics*, **7** (3) pp.211–24.
Parsons, Talcott (1951), *The Social System*, Glencoe, Ill: The Free Press.
Ranis, Gustav and John C. Fei (1988), 'Development Economics: What Next?', in Gustav Ranis and T. Paul Schultz (eds), *The State of Economic Development* Oxford: Basil Blackwell, pp. 100–36.
Smelser, Neil J. 1963, *The Sociology of Modern Life*, Englewood, NJ: Prentice Hall.
United Nations (1981), *World Economic Survey*, New York: United Nations.

PART III

The United States

9. Low Saving Rates and the 'Twin Deficits': Confusing the Symptoms and Causes of Economic Decline

Robert A. Blecker*

I INTRODUCTION

While the cold war may be ending, a new kind of spectre is haunting American capitalism: that of a 'saving shortfall'. From Boskin to Summers, from Darman to Rostenkowski, economists and politicians alike decry the United States' low saving rate. While some economists cite the federal budget deficit as the prime culprit, others allege that there is a serious problem of 'over-consumption' in the private sector.[1] According to a typical rendition (albeit from an untypical source):

> On the basis of massive borrowing and massive sales of national assets, Americans have been squandering their heritage and impoverishing their children. They have done so for the sake of present consumption ... (Daly and Cobb, 1989, p. 367)

The question of whether the US saving rate is really 'low' by either historical or international standards has been treated elsewhere by the present author (Blecker, 1990a and 1990b) and by others (for example, Hayashi, 1986; Lipsey and Kravis, 1987; Eisner, 1989a and 1991; Block, 1990; Steindl, 1990). These studies have shown that different ways of measuring saving have radically different implications about both the trends in US saving rates and how those rates compare with other countries'. This chapter will seek to go beyond questions of measurement in order to focus on the causes of the changes in observed saving rates in the

---

*This paper was written while the author was a Research Economist at the Economic Policy Institute (EPI). The author would like to thank EPI for permission to reproduce material published elsewhere and David Bunting for advice on the Consumer Expenditure Survey. The analysis and views in this paper are solely the responsibility of the author.

1980s and their implications for US economic policymaking in the 1990s.

The popular press has interpreted the falling saving rates of the last decade as the result of attitude shifts in the 'me generation'. Economists have sometimes also adopted moralistic terminology in describing a 'consumption binge' or 'spending spree' in the 1980s. Nevertheless there is little support in the economic analyses for the popular impression of a sudden change in individual attitudes toward thrift. The serious analyses have focused on identifying changes in the objective conditions (constraints) governing individual consumers' behaviour. While many explanations have been given for the falling saving rate, at least one advocate of the 'saving crisis' view (Kotlikoff, 1990, p. 9) admits that 'there is no "smoking gun" explanation for the critically low level of U.S. saving'.

Given the lack of direct proof of a massive consumption binge by American households, the trade deficit is often cited as circumstantial evidence that the entire country is 'living beyond its means'. This assertion is based on the fact that a country with a trade deficit must, by definition, have domestic expenditures in excess of its national income. But this is the fallacy of inferring a causal relationship from a tautology. One could just as well say that a country has a trade deficit because it is not producing enough income to pay for its expenditures owing to a lack of international competitiveness or of foreign demand. And even if aggregate domestic expenditures are considered excessive, it remains to be seen who or what is responsible for these expenditures.

Often the correlation of high budget and trade deficits is held to demonstrate that government dissaving is the primary factor causing the nation to 'live beyond its means'. In this view, government borrowing depletes national saving, thus drawing in the net inflows of foreign capital which are required to finance the trade deficit. As we shall see, the fiscal deficit does explain part of the trade deficit, but not because government borrowing depletes private saving. Rather government deficit spending generates the savings required to finance itself; however in an open economy part of these savings may come from abroad.

All the different versions of the saving shortfall argument are based on the fundamental logic of neoclassical capital theory, according to which economic growth results from individuals sacrificing current consumption in order to provide for the future. In this view, it is assumed that more saving (refraining from consumption) necessarily results in additional investment (accumulating new means of production). Causality runs one way only, from saving to investment to growth and competitiveness. I shall argue in this chapter that in fact the causality is mainly the reverse: the low US saving rate is largely a *sympton*, not the underlying cause, of the problems with capital accumulation and economic growth in the US in the past decade. This *reverse causality* argument is based on the perspective of *cumulative causation* in the growth process which is found in the post Keynesian theoretical paradigm. From this perspective, the US economy is caught in a vicious circle of stagnation in productive investment and income growth and – as a result – has a low realized saving rate.

In the case of the US in the 1980s, the pre-existing growth slow-down contributed to low saving rates in two ways: by raising the proportion of depreciation allowances to current income, and by squeezing consumers who had been accustomed to continuous increases in their standard of living. In addition, the upward redistribution of income and concentration of wealth permitted the wealthy to raise their consumption expenditures in ways which created the misimpression of an overall consumer 'binge'. And, contrary to the conventional view that high interest rates give incentives to save more, the high real interest rates of the past decade actually contributed to *lower* saving rates. Finally, while it is undeniable that some part of the worsened trade deficit of the 1980s was caused by the US fiscal deficit (combined with monetary tightness at home and fiscal contraction abroad), the two deficits are far from being 'twins'. The magnitude and persistence of the US trade deficits also reflect another factor – a secular decline in US competitiveness, uncompensated by dollar depreciation – which has a negative impact on the domestic saving rate as well.

Section II of the chapter begins with a brief theoretical overview, contrasting the traditional neoclassical view of saving and economic growth with an alternative perspective emphasizing the cumulative nature of the growth process. Section III then analyses whether the low US saving rates in the 1980s were caused by a generalized bout of 'overconsumption'. Section IV turns to the 'twin' deficits. Both the effects of the budget deficit on trade and the independent causes of the trade deficit are considered. Section V concludes with a discussion of the alternatives for US economic policy in the 1990s.

II THE ROLE OF SAVING IN THE GROWTH PROCESS

In the simplest, descriptive neoclassical growth models, the saving rate is exogenously given. The higher the saving rate, the higher are the steady-state levels of capital and output per worker, and the higher is the steady-state real wage. The saving rate does not affect the 'natural rate of growth' (population growth plus exogenously given productivity growth) but an increase in the saving rate will raise the growth rate in the transition to a steady-state with higher capital per worker. This 'capital deepening' (increase in the 'quantity' of capital per worker) raises the productivity of labour and the equilibrium real wage (equal to labour's marginal product), thus increasing the sustainable standard of living for society as a whole.

Traditionally, neoclassical policy analysis has rested on this core logic, augmented by a set of exogenous factors used to explain the saving rate (for example, demographics, tax incentives). In more complex models, in which saving is distinguished from investment, taxes on capital income are seen as driving a 'wedge' between the (after-tax) rate of return to savers and the (before-tax) cost of capital to firms. In this case, the key to high investment and rapid growth is a low cost of capital, which requires both a high saving rate and a small tax wedge.

An alternative view, derived from the Marxian and Keynesian theoretical traditions (see Eichner and Kregel, 1975; Harris, 1978; Marglin, 1984) conceptualizes saving as an endogenous variable in the growth process. In this view, the driving force behind economic growth is the accumulation of industrial capital in the form of productive investment. The desired rate of investment depends fundamentally on expectations about the growth of markets for firms' products and the profitability of investment projects (Eisner, 1978). Adding a Schumpeterian perspective, desired investment may also be an increasing function of the rate of technological progress (Steindl, 1979; Cooper, 1988) – and the definition of 'investment' can be expanded to include intangibles such as research and development (Eichner, 1976). The actual rate of investment may be constrained by the availability of finance, especially firms' internal funds or cash flow (see Kalecki, 1971; Fazzari and Mott, 1986–7). While the 'cost of capital' may also influence investment, its effects are seen as strictly subsidiary to the effects of expectations about demand, profits, and technology, as well as the ability of firms to generate internal finance.

Capital accumulation has the same effects in this view as in neoclassical theory: increased value of capital per worker, higher productivity of labour and higher real wages consistent with constant relative shares. However, neo-Marxian and post Keynesian theories do not derive these results from an aggregate production function in which merely increasing the amount of (homogeneous) capital per worker causes the marginal productivity of labour to rise. Rather these theories assume that capital accumulation increases labour productivity mainly via embodied technical progress and other forms of dynamic scale economies (such as specialization and learning effects) which were ignored by traditional neoclassical growth models (see, for example, Kaldor, 1972).

Most importantly for present purposes, the alternative theories recognize that *the effects of rapid capital accumulation in turn stimulate the additional savings which are required to finance that accumulation.* The primary vehicle for this positive feedback is *profits* – a key variable in the world of business, but one that is conspicuously absent from most neoclassical growth models. Given rapid productivity growth and enhanced competitiveness, firms should be able to increase their flow of profits. As long as the growth of real product wages can be held below the growth of labour productivity, the profit share should rise.[2] As a large portion of corporate profits are retained, it may be expected that corporate saving will rise in proportion to national income – and gross corporate saving provides the lion's share of finance for business fixed investment.

Household saving should also be robust in such an environment. A high profit share implies a high share of capital income (dividends, interest, capital gains) in personal income and such income tends to flow to wealthy households with above-average saving rates. Even among waged and salaried workers, however, steadily rising real incomes can lead to relatively high personal saving rates, as consumption patterns take time to adjust.[3] One would therefore expect to find comparatively high rates of household saving in countries experiencing rapid capital accumulation.

This alternative framework does not deny that high saving rates are a *necessary* condition for sustained rapid economic growth. But this framework does deny that saving rates are *independent* variables in the growth process, determined by such exogenous factors as the age composition of the population and tax incentives. On the contrary, this framework implies the *reverse* causality from the conventional wisdom: high (low) saving rates can be an *effect* of rapid (slow) capital accumulation and economic growth, rather than a cause.

Recently 'new' neoclassical models of economic growth have appeared which incorporate increasing returns and endogenous technical progress (see, for example, Romer 1986, 1987, 1990). Since productivity growth is endogenous, growth is no longer fixed at a 'natural rate' in the long run. The new growth models generally have the property that there are multiple equilibria, and the 'free-market' growth path is often sub-optimal compared with some form of government intervention.[4] Fundamentally this is because individual agents do not perceive the external economies or spillovers which they can foster by saving and investing more.

If individual free choice cannot be relied upon to yield a socially optimal growth rate, then the government may be justified in inducing individuals to save and invest more than they would otherwise. The new neoclassical growth models thus have policy implications which are, at the same time, both revolutionary and yet highly conventional. The revolutionary implication is that public policy can potentially improve on the 'free market' in the long run. But since the models do not, in effect, distinguish saving from investment, and since investment is assumed to be determined by saving, the policy prescription ends up being the same as in the old models: save more.

III US SAVING RATES AND CONSUMPTION BEHAVIOUR IN THE 1980s

This section examines a concrete case of the importance of viewing saving as an endogenous variable in the growth process: the alleged over-consumption problem in the US economy. Two measures of saving in the US national income and product accounts (NIPAs) fell to post-war record lows in the late 1980s: the *net national* saving rate, and the *personal* saving rate. These are the measures which are usually invoked by those who claim that the American people are shortchanging their descendants by spending too much for present consumption.

Table 9.1 shows how various NIPA-based saving rates have changed over the last three decades. Since calendar decades do not correspond to the timing of business cycles, the data are averaged over three time periods which cover mid-to-late expansions in the business cycle: 1963–8, 1976–9 and 1984–9. Although net national saving is usually measured in proportion to net national product (NNP), and personal saving in proportion to disposable income, all the saving concepts are measured relative to GNP for consistency. While adjustments could be made for various deficiencies in the NIPA measures of savings (for example, imputed incomes and expenditures, and the inconsistent treatment of private and public pensions)[5] the standard definitions will suffice for present purposes.

The net national saving rate fell by more than two-thirds from the mid-1960s to late 1980s. This fall can be decomposed into three main sources: increased depreciation allowances, increased budget deficits and reduced personal saving. First, the depreciation rate increased by 2.0 per cent of GNP from the 1960s to the 1970s, and by another 0.6 per cent in the 1980s. Adding depreciation allowances back in yields gross national saving. This also fell in the 1980s, but by much less than net saving. Second, the overall government deficit increased by 1.9 per cent of GNP from the late 1970s to the 1980s, resulting in lower (negative) government saving.[6] Taking out government saving, we obtain *gross private saving*, which *was only slightly lower* in 1984–9 than in 1963–8 (15.9 per cent of GNP versus 16.9 per cent). Third, the personal saving rate decreased by 1.6 per cent of GNP between 1976–9 and 1984–9, which accounts for most of the 2.0 per cent of GDP fall in gross private saving. Note that about half of gross

Table 9.1 Average US saving and investment rates in mid-to-late cyclical expansions (in per cent of GNP)

Concept	1963–8	1976–9	1984–9
Net national saving	8.2	7.0	2.5
Plus depreciation[a]	8.2	10.2	10.8
Equals gross national saving	16.5	17.3	13.3
Less government saving	(−0.5)	(−0.7)	(−2.6)
Equals gross private saving	16.9	17.9	15.9
Sum of			
Personal saving	4.8	4.9	3.3
Gross corporate saving	8.6	8.9	8.6
Non-corporate depreciation[b]	3.5	4.1	4.1
Memoranda			
Gross fixed investment	14.6	16.4	15.1
Gross fixed non-residential investment	10.1	11.1	10.3

Source: US Department of Commerce, Bureau of Economic Analysis (BEA), National Income and Product Accounts (NIPAs).
Notes:
[a] Depreciation is measured by capital consumption allowances, not by taxable depreciation.
[b] Includes unincorporated businesses as well as residential depreciation.

private saving is corporate, and *the gross corporate saving rate hardly changed at all* – it was the same in the late 1980s as in the mid-1960s.

Let us consider each of these components of net national saving more closely. NIPA estimates of economic depreciation ('capital consumption allowances') are based on assumed service lives for the various classes of plant and equipment. Since changes in technology and investment patterns have led to a greater proportion of short-lived types of equipment (such as computers) in the capital stock, the result is more rapid depreciation. Also, as Pieper (1989) has shown, a high depreciation rate (relative to current national income) can result from a growth slow-down, even with unchanged average service lives. The reason is that, when growth slows down, the depreciation on the old capital equipment from the previous period of rapid growth is large in relation to current output. Pieper finds that a substantial part of the increased depreciation rate in the US economy can be attributed to the post-1973 growth slow-down. Thus the depreciation factor is an example of reverse causality: *prior* changes in the rate and pattern of capital accumulation cause a *subsequent* fall in the net saving rate.

The budget deficit rose in the 1980s because, as is well known, the Reagan Administration pushed through simultaneous income tax cuts and military spending increases which were not matched by fully compensating cuts in social spending. While one could define military spending as 'social consumption' (as opposed to social investment), it clearly has nothing to do with individual families consuming more in the ordinary sense of the word. As for the tax cuts, it is often believed that these fuelled an across-the-board spending orgy by putting more disposable income in the hands of American taxpayers. But it has now been shown that only the taxpayers in the top decile enjoyed a significant effective tax cut in the 1980s, and that the largest tax cuts were received by the top 1 per cent (Pechman, 1990; US Congressional Budget Office, 1990; McIntyre, 1990). The vast majority of taxpayers had effective income tax rates (state, local, and federal combined, including social security) which were the same or higher at the end of the decade. Apart from the Pentagon, it was only the wealthy who could afford to 'over-consume' as a result of fiscal policy changes in the 1980s.[7]

Finally we come to the personal saving rate. If one examines the serious studies of why this rate fell, one finds a striking lack of support for the hypothesis of a generalized 'consumption binge'. The following are some of the factors which have been identified as contributing to the falling personal saving rate in the past decade:[8]

1. High interest rates led to more consumer spending as the income effect outweighed the substitution effect (Cantor, 1989).
2. High interest rates and the stock market boom led to overfunding of pension funds, and thus reduced private employers' contributions to defined-benefit pension funds, which are counted as imputed personal savings (Bosworth, 1989; Block, 1990; Christian, 1990; Steindl, 1990).
3. Households spent a large fraction of the cash payments they received from corporate takeovers (Summers and Carroll, 1987; Hatsopoulos *et al.*, 1989; Blecker, 1990a).
4. Reduced real income growth resulted in a high average propensity to consume due to slow adjustment of consumption spending (Bosworth, 1990).
5. A rise in the value of personal wealth relative to income from the 1970s to the mid-1980s had a positive effect on the average consumption–income ratio (Hatsopoulos *et al.*, 1989; Blecker, 1990a).

These factors suggest that the low personal saving rate was largely a function of changes in the overall economic environment and macro policies – not a result of the average consumer going on a spending 'binge'.

Indeed real personal consumption spending per capita actually grew more slowly in 1979–89 than in the previous two decades, as shown in Figure 9.1. However the growth of real personal disposable income per capita slowed down even more, resulting in a rising consumption–income

Figure 9.1 Growth of real disposable income and consumption per capita

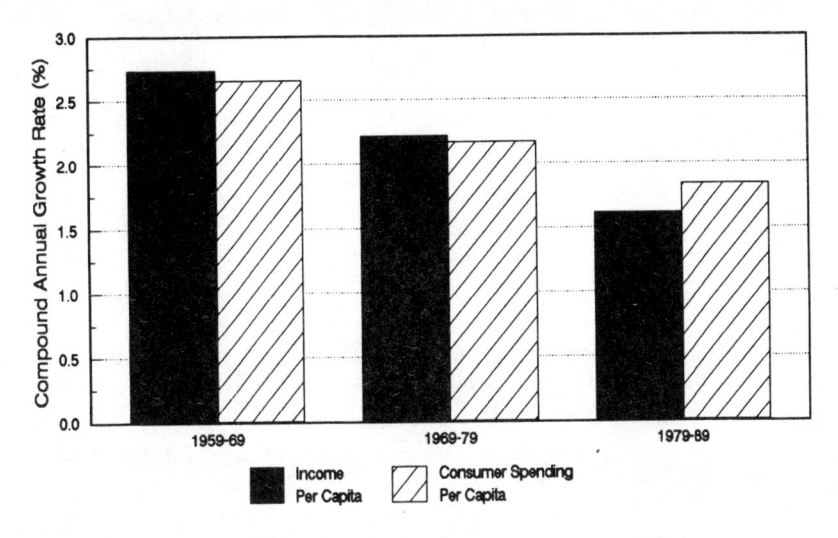

[Bar chart showing Compound Annual Growth Rate (%) for three periods: 1959-69, 1969-79, 1979-89. Income Per Capita and Consumer Spending Per Capita shown. 1959-69: both approximately 2.75%. 1969-79: both approximately 2.25%. 1979-89: income approximately 1.7%, consumer spending approximately 1.9%.]

Source: US Department of Commerce, BEA, NIPAs, and author's calculations.

ratio. This would seem to suggest an income squeeze rather than a consumption binge. More specifically it suggests that the falling personal saving rate is partly a function of the squeeze on working and middle-class families which has resulted from industrial decline and restructuring, stagnant or falling real wages and rising inequality in the distribution of income (see Mishel and Simon, 1988). And factors 1, 3, and 5 support the view that mainly the wealthiest households could have afforded to go on a major 'consumption binge' in the Reagan era.

These inferences are supported by the disaggregated data on consumption spending by income quintile shown in Table 9.2. The growth rates in this table must be interpreted with caution, since they are based on surveys of different households at different times. Also it was necessary to compare the most recent data available (1988) with a much older survey (1972–3), since no comparable survey was done in the late 1970s or early 1980s.[9] Nevertheless, the results are striking. Only the top quintile had positive growth of its real after-tax income between 1972–3 and 1988, and this quintile also had the highest growth rate of real consumption expenditures over the same period. The bottom 80 per cent clearly suffered from an income squeeze as nominal incomes failed to keep pace with inflation; the squeeze was most intense in the lowest quintiles. The fact that consumption grew more rapidly than after-tax income for all quintiles is, of course, just a reflection of the falling saving rate. Note that the gap between income and consumption growth diminishes from the bottom to

Table 9.2 Average annual growth rates of real after-tax income and consumer expenditures, 1972–3 to 1988 (per cent per year)

	After-tax income	Consumption expenditures[a]
All consumer units[b]	−0.04	1.61
By income quintile[c]		
Lowest 20%	−1.33	1.35
Second 20%	−0.99	1.09
Third 20%	−0.52	1.11
Fourth 20%	−0.08	1.61
Highest 20%	0.62	2.18

Sources: US Department of Labor, Bureau of Labor Statistics, Survey of Consumer Expenditures (Integrated Surveys) and Consumer Price Index (CPI-U-X1) and author's calculations.
Notes:
[a] Excluding cash contributions, personal insurance, pensions, and Social Security payments.
[b] Complete income reporters only.
[c] Quintiles are based on before-tax income.

the top quintile, indicating that the saving rate fell the most at the bottom where the income squeeze was greatest.[10]

Econometric estimates of consumption functions also yield results which are consistent with the view that mainly the rich were 'over-consuming' in the 1980s. Hatsopoulos, Krugman and Poterba (1989) found that about 70 per cent of the increase in the consumption–NNP ratio from 1970–9 to 1985–7 could be explained by three factors: increased personal interest income,[11] higher household net worth, and after-tax cash receipts from corporate takeovers. I re-estimated their equation with some modifications (in Blecker, 1990a)[12] and found that 55 per cent of the increase in the consumption–GNP ratio from 1970–9 to 1985–8 was explained by these same factors. Given the high concentration of bonds, stock and other assets in the population,[13] this finding corroborates the view that the high average propensity to consume in the 1980s was largely a result of increased spending by the wealthiest households.

These findings give specific content to the view that the decline in the NIPA personal saving rate is a symptom, rather than a cause, of the nation's true economic problems. The NIPA personal saving rate measures the gap or 'residual' between personal disposable income and consumption expenditures. In the 1980s, wealthy individuals did well, as real interest rates were high, and most assets rose substantially in value. In particular, the stock market boomed, partly as a result of the leveraged buy-out movement. And stockholders often found their corporate equity converted into cash by merger and acquisition activity. Thus high interest

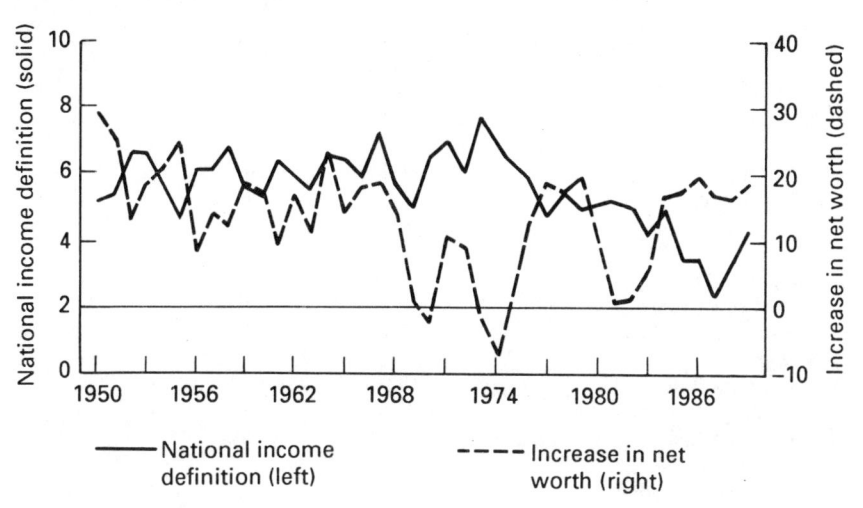

Figure 9.2 Inflation-adjusted personal saving rates (in per cent of disposable income)

Note: The increase in net worth is measured as a 3-year moving average.
Sources: FRB, BEA, and author's calculations.

income combined with capital gains on existing assets induced wealthy households (as well as companies contributing to defined-benefit pension plans) to save less of their current cash flow, without reducing the expected future value of their accumulated savings.[14]

The econometric evidence reveals that capital gains, both realized and unrealized, were used to finance part of the consumption growth of the affluent.[15] However capital gains are *not counted* in the Commerce Department's measure of personal income.[16] As a result, *the use of capital gains to finance wealthy consumers' spending has the effect of reducing the conventional measure of personal saving*, which is simply income minus consumption – even though the increase in household wealth should properly be regarded as *contributing* to savings. If we take a broader measure of personal saving – the increase in household net worth, adjusted for inflation – we find that the personal saving rate was *not* unusually low in the late 1980s, but in fact *recovered* from the losses due to inflation in the 1970s (see the dashed line in Figure 9.2).[17] This finding is also consistent with the fact that the highest income quintile had the smallest reduction in its saving rate, while still increasing its consumption at the highest rate.

The part of the saving story which is usually overlooked is the behaviour of non-financial corporate (NFC) profits. Table 9.3 gives data on non-financial corporate profits for the same three mid-to-late expansion

Table 9.3 *Non-financial corporate profits in mid-to-late cyclical expansions (per cent of non-financial corporate gross domestic product)*

	1963–8	1976–9	1984–9
Gross profits	26.3	24.4	24.5
Less:			
Depreciation[a]	8.2	10.4	11.1
Net interest	1.7	2.8	4.2
Equals net profits	16.3	11.2	9.2
Less:			
Dividends	3.9	2.8	4.2
Corporate taxes	6.7	5.2	3.4
Equals net cash flow[b]	5.7	3.1	2.6
Memoranda			
Gross cash flow[c]	13.9	13.5	13.7
Pay-out[d]	5.6	5.7	7.3
Household cash receipts from corporate takeovers[e]	0.8	0.9	2.6[f]

Source: US Department of Commerce, BEA, NIPAs, and author's calculations.
Notes:
[a] Measured by capital consumption allowances with capital consumption adjustment.
[b] Equal to retained earnings with capital consumption adjustment and inventory valuation adjustment.
[c] Equal to net cash flow plus depreciation.
[d] Sum of dividends and net interest.
[e] Calculated as explained in the Appendices to Hatsopoulos et al. (1989) and Blecker (1990a). Equals cash portion of merger and acquisition activity times an estimate of the household share of corporate stock.
[f] Average for 1984–8 only.

periods used in Table 9.1. NFC net profits declined by about 7 per cent of NFC GDP from the 1960s to the 1980s. Of this decline, only about 2 percentage points are due to lower gross profits, and the fall in gross profits occurred in the 1970s. The remainder of the decline in net profits is due (in roughly equal proportions) to higher depreciation allowances and net interest payments.[18] The NFC net cash flow was also reduced, as the reductions in tax liabilities were not sufficient to outweigh the fall in net profits. However, when depreciation allowances are added back in, we find that the gross cash flow – the total internal funds available to finance capital accumulation – stayed roughly constant at about 13–14 per cent of NFC GDP over these three periods.

The steady percentage of gross cash flow reveals that US businesses were hardly strapped for cash in the 1980s. On the contrary, the interesting question is, where did all the cash go? A large part of the answer is provided in a recent study of corporate restructuring by Blair and Litan (1990). They argue that the combination of low expected profitability of additional investment and high real interest rates on borrowed funds (as well as on financial assets) gave corporate managers incentives to get cash out of their firms rather than to reinvest it in expanded production capacity. Through such devices as leveraged buy-outs and debt-financed stock repurchases, 'free cash flow' (excess internal funds) was taken out of corporations and put in the hands of stockholders and creditors.

Although the NIPAs are not constructed to capture all the flows of funds involved in corporate restructuring, they do reflect some of these redirected flows. Table 9.3 shows that the total pay-out of dividends plus net interest from the NFC sector increased notably in the 1980s. This meant that the NFC sector was doing less net saving, while giving wealthy households more cash (either directly or through financial intermediaries) which could be spent on consumption. Moreover this NIPA-based measure of the pay-out rate does *not* include stock repurchases or leveraged buy-outs. The last line of Table 9.3 gives an estimate of household cash receipts from corporate mergers and acquisitions, also measured as a percentage of NFC GDP. This percentage nearly trebled from the 1970s to the 1980s. By 1988, these cash receipts were equal to 144 per cent of the NFC net cash flow and 24 per cent of the gross cash flow.

In short, the real problem with corporate capital accumulation in the US in the 1980s was a lack of profitable outlets for the reinvestment of corporate savings, not a lack of available savings. Or, more precisely, the problem was a lack of productive investment outlets which could pay better than high-yielding financial assets. Corporate managers were trying desperately to get funds out of their companies, rather than trying to reinvest their funds productively. Investment was not constrained by a shortfall of savings, but rather the lack of investment opportunities constrained the realized amount of savings in the NFC sector. This is a problem that has no name in the neoclassical lexicon, but it is familiar to post-Keynesians as the problem of economic *stagnation* (see, for example, Steindl, 1979).

IV DISENTANGLING THE TWIN DEFICITS

The literature on economic stagnation has long recognized the potential for government deficit spending to substitute for private demand, at least in the short run. While the US federal budget deficits of the Reagan–Bush era were not consciously intended to combat stagnation, there can be little doubt that they helped to foster and sustain the prolonged economic expansion from 1983 to the present (1990). It is often asserted, however, that the budget deficit has had the pernicious effect of depleting national savings, particularly by inducing the net capital inflow which is associated with a chronic trade deficit. This section will analyse the relationship between the fiscal deficit, private saving and the external balance, focusing once again on the direction of causality.

The view that the budget deficit worsens the trade balance by depleting national saving is based on the national income identity in the form:

(1)   Current Account = National Saving − Domestic Investment,

in which the government deficit appears as a negative part of national saving. But this way of posing the problem ignores the effect of deficit spending on private saving and therefore gives the misleading impression that a bigger budget deficit must either lower the current account or 'crowd out' investment. For this reason, it is more helpful to write the national income identity in the form:

(2)   Government Deficit = Private Saving − Domestic Investment + Net Foreign Saving,

where net foreign saving equals the current account *deficit*. There are thus *three* ways in which an increased government deficit must ultimately finance itself: a rise in private saving, a fall in domestic investment, or a rise in foreign saving (fall in the trade balance).

These possibilities may be understood in terms of several alternative theoretical models:[19]

1. In the Keynes–Kalecki view, private domestic saving will rise as a result of the multiplier effects of deficit-financed government spending on national income, corporate profits and cash flows. This assumes either an accommodative monetary policy which holds the interest rate constant, or else that investment is insensitive to interest rates. However, unless the economy is completely closed to imports, there will be some leakage of increased domestic spending to import demand. To this extent, domestic deficit spending raises foreign income and profits, resulting in a net inflow of foreign saving to finance the increased net imports.[20]
2. In the strict neoclassical–monetarist view, domestic investment will fall as a result of 'crowding out' by a rise in the interest rate. Essentially this assumes a monetary policy which holds the money supply constant by raising interest rates − and that (financial) capital is internationally immobile (or interest-inelastic). There is no effect on

the trade balance, as long as there is no increase in the money supply relative to money demand. A trade deficit will result if and only if the central bank monetizes the fiscal deficit, as this will create excess real balances which the public will spend on net imports.
3. The neoclassical–Keynesian (IS–LM) 'synthesis' allows for a partial increase in domestic income and saving and partial crowding out, in the short run. In an open economy with immobile financial capital and a fixed exchange rate, the trade balance falls temporarily until the net outflow of reserves lowers the money supply enough to restore income to the level consistent with balanced trade; investment ends up completely crowded out in the long run. If the exchange rate is flexible, however, the currency depreciates enough to permit sustained higher income without a trade deficit, and investment is only partially crowded out.
4. An important variant of the neoclassical–Keynesian synthesis view is the Mundell–Fleming model, which assumes perfect (financial) capital mobility (infinite interest-elasticity) along with a flexible exchange rate. Assuming that the central bank holds the money supply constant, raising the fiscal deficit puts upward pressure on the interest rate, thus attracting an inflow of foreign funds that causes the currency to appreciate and keeps the actual interest rate from rising. As a result of the currency appreciation, net exports rather than domestic investment are 'crowded out'. There is no increase in domestic income and the entire rise in the fiscal deficit is financed by increased net foreign saving. The entire trade deficit is caused by a price effect rather than an income effect. This is the most extreme case, however. With imperfect capital mobility (or in the large country case) some expansion of domestic income (and saving) will occur and only part of the fiscal deficit is financed by foreign saving (trade deficit).
5. Finally, in an important variation on the Mundell–Fleming theme, we have the case of perfect capital mobility with a fixed exchange rate.[21] In this case, the capital inflow induced by a rise in the fiscal deficit causes the central bank to accumulate additional reserves (in order to prevent the domestic currency from appreciating) which, if not sterilized, permit full accommodation of the fiscal expansion. Given the effective endogeneity of the money supply in this case, it is not surprising that the end result is similar to the Keynes–Kalecki model. Domestic income and saving rise, offset only by the leakage to import demand which causes some increase in net foreign saving (the trade deficit).

While this is not an exhaustive list of the possibilities, it suffices to make the point that there is no theoretical necessity for an increased budget deficit to cause an equal and offsetting rise in the trade deficit. This extreme result obtains only in the simplest Mundell–Fleming small country model, under very strong assumptions. On the other hand, almost every model allows for a partial response of the trade deficit as a result of some combination of income and price effects. Indeed such a response could hardly be ruled out, as it is really nothing more than *the open economy generalization of the basic Keynesian principle that a government deficit finances itself by raising savings*; the only issue is the extent to which net foreign saving rather than domestic private saving is raised. Furthermore how much the trade deficit increases – as well as *how* it increases (via price or income effects) – depends on several factors: whether foreign countries simultaneously expand; the price- and income-elasticities of import and export demand; the exchange rate regime; the degree of integration of international financial markets; and the monetary policy response of the central bank.

Some worsening in the US trade balance was probably inevitable as a result of the 1980s fiscal expansion, unless foreign countries simultaneously adopted expansionary fiscal policies or increased their investment rates. In fact the opposite took place, as many of the United States' leading trading partners (especially Japan and the Latin American debtors) contracted both private investment and fiscal policy. This made matters much worse than they had to be.

Table 9.4 compares the changes in the saving-investment, budget and trade (current account) balances between the late 1970s and the 1980s in the US, Japan and West Germany. The gross private saving rate fell much more in Japan than in the US, but this was more than offset by an even greater fall in Japanese gross domestic investment which freed funds to finance a trade surplus *cum* capital exports (see US Congress, Joint Economic Committee, 1988). Also, while the US government surplus fell by 1.9 per cent of GDP, the Japanese government surplus rose by 1.0 per cent of GDP and the German government surplus rose by 0.4 per cent. *It was this opposite thrust in fiscal policies which led to such massive trade imbalances*, especially with Japan, not the increased US fiscal deficit alone. Indeed the increased US budget deficit made it possible for Japan and, to a lesser extent, Germany to tighten their budgets without suffering aggregate demand problems, as their growing external surpluses (mainly with the US) substituted for domestic demand. Had Japan and Germany (along with other surplus nations) expanded rather than tightened their budgets in the 1980s, the global imbalances problem would have been much smaller.

But the *way* in which the US trade deficit increased was not due to fiscal policies alone. What happened in the US in the 1980s was a mixture of

Table 9.4 Current account, saving-investment and budget balances for the US, Japan and West Germany, 1974–9 to 1980–7 (per cent of GDP)

Country	Period	Current Account	=	Gross Private Saving[a]	−	Gross Domestic Investment[b]	+	Government Budget Surplus[c]	Statistical Discrepancy[d]
US	1974–9	0.3		19.7		(17.7)		−1.8	0.1
	1980–7	−1.6		18.9		(16.8)		−3.7	0.0
	Change[e]	−1.8		−0.8		(−0.8)		−1.9	+0.1
Japan	1974–9	0.3		29.4		(27.1)		−2.2	0.2
	1980–7	2.1		27.0		(24.1)		−1.2	0.4
	Change[e]	+1.7		−2.5		(−3.0)		+1.0	+0.2
Germany	1974–9	1.0		20.2		(18.0)		−1.2	0.0
	1980–7	1.3		20.0		(17.9)		−0.8	0.0
	Change[e]	+0.3		−0.1		(−0.1)		+0.4	−0.1

Source: OECD, *National Accounts, Volume II, Detailed Tables, 1974–1987*, Paris, 1989, and author's calculations.

Notes:
[a] Sum of net national saving plus consumption of fixed capital (including public corporations, but excluding general government).
[b] Gross fixed capital formation (including public corporations, but excluding general government) plus increase in stocks.
[c] General government net saving plus depreciation allowances minus fixed capital formation (excluding public corporations).
[d] Includes rounding error.
[e] Equals 1980–7 average minus 1974–9 average. Changes were rounded separately.

cases 4 and 5, varying from year to year as the Federal Reserve alternated between its general devotion to tight money and high interest rates on the one hand, and the need to prevent a financial collapse (in 1982 and again in 1987) and to keep the dollar from rising too far (in 1985) on the other. When the Reagan tax cuts took effect in 1982–4, the Federal Reserve shifted from a relatively accommodative stance (designed to rescue the banking system from the 1982 recession and debt crisis) to an extremely restrictive stance (designed to prevent a putative revival of inflation). As the real interest rate soared in 1984, the result was a Mundell–Fleming-like sharp appreciation of the dollar and rise in the trade deficit (see Dornbusch, 1985).

By late 1984 and early 1985, however, the dollar began to rise far more than could be explained by any 'fundamentals' such as interest rate differentials (Dornbusch, 1988; Krugman, 1989). It is now generally acknowledged that the final ascent of the dollar was the product of a speculative bubble in the foreign exchange market, a bubble which was punctured only when the US announced its commitment to lower the dollar in March 1985.

In order to bring down domestic real interest rates as well as the dollar, the Fed was forced to allow the money supply to grow far above its official targets in 1985–6. The dollar did come down, bottoming out in 1988, after the Fed raised interest rates once again in a revival of its anti-inflationary crusade (in spite of the lack of evidence for acceleration of inflation).[22] As the dollar stabilized, the US economy behaved more like case 5,[23] with the budget deficit supporting continued domestic expansion and with considerable leakage to imports due to a very high income-elasticity of US import demand (Cline, 1989). Although the lower dollar succeeded in stimulating exports, imports continued to grow rapidly, and the trade deficit declined only to about 2 per cent of GNP by 1989.

It has been argued (for example, by Helkie and Hooper, 1988, and Sachs, 1988) that monetary policy has little net effect on the trade deficit, since the interest rate effects on investment demand offset the exchange rate effects on competitiveness. But even if tight monetary policy merely shifts the proximate cause of the trade deficit from income to price effects, as these economists claim, this would not imply that monetary policy was benign in its effects on the US international trade position.

If a trade deficit results simply from domestic demand stimulus – as in the case of a fiscal deficit accommodated by monetary expansion – then the trade deficit will be due mainly to the income effects of the fiscal deficit on import demand. Neither export producers nor import-competing firms need suffer in this case. But if the currency becomes overvalued as a result of tight monetary policy, then the trade deficit is due mainly to a loss of price competitiveness which adversely affects both export producers and import-competing firms who would otherwise be able to compete effectively.

Indeed this is exactly what happened in the early 1980s, according to Helkie and Hooper (1988), who found that $121 billion out of the total $165 billion decline in the merchandise trade balance (excluding agricultural exports and oil imports) from 1980 to 1986 could be explained by relative price changes which were mainly the result of exchange rate changes.[24] Thus the devastating consequences of the 1980s trade deficits on such sectors as agriculture and capital goods – both of which are relatively efficient and intrinsically competitive – must be attributed mainly to tight monetary policy, not to loose fiscal policy.

In any case, most empirical estimates show that only a fraction of the increased budget deficit was financed by foreign saving inflows (rise in the trade deficit). For example, both Sachs (1988) and Bernheim (1988) found that the US current account declines by only about $0.30 for every $1.00 increase in the budget deficit – in spite of using very different methodologies.[25] These estimates suggest that the two deficits are more like cousins than twins. These results also raise the question, how was the rest of the budget deficit financed?

There is no evidence that government borrowing *per se* crowded out domestic investment in the past decade.[26] Gross fixed investment spending followed a fairly normal course over the business cycle, recovering to historically normal levels (in proportion to GNP) in the mid-to-late expansion phase (see Table 9.1, above). Moreover there is no evidence that private borrowers had any difficulty in raising external funds (after the credit crunch of the 1979–82 period), in spite of persistent high real interest rates, and internal funds (cash flows) were robust, as we have seen. Given that the 1983–90 economic expansion was largely maintained by federal deficit spending, it seems more reasonable to conclude that the budget deficit crowded investment in rather than out (see Eisner, 1989b).[27]

Since there was virtually no crowding out of domestic investment, the rest of the budget deficit must have been financed by higher private domestic saving, relative to what it would have been otherwise – in spite of the apparent decline in some of the NIPA measures of private saving. On the corporate side, both gross corporate saving and NFC gross cash flow were reasonably robust, as shown in Tables 9.1 and 9.3. The relatively good performance of gross corporate saving in the 1980s recovery was undoubtedly helped by government deficit spending – indeed, it was directly fuelled in part by the cut in effective corporate taxation (see Table 9.3).

It might seem from the decline in the NIPA personal saving rate that personal savings did not contribute to financing the budget deficit. However this impression is certainly misleading, as individuals bought large amounts of government debt in the 1980s – either directly or through intermediaries such as pension funds and money market funds. As noted previously, NIPA personal savings do not measure these increases in holdings of government securities. Direct household holdings of US government securities alone (excluding indirect holdings through intermediaries) nearly doubled in proportion to total household net worth, from 3.0 per cent in 1979 to 5.4 per cent in 1989.[28] Moreover, the annual increases in these holdings, which averaged about $90 billion from 1985 to 1989, are large in relation to the federal deficits. Thus the household sector did contribute substantially to financing the government deficit through increased holdings of government debt, even though this financing is not reflected in the NIPA personal saving figures.

The reverse side of the coin is how much of the increased US trade deficit in the past decades can be attributed to the increased US budget deficit. The *highest* estimates are less than half. For example, Helkie and Hooper (1988) found that domestic fiscal expansion accounted for $70 billion out of the $143 billion deterioration in the current account between 1980 and 1986, while foreign fiscal contraction accounted for another $25 billion.[29] And the model used by Helkie and Hooper is at the *high* end of international macro models in terms of the predicted effects of US fiscal expansion on the current account deficit; most other models show *smaller* long-term effects.[30]

If the increased fiscal deficit accounts for less than half of the increased trade deficit, then to what should the remainder of the latter be attributed? Most international economists now concede that there has been a secular deterioration in US international competitiveness dating back at least to the early 1970s, if not earlier. This secular decline was reflected in the downward trend in the real value of the dollar during the 1970s (see Figure 9.3), while the current account remained roughly in balance. In the 1980s, both indexes in Figure 9.3 show the dollar falling back to nearly its 1980 real value by 1988, yet the current account deficit remained over $100 billion (about 2 per cent of GNP) by the end of the decade. The stagnation of US real wages since the early 1970s is further evidence for competitive decline. Indeed a common definition of competitiveness is the ability of a country to maintain balanced trade while 'achieving an acceptable rate of improvement in its standard of living' (Hatsopoulos *et al.*, 1988, p. 299).[31]

Elsewhere (Blecker, 1990c) I have estimated the cumulative effect of the structural decline in US competitiveness on the merchandise trade balance for the 1980s. My mid-range estimates show that constant-dollar non-petroleum imports (in 1982 prices) were roughly $90 billion higher in 1989

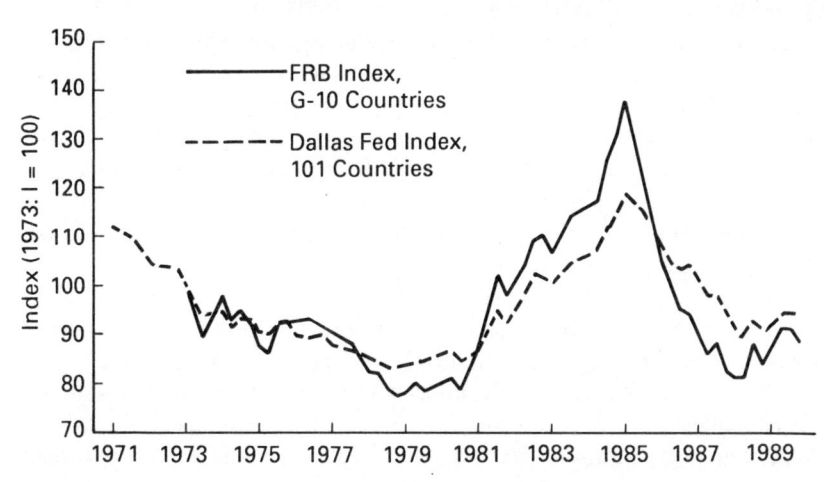

Figure 9.3 Alternative measures of the real value of the US dollar, quarterly, 1971–89

Source: Federal Reserve Board of Governors and Federal Reserve Bank of Dallas.

than would be expected as a result of increasing US income (or expenditures) and the changing relative price of imports (even with two years of quarterly lags) from 1980 to 1989. Since the total merchandise trade deficit for 1989 was $126 billion in 1982 dollars, as much as three-quarters of that deficit may be attributable to a structural tendency towards rising imports.[32] While these estimates may be exaggerated because of problems in the NIPA measure of real import volume,[33] even if they were off by a substantial margin they would still reveal a considerable secular decline.

It is often argued that any structural change in competitiveness must be offset by exchange rate adjustment, at least in the 'long run' (see, for example, McCulloch, 1985; Lawrence, 1989). This seems to be based on the old view that flexible exchange rates will automatically adjust to prevent current account imbalances, a view which essentially ignored the international mobility of financial capital. It is now generally recognized that the main determinants of currency fluctuations are located in international financial markets, not goods markets.[34]

After almost two decades of experience with floating exchange rates, international monetary economists have had to admit that they have no generally valid models that can explain the actual currency fluctuations better than the assumption of a random walk (Meese, 1990). Foreign exchange markets exhibit speculative runs which cannot be explained by any objective economic conditions; therefore even 'the hypothesis of informed, rational speculation must be rejected' (Dornbusch, 1989). There is no generally accepted exchange rate theory today which predicts a simple or automatic adjustment of exchange rates to offset real competitive advantages or disadvantages over any specific time horizon.

Scepticism about the prospects for automatic and effective exchange rate adjustment is also justified by the historical record of the past two decades of floating rates. The dollar depreciation of the 1970s was not automatic. Rather, it was deliberately induced by policymakers under the Nixon and Carter administrations. This policy had to be abandoned in 1979 because of its destabilizing consequences for US inflation and the global monetary system. As a result, US competitive decline ceased to be offset by dollar depreciation in the 1980s.

Even if one postulates that real exchange rates must eventually offset competitive shifts in a hypothetical 'long run' equilibrium, however, two difficulties remain. First, if a nation's currency does not adjust to its equilibrium value faster than the underlying competitive conditions themselves change, then actual trade deficits can be continuously affected by those changing conditions for an indefinite period of time. Second, if one relies entirely on real exchange rate adjustment to counteract a competitive decline, then the problem is 'solved' at the cost of a permanent reduction in the nation's real wages and standard of living.

The sources of US competitive decline may be conceptualized in term of the product-cycle and technological-gap views of international trade (see Vernon, 1966; Dosi and Soete, 1983). While the US traditionally exported innovative manufactured products in which it had absolute advantages, US technological leadership has now been challenged by the convergence of Japan and other advanced industrialized nations (Soete, 1985). At the same time, the accelerated transfer of industrial technology to the newly industrialized countries (NICs), together with revolutionary changes in production methods, international communications and global transportation, has left the US more vulnerable to competition from low-wage countries even in relatively sophisticated manufactures (Mead, 1990). These twin trends imply a squeeze on US real incomes as the 'monopoly rents' to its dwindling technological leadership decline.[35]

While these trends have been going on for some time, the overvaluation of the dollar in the 1980s may have exacerbated them. For example, Baldwin's (1988) model of the 'beachhead effect' shows how the market share of imports can be permanently increased by a sufficiently large transitory overvaluation of the home currency when there are large sunk costs of market entry. This phenomenon of permanent or irreversible effects of a temporary change in a variable has come to be known as 'hysteresis'.

To close the circle of cumulative causation, it is necessary to recognize how declining competitiveness affects domestic incomes and savings. One way or another, declining competitiveness implies slower growth of real incomes. This may come about through currency depreciation and real wage cuts, or it may come about through the negative employment effects of trade deficits, but either way, the impact of worsened competitiveness is to reduce domestic production and national income relative to what they would be otherwise.

Declining competitiveness also affects the distribution of income. Domestic firms cannot pass on increases in labour or other costs as readily when their products are less competitive (Kalecki, 1971). As a result profit margins may be squeezed by relatively rapid increases in domestic unit labour costs relative to foreign, if not offset by currency depreciation (see Blecker, 1989; You, 1990). Alternatively wages may be depressed in sectors that become less competitive, or high-wage industrial jobs may simply be eliminated and replaced by low-wage jobs in non-tradable services. Lower wages tend to offset the negative effects on profit margins and thus help to prevent the corporate saving rate from falling. But lower wages also imply an income squeeze on working-class households which can lower the personal saving rate. In the US economy, the effects of reduced competitiveness seem to have shifted in the past two decades. It appears that corporate profitability was squeezed in the 1970s (see Table 9.3 above), while personal incomes and savings were squeezed in the 1980s (see Tables 9.1 and 9.2 above).

To the extent that either real income growth slows down or the profit share of income falls, the private saving rate would be expected to decline. In addition the government will lose revenue on forgone national income. Once this point is recognized, the neoclassical 'saving shortage' view is completely stood on its head. A low saving rate can be a sympton of an underlying competitive decline which is simultaneously reflected in a trade deficit. In this case, a trade deficit is not caused by excessive domestic spending, but rather by the inability of domestic producers to compete with foreign rivals while still providing adequate wages and profits to domestic workers and investors, respectively.

V ALTERNATIVE POLICIES FOR CAPITAL ACCUMULATION IN THE 1990s

The above analysis brings into sharp focus the policy alternatives for reviving US economic growth in the next decade. The conventional wisdom, based on neoclassical growth theory and the 'saving shortfall' analysis, asserts that the US needs to focus mainly on increasing the national saving rate. The only disagreement among proponents of this perspective is over the best means for achieving this end. The prime candidates are fiscal tightening, saving incentives and consumption taxes. Often the need for such measures is portrayed as a desperate national necessity for reversing the country's 'mortgaging of its future'. Even those (such as Hatsopoulos *et al.*, 1988; Dornbusch *et al.*, 1989) who acknowledge the importance of underlying competitive decline still maintain that the solution requires pro-saving measures to foster more sacrifice for the future.

The analysis in this chapter shows that such a fixation on raising the saving rate is misguided. The low private saving rate (to the extent that it really is low) is more a consequence than a cause of the nation's underlying economic problems: inadequate productive investment, slow productivity growth, increased financial speculation, rising inequality, stagnant real wages and slow growth of average real incomes. To this extent, the saving shortfall view mistakes a symptom of the nation's economic problems for their root cause. The constant harping on the theme of an intergenerational (future to present) transfer serves to obscure the enormous *intra*generational transfer (from workers, the poor and the middle class to the wealthy) which was caused by the fiscal policies and structural changes of the 1980s. Yet most of the proposed remedies for the 'saving shortfall' (for example, consumption taxes) are distributionally regressive, and would thus place most of the burden on those whose incomes grew the least in the past decade – and who contributed the least (if at all) to the alleged consumption excesses of the 1980s.

To a considerable extent the decline in US private saving has been caused by the unprecedented high real interest rates of the past decade. Contrary to the standard presumption that high interest rates give incentives to raise savings, it turns out that high interest rates have in fact reduced national savings – at least as they are conventionally measured. The reasons for this outcome include not only the positive income effect on current consumer spending, but also the squeeze on corporate profits from high net interest payments, the disincentives given to the retention and reinvestment of corporate profits, and the appreciation of the dollar which contributes to the trade deficit. Even the government deficit itself is increased by the high interest rates which the government must pay on its rising debt.[36]

While high interest rates are usually blamed on government borrowing, other sectors (households and corporations) have also borrowed heavily in the past decade (see Pollin, 1991). Moreover responsibility for determining interest rates lies mainly with the Federal Reserve. However, apart from the Fed's ideological commitment to tight money as an anti-inflationary device, it is important to recognize the constraints (both structural and conjunctural) under which the Fed has been operating. Financing large government deficits does pose a difficult challenge for the Fed in a world of highly integrated, unregulated and volatile financial markets. For example, accommodating the budget deficit with easy money could make the dollar fall rather than rise, possibly precipitating a destabilizing speculative flight from the dollar in foreign exchange markets. While monetary policy may have been unnecessarily restrictive even from this perspective, the Fed clearly has to walk a knife-edge in regard to the value of the dollar.

It is therefore too simple just to call for the Fed to lower interest rates. US interest rate reductions must be accompanied by other measures to prevent destabilization of the domestic and global financial systems. One such measure would be the announcement of credible target zones for the dollar relative to other major currencies, as advocated by Williamson (1987) among others. A coordinated reversal of international fiscal imbalances, with the surplus countries expanding while the US contracts, would also be appropriate for fostering an environment in which more expansionary monetary policy would not be destabilizing.

This raises the always controversial topic of US fiscal policy. This chapter has shown that there is no cause for alarm about the budget deficit from the standpoint of a 'saving shortfall'. There is certainly no justification for the idea that the federal government should run unprecedented surpluses in order to compensate for low private saving (see, for example, Summers and Carroll, 1987; Bosworth, 1989). Nevertheless there are at least five valid reasons for concern about a sustained structural budget deficit: (1) it contributes at least partially to the trade deficit; (2) it motivates the Fed to keep real interest rates high; (3) it redistributes income from average taxpayers to wealthy bondholders; (4) it creates a liability structure for the federal government which may become increasingly costly to finance; and (5) it distracts political energies from more important issues.[37] While unilateral US fiscal tightening by itself could trigger a severe recession, sufficient doses of monetary expansion, foreign demand growth and continued domestic growth could permit a gradual reduction in the US fiscal deficit (as a percentage of GNP) without undue hardships.

It is also important that any efforts to reduce the US budget deficit be aimed at reversing, rather than exacerbating, the deeper underlying problems of the US economy. First, given the regressive effects of the 1980s changes in US fiscal policy, it would be perverse to impose further regressive taxes such as consumption taxes. If any taxes should be raised, they should be mainly the marginal income tax rates on the upper brackets. Given that much of the decline in the personal saving rate is attributable to the consumption spending of the rich, restoring at least the pre-1980 degree of progressivity of the income tax is justified on economic as well as ethical grounds. Second, given the problems of slow productivity growth and declining competitiveness, it would be disastrous to further cut back public investment spending.[38] The nation needs to invest more, not less, on infrastructure, education and other public needs, even at the expense of larger current deficits – although this may not be necessary if we take advantage of the 'peace dividend' (see Faux and Sawicky, 1990).

In the final analysis, however, it is important not to over-emphasize the importance of US fiscal policy. Indeed the obsession with eliminating the budget deficit at all costs has been one of the most pernicious effects of adopting the saving shortfall perspective. The US needs to stop fixating on saving rates and the budget deficit, and instead confront the fundamental problems of industrial decline, loss of technological leadership, elimination of high-wage jobs, poor basic education, deteriorating infrastructure, rising inequality, excessive financial speculation and increasing financial fragility. If these problems are successfully addressed (and that is no small task) the national saving rate will take care of itself. If these problems are ignored, efforts to treat the symptom of a low realized saving rate will not cure the disease of economic stagnation.

NOTES

1. For various shades of opinion on the saving shortfall see Summers and Carroll (1987), Friedman (1988), Bosworth (1989), Nordhaus (1989), Guttman (1989), Hatsopoulos *et al.* (1989), Walker *et al.* (eds) (1990) and Kotlikoff (1990).
2. Over the business cycle, the profit share will first rise and then fall as rapid expansion eventually drives up costs (wages, raw materials, interest) and thus cuts profit margins. Nevertheless, over the long run, sustained rapid productivity growth is generally associated with a high profit share.
3. This factor is recognized by neoclassicals such as Bosworth (1990).
4. The new growth models yield welfare implications through the assumption that saving is determined by intertemporal optimizing behaviour, which allows a distinction to be drawn between private and social optimization. This assumption had already been incorporated in models of optimal growth with traditional static assumptions about technology (see Burmeister, 1980; Marglin, 1984).
5. See Block (1990) for an analysis of personal saving which focuses on these types of deficiencies.
6. Actually the federal deficit increased somewhat more, but this was offset by increased state and local surpluses which were mainly due to contributions to public pension funds which would be counted as 'personal saving' if they were made by private companies.
7. In addition to the obvious effects of changes in effective tax rates, there is the less obvious effect of higher interest payments on the government debt redistributing income from average taxpayers to wealthy bondholders (see Michl, 1990).
8. To be sure, other factors have been suggested. Some (for example, Christian, 1990) point to the declining percentage of 'prime savers' (ages 45–64) in the population since

the early 1970s. However evidence for the life-cycle view in cross-sectional studies is weak, as shown by Danziger et al. (1982–3) and Summers and Carroll (1987). Summers and Carroll emphasize institutional changes such as increased availability of consumer credit, improved insurance coverage and increased well-being of the elderly. But there is no direct evidence that such changes can explain the timing or extent of the decrease in the personal saving rate. Kotlikoff (1990) hypothesizes that 'there has been a decline in the bequest motive for saving' but offers no evidence in support of this view.

9. Integrated (interview and diary) Consumer Expenditure Surveys are available only for 1972–3 (combined) and 1984–8 (annually); the 1980–1 interview and diary surveys were never integrated. This makes it impossible to distinguish changes in the decades of the 1970s and 1980s accurately. If one compares 1984 with 1988, one finds that the greatest consumption growth was in the fourth quintile (second from the top) while the lowest quintile had negative real consumption growth; after-tax income growth from 1984 to 1988 was inversely related to income. However comparing 1988 with 1984 is misleading. First, most of the upward redistribution of after-tax income due to Reagan's tax changes had already taken place by 1984. Second, 1984 was an early recovery year while 1988 (like 1972–3) was a late expansion year; the pattern of income growth from 1984–8 could thus reflect a cyclical recovery pattern. Third, the four-year burst of upper-middle class (fourth quintile) consumption could be just a transitory catch-up, rather than a permanent acceleration.

10. For a detailed disaggregated analysis of saving rates see Bunting (1991).

11. In fact, the rise in interest income relative to NNP more than accounts for the entire increase in disposable income relative to NNP, as both labour and other capital income fell relative to NNP. Since the 70% figure only includes the net effect of higher disposable income relative to NNP, this figure is really an underestimate of the combined effects of these three factors. The same consideration applies to the 55% figure cited in the next sentence.

12. In addition to adding one year to the sample, I replaced NNP with GNP (to avoid spurious inferences from the effects of increased depreciation). Hatsopoulos et al. used the percentage of the population under 16 as a demographic proxy. I replaced this variable with Christian's (1990) ratio of 'prime savers to prime borrowers' (population aged 45–64 over population aged 25–44). This not only increased the explanatory power of the demographic proxy, but also eliminated the serial correlation of the residuals. It is possible that this ratio has such a big effect because it is correlated with some unobserved, missing variable. However efforts to identify such a variable (such as the growth slowdown) did not prove fruitful.

Omitting a demographic variable results in implausible values for the coefficients on the other variables, as well as first-order serial correlation of the residuals. However the significance of this demographic variable does not necessarily confirm the strict 'life-cycle' view, which requires that the elderly dissave (see Danziger, et al., 1982–3). The population aged 45–64 can be regarded as the prime *earners*, and it is not surprising that the saving rate is higher when the proportion of the population in this bracket is higher – regardless of their motives for saving.

13. According to Mishel and Simon (1988), based on data from the 1983 Survey of Consumer Finances, the top 10 per cent of households own 51 per cent of liquid assets (bank deposits), 72 per cent of corporate stock, 86 per cent of tax-exempt municipal bonds, and 70 per cent of other bonds.

14. To the extent that upper-middle class households own real estate and financial assets which appreciated in value, their consumption rate was also increased by wealth effects. See note 9 above on the behaviour of the second-highest income quintile in 1984–8.

15. Both Hatsopoulos et al. (1989) and Blecker (1990a) found that nearly $0.60 of every $1 of after-tax cash receipts from corporate takeovers were spent on consumption, holding other factors constant. This is in addition to the ordinary wealth effect of higher personal net worth.

16. This point is also made by Steindl (1990).

17. The national income definition of personal saving was adjusted by subtracting the

188   *The United States*

product of the inflation rate (measured by the change in the GNP implicit deflator) and the stock of household net interest-bearing assets at the end of the previous year. The annual increase in household net worth was adjusted by subtracting the product of the inflation rate and household net worth at the end of the previous year.
18. These depreciation allowances are NIPA capital consumption allowances, not the accounting depreciation allowances used for tax purposes.
19. For a survey of these and other models see Dernburg (1989).
20. If the exchange rate is flexible and financial capital flows are relatively interest-inelastic, the currency would be expected to depreciate, thus offsetting at least some of the fall in the trade balance. If the exchange rate is fixed, however, an accommodative monetary policy might be impossible to maintain, as interest rates might have to be raised in order to defend the currency. This in turn would weaken if not eliminate the domestic stimulus from the deficit spending, unless other countries also expand their demand.
21. Note that a country need not have an official peg for this case to obtain. A managed float with a monetary policy that targets the exchange rate will accomplish the same result.
22. It is also possible that the Fed's action was prompted in part by a desire to keep the dollar from falling any further.
23. The suggestion that case 5 applies to the US in the late 1980s is due to Alan Isaac. In the US case, the monetary base does not expand through the accumulation of foreign currency reserves by the Fed. Rather, the Fed has to keep US interest rates low enough to prevent the dollar from rising, which requires a relatively rapid rate of domestic credit expansion.
24. These figures (which include lagged effects) are adapted from Helkie and Hooper's Table 2–12, p. 41. The results are not substantially affected if agricultural exports and oil imports are included.
25. Sachs uses a general equilibrium model to simulate the effects of fiscal expansion, assuming that monetary policy is endogenously tightened when the budget deficit rises. Bernheim simply regressed changes in the current account on changes in the budget deficit and a distributed lag of GNP growth rates.
26. See Pollin (1991) for additional arguments on this point.
27. This may explain the apparent conflict between the earlier assertion that productive investment was displaced by financial speculation due to high interest rates, and the present assertion that investment was not crowded out by government borrowing. There is no inconsistency if we recognize that a government-led demand expansion could keep investment up at the same time as the low net profit rate tended to discourage investment. This is simply to say that the accelerator effect dominated the profitability effect. This interpretation is also consistent with the shift away from long-term investments, especially in industrial equipment and structures, and towards more short-term investments, especially in information processing equipment and commercial structures (see Blecker, 1990a, Table 16, p. 44).
28. The data in this paragraph are derived from Federal Reserve, *Balance Sheets for the U.S. Economy 1945–89*, April 1990; BEA, National Income and Product Accounts (NIPAs); and author's calculations.
29. See Helkie and Hooper (1988), Table 2–17, p. 48. Note that, while they attribute most of the current account decline to fiscal imbalance, they also attribute most of the merchandise trade deterioration to dollar overvaluation (see above). There is no inconsistency in these findings, given their view that monetary tightness displaced the income effects of the fiscal imbalance with price effects through the dollar appreciation.
30. See Bryant *et al*. (eds) (1988). According to Table 4–7 (p. 74), of the eight models surveyed, the Federal Reserve Multi-Country Model (MCM) used by Helkie and Hooper predicts the biggest cumulative effect of US fiscal expansion on the US current account deficit over a six-year period.
31. Similar definitions are found in McCulloch (1985) and Lawrence (1989).
32. For econometric reasons, I was not able to obtain statistically reliable estimates of a secular decreasing tendency of US exports, although there is some evidence for such a

trend in the 1980s. See the Appendix to Blecker (1990c) for more details.
33. In particular, 'real' imports of computers are valued at the 1982 prices of the 'hedonic' attributes of the computers (such as memory capacity). Since the prices of these attributes fell rapidly in the mid-1980s, real quantities for the late 1980s are exaggerated.
34. The value of international financial flows dwarfs the value of trade flows. Foreign exchange transactions in the three largest trading centres (London, New York and Tokyo) alone totalled $188 billion *per day* as of March 1986, and 'worldwide foreign exchange could possibly exceed $250 billion per day or more than $60 trillion per year' (Levich, 1988, p. 220). In contrast, the total value of US merchandise trade in 1986 was $592 billion for the *entire year*, or less than $2 billion per day.
35. In Krugman's (1979) formalized model of North-South product-cycle trade, a decline in the rate of innovation in the North combined with an increase in the rate of technology transfer to the South will lower Northern wages relative to Southern, and may even reduce the former absolutely.
36. The amounts involved are not trivial: by fiscal 1989, federal net interest payments of $169 billion exceeded the total (on- and off-) budget deficit of $152 billion (*Economic Indicators*, May 1990). With such a large interest burden, and much of the national debt turning over frequently, the current interest rate has a substantial impact on government outlays.
37. Point (2) is discussed by Wray (1989) and point (3) by Michl (1990). Point (4) was suggested by Hyman Minsky in a discussion of an earlier version of this paper. Point (5) is suggested by James Galbraith in Bosworth *et al.* (1990).
38. This point has been recognized by some economists associated with the saving shortfall view (for example, Nordhaus, 1989). The contribution which public investment spending can make to private productivity and profitability is now recognized by neoclassicals such as Aschauer (1988, 1989).

REFERENCES

Aschauer, David A. (1988), 'Government Spending and the "Falling Rate of Profit" ', *Federal Reserve Bank of Chicago Economic Perspectives*, vol. 12, May/June, pp. 1–17.
Aschauer, David A. (1989), 'Is Public Expenditure Productive?', *Journal of Monetary Economics*, vol. 23, pp. 177–200.
Baldwin, Richard E. (1988), 'Hysteresis in Import Prices: The Beachhead Effect', *American Economic Review*, vol. 78, no. 4, September, pp. 773–85.
Bernheim, B. Douglas (1988), 'Budget Deficits and the Balance of Trade', *Tax Policy and the Economy*, NBER, vol. 2, pp. 1–31.
Blair, Margaret M. and Robert E. Litan (1990), 'Corporate Leverage and Leveraged Buyouts in the Eighties', in John B. Shoven and Joel Waldfogel (eds), *Debt, Taxes, and Corporate Restructuring*, Washington, DC: Brookings.
Blecker, Robert A. (1989), 'International Competition, Income Distribution and Economic Growth', *Cambridge Journal of Economics*, vol. 13, no. 3, September, pp. 395–412.
Blecker, Robert A. (1990a), *Are Americans on a Consumption Binge? The Evidence Reconsidered*, Washington, DC: Economic Policy Institute.
Blecker, Robert A. (1990b), 'The Consumption Binge Is a Myth', *Challenge*, vol. 33, no. 3, May/June, pp. 22–30.
Blecker, Robert A. (1990c), 'The US Trade Deficit: Competitive Decline and Macro Performance', Washington, DC: Economic Policy Institute, September (unpublished).

Block, Fred C. (1990), 'Bad Data Drive Out Good: The Decline of Personal Savings Reexamined', *Journal of Post Keynesian Economics*, vol. 13, no. 1, Fall, pp. 3–19.

Bosworth, Barry (1989), 'There's No Simple Explanation for the Collapse in Saving', *Challenge*, vol. 32, July–August, pp. 27–32.

Bosworth, Barry (1990), 'International Differences in Saving', *American Economic Review Proceedings*, vol. 80, no. 2, May, pp. 377–81.

Bosworth, Barry et al. (1990), *Seminar: Macroeconomic Policy*, Washington, DC: Economic Policy Institute.

Bryant, Ralph C., Dale W. Henderson, Gerald Holtham, Peter Hooper and Steven A. Symansky (eds) (1988), *Empirical Macroeconomics for Interdependent Economies*, Washington, DC: Brookings.

Bunting, David (1991), 'Savings and the Distribution of Income', *Journal of Post-Keynesian Economics* (forthcoming).

Burmeister, Edwin (1980), *Capital Theory and Dynamics*, Cambridge: Cambridge University Press.

Cantor, Richard (1989), 'Interest Rates, Household Cash Flow, and Consumer Expenditures', *Federal Reserve Bank of New York Quarterly Review*, Summer, pp. 59–67.

Christian, James W. (1990), 'Prospects and Policies for Higher Personal Saving in the 1990s', in Charls E. Walker et al. (eds), *The U.S. Savings Challenge: Policy Options for Productivity and Growth*, Boulder: Westview Press.

Cline, William R. (1989), *United States External Adjustment and the World Economy*, Washington: Institute for International Economics.

Cooper, Ronald S. (1988), 'An Empirical Model of the Role of Technological Change in Industry-Level Investment Dynamics', unpublished PhD dissertation, American University.

Daly, Herman E. and John B. Cobb, Jr. (1989), *For the Common Good: Redirecting the Economy toward Community, the Environment, and a Sustainable Future*, Boston: Beacon.

Danziger, Sheldon, Jacques van der Gaag, Eugene Smolensky and Michael K. Taussig (1982–3), 'The Life-Cycle Hypothesis and the Consumption Behavior of the Elderly', *Journal of Post-Keynesian Economics*, vol. 5, no. 2, Winter, pp. 208–27.

Dernburg, Thomas F. (1989), *Global Macroeconomics*, New York: Harper & Row.

Dornbusch, Rudiger (1985), *Dollars, Debts, and Deficits*, Cambridge: MIT Press.

Dornbusch, Rudiger (1988), 'The Adjustment Mechanism: Theory and Problems', in Norman S. Fieleke (ed.), *International Payments Imbalances in the 1980s*, Boston: Federal Reserve Bank of Boston.

Dornbusch, Rudiger (1989), 'The Dollar, US Adjustment and the System', unpublished, MIT, paper presented at American Economic Association Meetings, Atlanta, December.

Dornbusch, Rudiger, Paul Krugman and Yung Chul Park (1989) *Meeting World Challenges: U.S. Manufacturing in the 1990s*, Rochester: Eastman Kodak Company.

Dosi, Giovanni and Luc Soete (1983), 'Technology Gaps, International Specialization, and Cost-Based Adjustment: Some Explorations on the Determinants of International Competitiveness', *Metroeconomica*, vol. 35, October, pp. 197–222.

Eichner, Alfred S. (1976), *The Megacorp and Oligopoly*, Cambridge: Cambridge

University Press.
Eichner, Alfred S. and J. A. Kregel (1975), 'An Essay on Post-Keynesian Theory: A New Paradigm in Economics', *Journal of Economic Literature*, vol. 13, December, pp. 1293–1314.
Eisner, Robert (1978), *Factors in Business Investment*, Cambridge, Mass.: NBER and Ballinger.
Eisner, Robert (1986), *How Real Is the Federal Deficit?*, New York: Free Press.
Eisner, Robert (1989a), 'Divergences of Measurement and Theory and Some Implications for Economic Policy', *The American Economic Review*, vol. 79, no. 1, March, pp. 1–13.
Eisner, Robert (1989b), 'Budget Deficits: Rhetoric and Reality', *Journal of Economic Perspectives*, vol. 3, no. 2, Fall, pp. 73–93.
Eisner, Robert (1991), 'The Real Rate of U.S. National Saving', *Review of Income and Wealth*, Series 37, March.
Faux, Jeff and Max Sawicky (1990), *Investing the Peace Dividend: How to Break the Gramm–Rudman–Hollings Stalemate*, Washington, DC: Economic Policy Institute.
Fazzari, Steven M. and Tracy L. Mott (1986–7), 'The Investment Theories of Kalecki and Keynes: An Empirical Study of Firm Data, 1970–1982', *Journal of Post Keynesian Economics*, vol. 9, Winter, pp. 171–87.
Friedman, Benjamin M. (1988), *Day of Reckoning: The Consequences of American Economic Policy Under Reagan and After*, New York: Random House.
Guttman, Robert (1989), 'The Saving Shortfall Reconsidered', *Challenge*, vol. 32, September–October, pp. 47–51.
Harris, Donald J. (1978), *Capital Accumulation and Income Distribution*, Stanford: Stanford University Press.
Hatsopoulos, George N., Paul R. Krugman and Lawrence H. Summers (1988), 'U.S. Competitiveness: Beyond the Trade Deficit', *Science*, vol. 241, 15 July, pp. 299–307.
Hatsopoulos, George N., Paul R. Krugman and James M. Poterba (1989), *Overconsumption: The Challenge to U.S. Economic Policy*, New York and Washington: American Business Conference and Thermo-Electron Corporation.
Hayashi, Fumio (1986), 'Why is Japan's Saving Rate So Apparently High?', National Bureau of Economic Research, *Macroeconomics Annual*, pp. 147–211.
Helkie, William L. and Peter Hooper (1988), 'An Empirical Analysis of the External Deficit', in Ralph C. Bryant *et al.* (eds), *External Deficits and the Dollar: The Pit and the Pendulum*, Washington: Brookings.
Kaldor, Nicholas (1972), 'The Irrelevance of Equilibrium Economics', *Economic Journal*, vol. 82, December, pp. 1237–55.
Kalecki, Michal (1971), *Selected Essays in the Dynamics of the Capitalist Economy*, Cambridge: Cambridge University Press.
Kotlikoff, Laurence J. (1990), 'The Crisis in U.S. Saving and Proposals to Address the Crisis', unpublished, Boston University/NBER, May.
Krugman, Paul R. (1979), 'A Model of Innovation, Technology Transfer, and the World Distribution of Income', *Journal of Political Economy*, vol. 87, no. 2, April, pp. 253–66.
Krugman, Paul R. (1989), *Exchange-Rate Instability*, Cambridge, Mass.: MIT Press.
Lawrence, Robert Z. (1989), 'The International Dimension', in Robert E. Litan *et*

al. (eds), *American Living Standards: Threats and Challenges*, Washington, DC: Brookings.

Levich, Richard M. (1988), 'Financial Innovations in International Financial Markets', in M. Feldstein (ed.), *The United States in the World Economy*, Chicago: University of Chicago Press/NBER.

Lipsey, Robert E. and Irving B. Kravis (1987), *Saving and Economic Growth: Is the United States Really Falling Behind?*, New York: The Conference Board.

Marglin, Stephen A. (1984), *Growth, Distribution, and Prices*, Cambridge: Harvard University Press.

McCulloch, Rachel (1985), 'Trade Deficits, Industrial Competitiveness, and the Japanese', *California Management Review*, vol. 27, no. 2, pp. 140–56.

McIntyre, Robert S. (1990), *Inequality and the Federal Budget Deficit*, Washington, DC: Citizens for Tax Justice.

Mead, Walter Russell (1990), *The Low-Wage Challenge to Global Growth*, Washington, DC: Economic Policy Institute.

Meese, Richard (1990), 'Currency Fluctuations in the Post-Bretton Woods Era', *Journal of Economic Perspectives*, vol. 4, no. 1, Winter, pp. 117–34.

Michl, Thomas R. (1990), 'Debt, Deficits, and the Distribution of Income', unpublished, Colgate University, January.

Mishel, Lawrence and Jacqueline Simon (1988), *The State of Working America*, Washington: Economic Policy Institute.

Nordhaus, William D. (1989), 'What's Wrong with a Declining National Saving Rate?', *Challenge*, vol. 32, July–August, pp. 22–6.

Pechman, Joseph A. (1990), 'The Future of the Income Tax', *American Economic Review*, vol. 80, no. 1, March, pp. 1–20.

Pieper, Paul (1989), 'Why Net Investment Has Fallen', paper presented at Western Economic Association Meetings, June.

Pollin, Robert, (1991), 'Budget Deficits and the U.S. Economy: Considerations in a Heilbronerian Mode', in Ronald Blackwell et al. (eds), *Social Forces and Economic Questions: Essays in Worldly Philosophy*, New York: Macmillan (forthcoming).

Romer, Paul M. (1986), 'Increasing Returns and Long-Run Growth', *Journal of Political Economy*, vol. 94, October, pp. 1002–38.

Romer, Paul M. (1987), 'Growth Based on Increasing Returns Due to Specialization', *American Economic Review Proceedings*, vol. 77, no. 2, May, pp. 56–62.

Romer, Paul M. (1990), 'Are Nonconvexities Important for Understanding Growth?', *American Economic Review Proceedings*, vol. 80, no. 2, May, pp. 97–103.

Sachs, Jeffrey D. (1988), 'Global Adjustments to a Shrinking U.S. Trade Deficit', *Brookings Papers on Economic Activity*, no. 2, pp. 639–74.

Soete, Luc (1985), 'International Diffusion of Technology, Industrial Development and Technological Leapfrogging', *World Development*, vol. 13, no. 3, pp. 409–22.

Steindl, Josef (1979), 'Stagnation Theory and Stagnation Policy', *Cambridge Journal of Economics*, vol. 3, no. 1, March, pp. 1–14.

Steindl, Josef (1990), 'Capital Gains, Pension Funds, and the Low Saving Ratio in the United States', *Banca Nazionale del Lavoro Quarterly Review*, June, pp. 165–77.

Summers, Lawrence and Chris Carroll (1987), 'Why Is U.S. National Saving So Low?', *Brookings Papers on Economic Activity*, no. 2, pp. 607–42.

U.S. Congress, Joint Economic Committee (1988), 'Restoring International Balance: Japan's Trade and Investment Patterns', Staff Study, July.

U.S. Congressional Budget Office (1990), *The Changing Distribution of Federal Taxes, 1977–1990* (February update).

Vernon, Raymond (1966), 'International Investment and International Trade in the Product Cycle', *Quarterly Journal of Economics*, vol. 80, May, pp. 190–207.

Walker, Charls E., Mark A. Bloomfield and Margo Thorning (eds) (1990), *The U.S. Savings Challenge: Policy Options for Productivity and Growth*, Boulder: Westview Press.

Williamson, John (1987), 'Exchange Rate Management: The Role of Target Zones', *American Economic Review Proceedings*, vol. 77, no. 2, May, pp. 200–4.

Wray, L. Randall (1989), 'A Keynesian Presentation of the Relations Among Government Deficits, Investment, Saving, and Growth', *Journal of Economic Issues*, vol. 23, no. 4, December, pp. 977–1002.

You, Jong-il (1990), 'Income Distribution, Growth, and Economic Openness', unpublished, Harvard University, March.

10. Efficiency, Rent-seeking and Privatization: Ten Propositions

John D. Donahue

A set of criteria are proposed for assessing a publicly-funded task's eligibility for delegation to private suppliers. The potential gains from privatization come in part from technical efficiency improvements, in part from reductions in rents, and in part from improved allocation of resources among public tasks and between the public and private sectors. Tasks *differ* substantially in their suitability for privatization. Indeed for some functions profit-seekers are more likely than civil servants to extract rents. Since the interplay of political advocacy and resistance often shapes the choice between contractors and public workers, and since incentives to political activism tend to vary with the rents at stake, a political decision-making process will often yield a suboptimal, or even perverse, pattern of privatization.

THE PUBLIC–PRIVATE CHOICE IN A COUNTER-FACTUALLY SIMPLE WORLD

The privatization debate, at base, concerns the proper form of organization for the agents who carry out the public's business. Consider first the strengths and weaknesses of profit-seeking agency versus bureaucratic agency, each in its ideal form. Suppose, at the outset, that our political and economic institutions were accurately described by the cheeriest of primers on microeconomics and public administration. Public employees – although lacking any inherent interest in minimizing costs – faithfully obey mandates and follow prescribed procedures. Private firms carrying out contracts with the government – while ready to charge what the market will bear – bid competitively and endeavour to deliver as promised. What considerations should govern officials' choices between profit-seeking and bureaucratic agents in this simpler world? For which kinds of tasks does it make sense to *contract for results* (the defining characteristic of profit-seeking agency) and for which to *contract for allegiance* (the defining characteristic of bureaucratic agency)?

Proposition 1 Profit-seeking agency is more appropriate to the extent that:

1. the product desired can be fully defined in advance;
2. the government can choose among several competing agents;
3. the product delivered can be evaluated unambiguously;
4. poorly-performing agents can be replaced or otherwise penalized;[1]
5. the costs of poor performance (in any one contract) are limited;
6. the government neither knows nor cares much about the *means* of achieving public goals.

The product must be definable – in detail and in advance – so that agents can predict their requirements for meeting the specifications and submit bids accordingly. The second condition is crucial: only competition can be expected to restrain costs.[2] Unless performance can be evaluated, the public's representatives cannot determine that specifications have been met, or make informed judgements about whether to keep or replace the original agent. If agents face no reliable penalties for failing to deliver as promised, competition and contracts become meaningless. The fifth condition – the costs of poor performance are relatively small – simply means that the sanctions which can be brought to bear against agents who disappoint are commensurate with the potential consequences of poor performance. (Suppose private contractors handle air-traffic control, for example. Simply forfeiting the contract would generally be considered an inadequate sanction for negligently allowing two 747s to collide.) Finally, if the public cares only about the price and quality of the product, officials can leave the means of producing the result to the ingenuity of profit-seeking agents.

Proposition 2 Bureaucratic agency is more appropriate to the extent that:

1. requirements are uncertain and subject to revision;
2. competition is difficult or impossible to arrange;
3. *results* are harder to evaluate than *activity*;
4. activities believed to produce value can be made routine, and agents can be sanctioned for departures from routine;
5. the costs of failure (in any one project) are high;
6. means as well as ends matter.

When the task to be accomplished is liable to redefinition, contracts based on tentative specifications may have to be cancelled or renegotiated;

bureaucracy preserves for the government the valuable right to revise mandates.[3] If selecting among competing agents is impractical or impossible – either from the start, or once a long-lived project gets under way – formal authority systems must substitute for the discipline of competition. When output cannot be clearly evaluated, contracts cannot be based on results. But if the relationship between agents' activities and desired results is predictable, and if activity *can* be observed, rules can be set and agents rewarded for their fidelity to the rules. If the costs of failure are relatively high, close control over agents becomes more valuable, and reliance upon after-the-fact sanctions becomes risky. Finally, if the public's representatives already know the best way of achieving desired results, or if the public cares about means as well as ends, there is less to lose and more to gain by contracting with agents to keep to a specified programme, rather than achieving a specified result by means of their own design.

In a simple world where both markets and bureaucracies work well, in essence, what the public *loses* by choosing a bureaucratic over a profit-seeking agent is the cost discipline of competition, and the benefits of innovation by agents motivated to discover better, cheaper ways to deliver value. What it *gains* is control over methods, and the right to change mandates as circumstances require. Bureaucratic agents are neither inspired nor empowered to exercise initiative in pursuit of greater cost efficiency. Profit-seeking agents cannot be expected to limit prices unless competition requires them to do so, nor to attend – at any significant cost – to dimensions of value other than those contractually specified.

Suppose the White House needs repainting. *With profit-seeking agency*, Conditions (1) and (3) hold if the building manager can specify the scope of the renovation and the durability required of the finish, and can verify – by checking the grade of paint used, inspecting the trim, and so on – the quality of the job. Condition (2) holds if several contractors submit sealed, final bids. Condition (4) holds if contractors put up a performance bond, or the contract provides for cancellation if specifications are not met in the course of the project. Condition (5) holds if a botched job is readily fixable, and no state ceremony or inauguration looms which would render it costly if a low-bidding but unexpectedly incompetent contractor left ugly streaks on the West Wing. Condition (6) holds if the building manager has no special insights into the best way to paint the White House and does not care whether the contractor uses brushes, rollers or spray guns, ladders, scaffolds or hydraulic lifts, big crews or small crews, union or non-union labour, so long as the job is done cheaply and well. In these circumstances, the sensible choice is to write up specifications, solicit bids, pick the lowest-bidding contractor, and let him figure out the best way to paint the White House and pocket the profit if he does it efficiently.

Consider another public task, protecting the President against assassination. *With bureaucratic agency*, condition (1) holds if the President's schedule and itinerary are uncertain and subject to revision; the nature of the task cannot be specified with enough detail to allow realistic cost predictions or meaningful bids. Condition (2) holds if it is impossible (because of condition (1) or unwise (for secrecy reasons) to distribute specifications for a month's worth of bodyguarding and solicit bids from competing firms, or if only one or a few firms are equipped for the job, or if it would be difficult to switch security firms after an initial contract. Condition (3) holds if it is hard to gauge different degrees of risk short of an actual attack, or to count the number of assassination plots deterred, but relatively easy to tell if a bodyguard is on hand and alert. Condition (4) holds to the extent that an agent's task can be specified as a routine – stick close to the President, watch for assassins, and use the tactics you have been trained in to frustrate attacks – and where departures from routine are more likely to reduce performance than to increase efficiency.[4] Condition (5) means that it would be imprudent to hire a low-bidding security firm, see how they do for six months, and renew the contract if the President stays intact. Condition (6) holds if it matters *how* the President is protected; some low-cost security methods – keeping crowds a half-mile back, transporting the President in an armoured car, opening fire on all shady-looking characters – are undesirable. Under these circumstances, the potential gains from contracting out – cost savings and innovation – are swamped by the potential losses. It makes sense to set up a security bureaucracy, establish rules and routines, hire and train agents to follow them, and evaluate agents by their fidelity to procedure.[5]

One could imagine reversing the choice in each of these hypothetical situations. Suppose the building manager at the White House for some reason preferred to have the paint job done by civil servants. Since bureaucratic agents have no stake in efficiency, the costs would very likely be higher than for a contractor selected through competitive bidding. If the building manager aspired to a bureaucratic arrangement without sacrificing efficiency, and if he were authorized to use any form of contracting he chooses, he might set up a bureaucracy with these characteristics: the painting staff is not constrained by any standard procedures; they are encouraged to think of different approaches to painting the White House; each worker can propose an approach and submit a budget; the building manager selects the most attractive proposal, and appoints its author as leader of the painting team, with authority over the members; if the team's innovations let it do the paint job as specified for less than the budgeted sum, it gets to keep the remainder, and the leader decides how this surplus will be shared among the members.[6] Similarly, if the President's security director strongly prefers private-sector protection services, he could in principle write a contract enumerating the job's complex requirements. Since the output – protection from a range of imperfectly observable risks – cannot be completely specified, the payment would have to be based in large part on *activity* rather than *results*. The security firm would provide bodyguards to accompany the president as needed, using an agreed-upon set of acceptable security tactics, and would be paid a specified fee for the time spent on the job.

But in the first case, obviously, the result is a bureaucracy that mimics private contracting, and in the second case a private contractor that resembles a bureaucracy. The civil-service painting contract, to the extent that incentives are arranged to achieve low costs and innovation, surrenders control over means and the principal's right to revise the contract. The private-sector security arrangement, to the extent that the contract specifies protocol and is based on activity rather than results, will lose the virtues of cost-based competition and innovation. Hence:

Proposition 3 The fundamental distinction is between output-based contracts and input-based contracts, not between profit-seeking and bureaucratic agents *per se*.

The efficiency gains of competition can usually only be purchased at the expense of full control over means and the right to revise mandates without recontracting. The inherent tension, in other words, is between paying for activity and paying for results, contractual arrangements that are typically *but not necessarily* associated with government agencies, in the one case, and outside contractors, in the other. To the extent that a public institution is organized instead around output-based agency contracts it will tend to lose both the virtues and the defects of bureaucracy and display the virtues and defects of profit-seeking agency. To the extent that a private firm contracts to accept the instructions of public officials, rather than to deliver a specified result, it will tend to take on characteristics of bureaucracy. If the White House building manager insists on the option to change the specifications on the paint job once the contractor has been selected, or reserves the right to suspend work during unanticipated state functions, or requires that the paint be American-made, or the workers be unionized, or Republicans, or subjected to security checks, or that specified numbers be minorities or women, each restriction on *how* the White House should be painted will tend to erode the cost advantages of outside contracting. The rationale for profit-seeking agency is competition among agents to develop more efficient means to create value; as their discretion to do so is restricted, the benefits of competition are lost. Analogously, if the security director seeks to cut the costs of protecting the

President by minimizing formal monitoring and evaluation, suspending procedural routine and offering bonuses to agents who experiment with ways to foil assassins more expeditiously, many of the advantages of bureaucracy disappear. The rationale for bureaucratic agency is control over means, when means are more definable or observable than ends, or when means are important ends in themselves. Ceding control to agents, to encourage economies or innovation, undercuts the advantages of hierarchical authority systems.

A focus on procedure rather than product is not a remediable *defect* of bureaucracy, but a *description* of input-based contracts. An exclusive devotion to measured costs and revenues is not a failing of profit-seekers, but the predictable result of output-based contracts. This is by no means to say that bureaucracies cannot be made more efficient or profit-seeking firms be made more broadly accountable, through carefully balanced contracts that tailor the mix of incentives to the task at hand. But it does suggest caution in efforts to make public agencies more business-like, or to make private contractors responsive to unpriced considerations. Hybrid contracts – which are what we generally see in both private and collective endeavours – tend to merge both the virtues and the defects of each form of contract, in varying proportions and with varying results.

To ask whether bureaucrats or private contractors perform better *in general* is a meaningless question, rather like asking if an axe or a shovel is the better tool: it depends on the job. But it also depends on the *quality* of each alternative. 'Which type?' matters, but 'how good?' matters, too; in some cases, it might matter more. A very good shovel may be more useful for felling a tree than a very bad axe; a sharp, sturdy axe might do better for digging a hole than a bent and flimsy shovel. The second set of issues governing the choice of agents concerns how closely each organizational alternative can be expected to approximate its ideal.

This chapter has dealt so far with more or less idealized versions of each organizational form in order to isolate the relative advantages of well-functioning bureaucratic and profit-seeking agency contracts from the relative tendency of each type of relationship to break down. (These two issues are frequently confused.) But in the real world, political representatives frequently have an imperfect understanding of the public interest, and are only weakly motivated and enabled to define public tasks meaningfully or to hold agents to account. Bureaucrats do not reliably defer to authority or subordinate their own interests to the organization's mandate. Profit-seekers do not always submit to the discipline of competition, or dedicate their ingenuity solely to cutting costs and improving quality. And neither type of agent can be expected passively to adapt to public spending decisions without exercising – in their roles as political principals

– their power to shape the collective choices from which they stand to benefit.

BUREAUCRATIC AND PROFIT-SEEKING AGENCY BREAKDOWNS

Inefficiency

Efficiency is an institutional artifact. The set of institutions called the market has two engines of efficiency. The first is consumers' understanding of their own interests and their ability to signal and sanction producers through their buying decisions. The second is ownership claims on the net revenues of a private enterprise, and owners' rights to collect the gains from cost control. Together these tend, when markets work well, to push resources into alignment with people's desires. But for undertakings that cannot be organized through the market, these forces are altered, weakened or absent. Individuals express their priorities through the political process, and information about demand is aggregated, imprecise and only indirectly conveyed to agents. Ownership is widely dispersed. Citizens' interests, as owners, in encouraging efficiently defined and performed public undertakings are real, but diluted. Their ownership rights are correspondingly attenuated and exercised indirectly through representatives. Public officials may not know very precisely how the public interest can be most efficiently advanced. Nor – because of each citizen's small stake in most of the details of public management, because of citizens' limited information about those details, and because of the large number of factors governing citizens' voting decisions – are even the most dedicated officials strongly motivated to practise vigilance against inefficiency in the details of public undertakings.

These points apply whether bureaucratic or profit-seeking agents do the work. The mandates assigned to either type of agents at best will be based on honest but error-prone definitions of the public interest. Public officials will tend to specify goals with less care and precision, monitor performance less vigilantly, evaluate less rigorously and sanction poor performance less sternly than would the owner of a closely-held firm. These are problems of collective action and not of any particular organizational instrument. But the basic problems are manifest in different ways with different types of agency relationships. These distinctions are explored here along two dimensions of efficiency. The first concerns getting the right things done; the second concerns getting them done cheaply and well.

Efficient Mandates: Ambiguity, Discretion and Honour

One source of inefficiency in public spending is vague mandates that fail to concentrate resources on the most promising sources of social value. When such vagueness results from negligence on the part of political agents, rather than from uncertainty at higher levels about just what needs to be done, shifting from bureaucratic to profit-seeking agents may offer a remedy. Agency relationships based on output require (or at least strongly encourage) officials to define mandates precisely. Writing contracts with profit-seeking agents generally involves developing specifications and defining the terms by which performance will be evaluated. When contracts are based on inputs rather than outputs, conversely, the ultimate goals may more easily be left obscure and the logic linking a particular undertaking to the public interest may remain unexamined. Agents, however faithful, may end up wasting their time and the public's money. If political officials find it tedious or politically distasteful to spell out the details of public endeavours, and are tempted to neglect the task, the discipline of writing output-based contracts can lessen the risk of slack originating in poorly thought-out or ambiguous mandates.

If attenuated responsibility leads public officials to neglect to define mandates *clearly*, however, they may for the same reason, when pressed to specify, neglect to define them *correctly* (by any reasonable definition of that complex notion). They may fail to single out the most valuable subset from a larger set of potential undertakings. The wrong road may be paved, the wrong disease researched, the wrong weapon developed. Here we confront the common dilemma alluded to above: what if *neither* valuable results nor value-creating behaviour can be spelled out precisely in advance? The dilemma presents a choice between two risky options. Public officials can specify mandates on the basis of incomplete information, which will frequently result in the wrong thing getting done – profit-seeking agents are assigned to produce the wrong output, or bureaucratic agents are assigned to follow an irrational productive routine. (Nikita Khrushchev once complained that the Soviet lighting-fixture industry produced massively ugly fixtures 'because the heavier the chandeliers produced, the more a factory gets since its output is calculated in tons'.[7]) The other option is to leave mandates open-ended, and grant agents discretion in their behaviour. The relative risks of inefficiency with vaguely defined mandates versus badly defined mandates depends on what occurs at lower levels when goals or procedures are left imprecise. When are agents *able* to fill in the details correctly – that is, to select the highest-value options contained within loose mandates? When, assuming they are able, are they *motivated* to do so?

Agents are able to interpret ambiguous mandates efficiently to the extent that, first, they appreciate the ultimate goals to be served and, second, they command either *technical expertise* or *information about context* which principals or higher-level agents do not share. A National Park Service wildlife specialist probably knows more than Congressmen do about how to encourage a proper balance of species within a park; a Federal Aviation Administration engineer knows more about the technical arcana of air-traffic control. Similarly a schoolteacher gains valuable information about context as he becomes familiar with the strengths and weaknesses of individual students, as does an infantry officer in the field as he gathers information about terrain and enemy positions that his rear-echelon superiors lack. In each case, agents are well-positioned to fill in efficiently the details of the vague mandates 'maintain ecological balance', 'ensure air safety', 'teach the children', or 'contain the enemy'.[8]

If agents are able to fill in efficiently the details of loosely defined mandates, under what circumstances will they act on that ability? One option is contractual incentives: rewards for efficient interpretation and penalties for bad choices. The notion of contractual incentives to interpret correctly a vague commission seems to have an element of paradox. If good performance can be defined, why leave mandates vague, instead of spelling out the results or behaviour by which agents will be judged? And if it cannot be defined, how can there be any sensible basis for rewarding agents?

These features describe much of the work to be done in the world, and an especially large proportion of public tasks, where multiple goals and contextual uncertainties combine to make advance prescriptions more difficult than judgements after the fact. When John Jay embarked for Europe in late 1779 to negotiate an end to the War of Independence, his instructions from Congress were a mixture of the vague and the unachievable. During four years of wrangling with the British, French and Spanish over the terms of America's separation from Britain, Jay and the rest of the delegation gained a vast amount of information and expertise that a distant and preoccupied Congress lacked. Jay exercised considerable discretion in setting and altering the details of the American position; indeed, he ignored explicit instructions when he judged that Congress, had it been privy to the details of the negotiations, would have instructed him otherwise. The Treaty of 1783 was recognized as a triumph for America on Jay's return – when the motives and machinations of the foreign interests became known – and his shrewd exercise of discretion earned him public esteem and further office.[9] One could argue that Jay, as the American people's agent, was 'contractually' motivated to harness his judgement to the public interest, and was duly rewarded for good performance. But it was an odd sort of contract, feasible only because of Jay's intrinsic desire to secure the best deal for America. Had he been motivated by self-interest alone, he would probably have balked at the contract 'use your judgement and accept evaluation by criteria to be determined later'.

In circumstances where good performance can only be defined in retrospect, the agent obviously faces the risk that, despite his best efforts, circumstances beyond his control (including ultimate goals that are incoherent or inconsistent) will lead to unfavourable evaluation. Prudent profit-seeking agents may be unwilling to undertake endeavours where their compensation depends so heavily on chance. It may be possible to write conditional contracts where payment depends on post-hoc evaluations which take into account unfolding events and assess agents' judgements in the light of the information available at each stage. Such contracts, though, are likely to be cumbersome, complex and expensive to adjudicate, and open to disputes about the favourability or otherwise of factors apart from the agent's performance. This amplifies the point that, when the product desired cannot be fully specified, there are serious impediments to profit-seeking agency arrangements. But there are problems as well with bureaucratic agency. If agents' compensation does *not* depend on results, and if no standard operating procedure can be laid out in advance, why should agents use their discretion to advance the public interest, instead of dissipating their efforts across the whole vague range of the mandate or concentrating on random portions of it?

This problem helps to explain why bureaucratic agents frequently end up doing the wrong things. It is hard to promote the common good if political officials cannot or do not specify just what this means. But it also highlights the immense social value of agents' *intrinsic* motivation to serve the public interest. To the extent that higher-level officials can rely on agents to exercise discretion efficiently, in the light of their special training or privileged grasp of circumstances, mandates can be left open; projects can be adapted as context requires; and monitoring costs can be spared. The public's business becomes much easier to accomplish if agents display a combination of informed fidelity to the public interest, initiative and integrity summarized by the term *honour*, an issue too complex to summarize neatly but too important to neglect.

Anthony Downs (1967, p. 2) wrote that the range of bureaucratic agents' goals includes power, money, security and convenience, but also 'loyalty to an idea, an institution, or the nation, pride in excellent work, and desire to serve the public interest'. Max Weber (1946a, p. 80) gave "social honor" equal weight with "material reward" in motivating bureaucrats. Even public choice theorist Gordon Tullock (1977, p. 282) granted a role for the bureaucrat's devotion to the public interest, albeit in a rather backhanded way, when he wrote that

> most civil servants live a relatively low-pressure existence. They have a fairly secure income and a great deal of freedom in planning their own activities ... The individual whose behavior is not likely to affect his future income very much is free to devote more of his effort to maximizing his own utility function. One argument in this utility function is normally a desire to benefit others which, in a government servant, may involve the public interest. Thus, the individual civil servant may do what in his view is the right thing for the government simply as a way of maximizing his own utility.

Bureaucratic honour here refers to an agent's intrinsic sympathy with organizational goals and propensity to advance them uncompelled and uncertain of material reward. In a soldier or diplomat it involves patriotism, in a teacher love of learning, in a judge a devotion to justice, and so on. It is particularly valuable when public officials' limited information requires that lower-level agents exercise discretion, and when extrinsic motivations are difficult to arrange.

Few would deny that bureaucratic honour is often useful and sometimes essential. But three complications remain. First, as suggested earlier, an agent may be sincerely motivated by a view of the public good that diverges from that of elected officials and has no reliable connection to the citizenry's desires. Rather than supplementing an incompletely specified agency contract, bureaucratic honour may conflict with it. Bureaucratic discretion, exercised with a sense of commitment to some vision of the social good but without effective accountability to the public, may *increase* the inefficiency of public undertakings by further distancing collective resources from collectively valued results.

Second, why should honour be counted valuable for bureaucratic and not for profit-seeking agents? Clearly society is better off when both sorts of agents display integrity, and indeed if profit-seekers were uniformly (and not just typically) honest and public-spirited many of the problems of contracting would disappear. But if profit-seekers are *differentially* honour-bound, the more public-spirited of them tend, by the logic of cost-based bidding, to lose contract competitions: if the honourable profit-seeker anticipates spending extra resources to produce value beyond the literal provisions of a contract, his costs and hence his bids will exceed those of competitors who attend to the letter of the contract and no more. (If his bids do not reflect such costs, he will steadily lose money and eventually go out of business.) If the superiority of his performance can be accurately measured after the fact, he may develop a reputational advantage that will counter this cost disadvantage in a series of similar contracts.[10] But when officials are unable or unmotivated to distinguish between minimal performance of contractual duties and the efficient exercise of discretion, the bias against honour-bound profit-seeking agents remains.

Third, it is easy but unhelpful to observe that bureaucratic honor is a good thing. A consensus on distributive justice would be a good thing, too, but is nonetheless elusive; to announce that it helps if bureaucrats are honourable does not make them so. Everyone has encountered some civil servants strongly devoted to the public interest, and some others conspicuously free of any such motivation. While it is wasteful to ignore bureaucratic honour where it exists, it may well be worse to rely on it where it does not. The potential for honour to bind bureaucratic agency relationships depends in part on the nature of the task and in part on broad cultural considerations.

While almost any undertaking may inspire intrinsic commitment, it seems more likely to be a significant factor for tasks that are clearly important, or surrounded by professional tradition, or which are charged with moral or emotional content. Agents performing military and diplomatic functions, or involved in teaching, research, social work, medicine and law enforcement may be highly motivated by honour and the opinions of their colleagues and the public. Clerks, street cleaners, road builders and other workers in functions with little visibility, prestige or autonomy are probably less likely to be so motivated.

The power of professional honour as a bureaucratic motivation also depends on the cultural status of bureaucrats. In many nations – Norway, France, Great Britain and Canada, for example – at least some civil servants enjoy a good deal of prestige. Carrying out official duties faithfully and efficiently earns high social regard and reinforces self-esteem. But when the civil service commands little prestige – as is generally true in the US today – there is less scope for honour and status as bureaucratic incentives. Max Weber (1946b, p. 200) noted this difference between European and American culture in 1918: '[T]he social esteem of officials as such is especially low when the demand for expert administration and the dominance of status conventions are weak. This is especially the case in the United States.' This suggests caution in relying on bureaucratic honour to buttress weak formal devices of accountability in this country. It also suggests that the opprobrium heaped upon civil servants in recent years – by further reducing the potential for honour as a motivate for bureaucrats – erodes our culture's ability to accomplish public tasks where close monitoring and extrinsic motivations are difficult to arrange.

In sum, the relative strengths of bureaucratic versus profit-seeking agency along the first dimension of efficiency – getting the right things done – depend crucially on whether public officials are technically able to specify mandates in detail and in advance. If they *can*, but tend not to, writing contracts with profit-seeking agents is likely to be a more useful discipline than drafting guidelines for bureaucratic agents. If officials are not equipped to define mandates, however, the advantage shifts to bureaucratic agency, *if* bureaucrats are capable of efficiently filling in the details of vague mandates *and* motivated to choose responsibly when their choices cannot be fully monitored or rewarded. And in cases where agents can neither be motivated extrinsically nor trusted to choose efficiently, society must either abandon the undertaking or resign itself to a measure of inefficiency.

Proposition 4 Profit-seeking agents generally cannot be expected to exceed the literal specifications of a contract. The more difficult it is to define mandates precisely in advance, and the more efficiency requires leaving agents some discretion, the more valuable are bureaucratic honour and internal commitment to public goals.

Efficient Performance: The Virtues of Ownership

The discussion above concerned the efficient *specification* of agents' tasks; the second dimension of efficiency concerns *performance*. This section is conceptually much simpler and can be summarized in a sentence:

Proposition 5 The more complete and more fully asserted are ownership rights, the less will the organization suffer from simple waste.

When the agents who control the productive organization are *owners*, or are effectively answerable to owners, the exercise of ownership rights (to determine the membership of the productive organization, direct its activities and claim net revenues) will limit random inefficiency or correctible departures from productive efficiency. (By 'random' I mean waste, muddle and confusion in the performance of accepted goals, as opposed to the inefficiency that results from the conflicting interests of principals and agents.) This tendency holds – albeit with different implications – whether or not government contracts are competitive and well-enforced: owners take up economic slack and convert it into lower prices or higher quality (if competition and officials' vigilance bridle profit ambitions) or elevated profits (if they do not.) Virtually every proposal urging a higher proportion of profit-seeking agents in the public realm turns on this point, and it is a real and often important advantage.[11]

In private firms, a layer of managers directly or indirectly interested in increasing profits controls the behaviour of lower-level employees. When a firm is commissioned to undertake a public task, the owners (or their agents) translate the *external* mandate into an *internal* mandate to generate revenue and limit costs.[12] There is no comparable function in a public bureaucracy, no link in the chain of agency relationships where incentives and authority to enforce efficiency are quite so potently concentrated.[13] Public managers also prefer efficiency to waste, but their interest in policing the details of subordinates' performance is usually less direct, less tangible and less focused. In particular, they lack any direct claim on cost savings. More important, even when public managers are motivated to enforce efficiency – by honour or by answerability to citizens or superior officials – they usually lack the rights to select and direct the productive team that private owners enjoy. Civil-service regulations, meant to guard against favouritism and corruption, often make it difficult to control agents through selective incentives or sanctions. Multiple mandates and constraints on management, even if imposed in sincere efforts to codify the complex criteria for public action, may so muddy accountability that no behaviour can be definitively evaluated.

Profit-seekers, then, are generally both motivated to eliminate random inefficiency and less constrained than bureaucrats in their capacity to do so. Three points qualifying this celebration of the virtues of ownership deserve emphasis, however. First, if the managers of a private contractor are not themselves owners and are weakly accountable to stockholders, there is room for the same kind of slack that saps the efficiency of governmental agencies. Second, profit-seekers perceive as slack *any* use of resources that does not boost net revenue, whether it is simple waste or attention to some public goal that is not made contractually explicit. Third, *random* inefficiency is not the only or necessarily the most damaging defect to which agency relationships are subject. Often the most important breakdowns of accountability involve not wasteful or rigid or inept performance, but the failure of agency contracts to subordinate agents' self-interest to the goals of the principals.

BUREAUCRATS, PROFIT-SEEKERS AND RENTS

Agents' self-interest can be bridled by two kinds of extrinsic forces: competition or institutional rules and procedures.[14] The first mechanism of accountability works best when the dimensions of competition can be specified. The second works when value-producing procedures can be clearly defined. Both approaches depend upon political agents to translate the public interest into contractual terms, monitor performance and enforce mandates. The section above discussed how the inability or negligence of political agents to carry out these duties can lead to inefficient performance. The same failures to define and enforce may grant agents scope for exercising self-interest at citizens' expense. Agents collect rents when they are paid more, in whatever currency, than the public should have to pay to get its business accomplished. Bureaucratic and profit-seeking agents differ significantly in the form of rents they tend to extract from the public.

Bureaucrats' Rents

A near-universal feature of bureaucracy is formal limits on monetary compensation. Even if the relevant legislators are sufficiently broad-minded, incompetent or corrupt to accede to his demands, the Secretary of Agriculture cannot arrange for his salary to be increased to a million dollars a year. In the US federal government, and in almost all state and local governments, salaries are set by legislation or ordinances, and can be changed only through a complex formal process. For example, it is unconstitutional (Articles II and III) to reduce federal judges' salaries, or to raise or cut the pay of a sitting President.

Government pay scales are also quite compressed: lower-level civil servants often make more than their private-sector counterparts, while top officials generally make less. One could argue, perhaps, that this pattern simply reflects relative worth: the public sector needs and gets better clerks and backhoe operators and worse top managers than the private sector. A more plausible explanation is that political considerations, and not economic ones alone, affect the compensation of public workers. Employees exercise political influence to push up wages and salaries. Public managers have little reason to resist such pressures and are generally happy to have their subordinates well paid. Government pay scales are constrained to some extent at all levels, however, and quite tightly at top levels, by public opinion. If average government salaries get very far out of line with average private-sector salaries, lawmakers will find it politically expedient to legislate freezes or reductions. And if top salaries exceed what the public perceives as reasonable – whatever their relation to top private-sector compensation – there is little to lose politically and much to gain from initiatives to limit them.

Bureaucrats generally, and higher-level bureaucrats especially, may be less constrained in their ability to collect *non-pecuniary* rents. The reasons are the same as those behind random inefficiency: the absence of competition makes performance difficult to evaluate; the absence of concentrated ownership dilutes the inducement to enforce accountability. When rents in cash are limited, self-serving agents may press for rents in kind – in the form of fringe benefits, pleasant working conditions, congenial associates, undemanding work loads, security against dismissal, and so on. These tend broadly to increase with the size of the bureau's budget, and to decrease with the energy of political agents' supervision, introducing a conflict of interest between bureaucratic agents and the public at large.[15] Non-pecuniary rents have two special problems. First, they are inefficient not just from the public's perspective, but from the agents' as well. Slack rule enforcement may benefit bureaucrats slightly at a large cost to the public; if rents could be collected in cash, bureaucrats could be made just as happy at less public expense. Second, non-pecuniary rents are difficult to identify. It may be very hard to tell whether a public organization has a 20-person accounting staff because the manpower is really needed or because the chief accountant enjoys the prestige of directing many subordinates.

Profit-Seekers' Rents

Bureaucratic rents result when political officials are unable or reluctant to drive a hard bargain with agents on the citizens' behalf. Profit-seekers collect rents for the same reasons, but in a different form. One member of the public choice school, which indicts bureaucracy as a prime source of wasteful government spending, charges that bureaucrats 'operate organizations which offer superior monopoly advantages. This unique monopoly position yields a relatively large fiscal residuum from which bureaucrats can indirectly extract wealth.'[16] It is not bureaucracy, however, but weakly-enforced accountability that exposes the public to exploitation. The public choice story strains credulity: public officials are unable or unwilling to assert the public's rights *vis-à-vis* bureaucrats, but when private agents do the work officials will somehow find the will and the means to vigilantly enforce competitive bidding, evaluate performance and impose penalties for incompetence, negligence or fraud.

Proposition 6 The attenuated accountability of public undertakings can permit both bureaucratic and profit-seeking agents to collect rents at the public's expense.

To the extent that a group of owners effectively controls the profit-seeking entity, rents will consist of extra net income, rather than extra pecuniary or non-pecuniary benefits accruing to lower level agents. If public officials' negligence limits competition or allows profit-seekers to save costs by misrepresenting quality, that is, the more frequent result will be higher profits, and not higher wages and salaries, more relaxed working conditions and so on. This will not be the case, however, when ownership rights are weakly enforced or challenged by subordinate agents. If a private firm's managers enjoy substantial autonomy from dispersed shareholders, they may capture rents for themselves, in the form of inflated salaries and elaborate perquisites, rather than passing them on as profits. If the firm's work force is organized, or if the firm is dependent on a few key subcontractors, then workers or suppliers may be able to claim part of the rents as higher wages or prices.

Four features of profit-seekers' rents are worth noting. First, there is an interesting discrepancy between economists' and laymen's interpretations of pecuniary and non-pecuniary rents. The average citizen would probably feel that, while both are deplorable, it is worse for a private contractor to overcharge the government by $10 000 than for an underworked civil servant paid ten dollars an hour to idly watch the clock for 1 000 hours over the course of a year. But an economist would consider the former a transfer – the funds can be saved and reinvested elsewhere, or at least spent on an enjoyable vacation – and the latter a clear waste of resources, since the bureaucrat doubtless gains less than $10 000 worth of pleasure from his idleness. Second, profit-seekers' rents, like bureaucratic rents, may be difficult to identify. A very profitable government contractor may be legitimately earning rich returns because it is innovative and efficiently run, or collecting rents because it is unharried by potential competition and able to raise prices or cut quality with impunity. Third, profit-seekers' rents are much more likely than bureaucratic rents to be highly concentrated, with important implications for the next section. Owners or those who exercise ownership rights – and not other members of the productive organization – will collect most of the available rents. Fourth, profit-seeking agents may have a greater interest than bureaucratic agents in misrepresenting the quality of their output, particularly if the perception of adequate quality means security against competitors, since owners can appropriate cost savings due to lower quality as well as those due to legitimately lower costs.

Proposition 7 Bureaucratic rents will generally be dispersed and (especially at higher levels) largely non-pecuniary. Profit-seekers' rents will generally be concentrated and pecuniary. The same ownership rights that encourage efficiency also concentrate incentives for rent-seeking.

This proposition, and the logic behind it, have one particularly distressing implication. If public endeavours differ in their 'natural' suitability for bureaucratic or profit-seeking agency – that is, if public officials can more tightly manage bureaucrats in one sort of undertaking and profit-seekers in another – each type of agent will probably tend to *prefer* employment in the endeavours for which it is *least* suited. Bureaucratic agents will find the richest rents in undertakings where it is especially hard to enforce accountability on bureaucrats; profit-seeking agents will find the richest rents where competition and evaluation tend to be weakest. The less scope there is for effective competition in a given function, for example, the more pressure we should expect from aspiring profit-seeking agents to shift that function from public to private suppliers. In the case-by-case choice between public and private delivery, the interests of agents, to the extent that they are self-serving and opportunistic, run counter to those of the citizenry at large.

AGENTS' INTERESTS AND THE POLITICS OF PUBLIC SPENDING

Inducements for Political Activism

A citizen's status as an agent in a collective undertaking is likely to affect his preferences about public spending and his propensity to act on those preferences. Along with his economic and moral interests, he will take his private benefits as an agent into account in exercising his rights as a principal to influence spending decisions. The owner of a construction company will consider her prospects for contracts, as well as her convictions about help for the homeless, as she reflects on a proposal for building emergency shelters. An official of the Drug Enforcement Administration will probably think differently about an anti-narcotics initiative than will his neighbour, even if they are equally appalled by drug abuse. A scientist's sense of national research priorities will generally have something to do with her own area of expertise. If citizens' interests as agents govern their political preferences, and if such interests are more politically potent – because more concentrated and better organized – than the interests favouring different spending patterns (or less collective spending) they may seriously distort public decisions. Self-interested agents, generally in coalition with groups who benefit disproportionately from public undertakings, may seize control of the spending agenda to the detriment of the dispersed and unorganized majority.

Two points qualify this generalization. The fact that an agent's employment interests coincide with her policy preferences need not mean that the former governs the latter. A citizen's choice of occupation and her spending preferences may both reflect the same underlying beliefs about socially valuable undertakings; a teacher's support for spending on education does not necessarily signal opportunism, nor does a doctor's support for public health care spending. It is conceptually difficult in most cases to disentangle a citizen's interests as a principal from his interests as an agent; the NASA worker whose vote goes to the candidate most supportive of the space programme probably does not know himself how much his position reflects his own enthusiasm for space exploration versus his eagerness to keep the job that his enthusiasm led him to select.

The second point is less obvious, but no less important, and is the reason for developing at such length the notion of economic rents. Incentives to distort spending arise *not* from mere involvement in some public undertaking, but from the availability of benefits, in cash or in kind, exceeding those otherwise obtainable. If a laser technician can choose among a number of equally attractive jobs across a range of industries, he has little stake – as a worker – in public spending on anti-missile defence systems. If the construction industry is booming and government contracts are no more lucrative than other projects, the building contractor has no material motive to push for more low-income housing. If a Securities and Exchange Commission lawyer knows he can easily find a comparable job in the private sector, his vote will probably not depend on candidates' positions on the budget for securities-law enforcement. In practice, of course, nearly everyone would rather not lose his job, nearly every contractor would prefer more business to less and, as I argue above, government contracts with either type of agents are especially likely to be rich in rents. But it is important to recognize that involvement in public projects does not automatically inspire a uniform type or degree of self-interested support for the budget behind the project.

A citizen usually takes several factors into account as she decides how, and how actively, to seek to affect public spending. She considers how various initiatives harmonize with her personal interests as a beneficiary of public spending. She considers how programmes promise to reflect and advance her moral and philosophical values. She examines her tax position and how heavily the burden of public spending falls on her. She considers as well the probability that her efforts will have an effect on spending decisions. These factors, along with her own taste or distaste for thinking about and getting involved in politics, determine how politically well-informed and active she will be. In general her interests as an agent will weigh more heavily, relative to other factors, the larger are the rents at stake, and the greater the probability that her own political activity can, at a cost commensurate with the rents she anticipates, significantly influence the relevant spending decisions. In other words, rents can be interpreted like any other source of revenues: the rational amount to invest in their pursuit – in time or money, or in other political concerns displaced – depends on the return expected.

Proposition 8 The importance of self-serving motives for an agent's political behaviour is roughly proportional to the rents at stake.

For example, if economic and institutional factors in the health-care industry are such that doctors make large rents and nurses earn little or nothing above their reservation wages, Proposition 8 predicts that we should see doctors, and not nurses, pushing for looser reimbursement rules and an expansion in government spending on health care. An agent's rent will be large if her situation as a public agent is especially favourable, or if her other options are especially bleak. If National Park Service maintenance workers are paid double the going wage, they will be inclined to resist proposals to shrink the park system or contract out maintenance work to private firms. A technician who is highly specialized in designing nuclear warheads would find few alternative uses for his skills, so that, even if his salary is not particularly high, he would have a lively interest in maintaining military spending and opposing disarmament. If his skills were more readily transferable, the importance of his self-interest as an agent would recede, relative to other political motives.[17]

The economic theory of groups (see especially Olson, 1965) predicts that large groups of moderately interested people will frequently be less organized and less politically effective than smaller groups of intensely interested people. This is precisely why we worry about the self-interest of agents: if information and organizational capacity were not potent instruments of political influence, agents' interest in slack and generous compensation would be countered by other citizens' interest in efficiency and low taxes. But organizational advantages may allow self-interested agents to prevail over dispersed and disorganized principals. The same logic suggests that small coalitions of agents will generally be more effectively organized than large ones. Policy influence is a 'public good' for the group that shares a common political goal; individual agents will be tempted to let others bear the burden of political action. It will be easier to overcome the public good problem if the group is small enough for mutual monitoring and persuasion, or if each agent anticipates rents that are large relative to the resources required to influence spending, or if the group has other organizational adhesives beyond a shared spending agenda.

Instruments of Political Influence

One obvious way in which agents can influence spending is through their *votes*. An agent may vote for the candidate promising the largest (or least tightly managed) version of the budget from which the agent's rents flow. Whether he uses his ballot in this way depends on at least three factors. First is the size of the rents at stake: the greater the agent's rents, the more likely his interest as an agent is to dominate his voting decision. Second is the relative importance of other issues on which candidates differ: a teacher might vote for a candidate based on his stand on abortion or some other highly salient issue, even if the candidate also proposes cutbacks in education spending. Third is the candidate's likely capacity, if elected, to affect the budget from which the agent's rents derive: if one candidate for the House favours more education spending but is unlikely to sit on the relevant committees, teachers will tend to cast their ballots by other criteria. In general the *cost* of voting on the basis of one's interests as an agent is the sacrifice of other political concerns, while the *benefit* depends on both the rents at stake and on the perceived link between the vote and the status of the relevant budget.

Agents' ballots are more likely to distort budget politics the greater is agents' propensity to vote according to their interests as producers and the greater the proportion of agents in the electorate. I argued above that profit-seekers' rents tend to be concentrated while bureaucratic rents are dispersed. If this is true, then with bureaucratic organization *many* agents will have *some* motivation to cast their votes according to their interests as agents, while with profit-seeking organization *a few* agents will have *strong* motives to defend their rents with their votes. If all the rents available in some public budget go to the owners of the profit-seeking entity that does the work, lower-level agents will have little interest in voting to preserve or increase the budget. Some military bases have replaced their canteens with private fast-food franchises. If the workers in those franchises are paid no more than they could get in comparable jobs off the base, they will have little financial stake in the size of the defence budget, although the franchise owners might. While rents will seldom be completely concentrated (few contractors' employees will be indifferent about keeping their jobs) bureaucrats should be more likely than contractors' employees to vote on the basis of their interest as agents.

Proposition 9 The more important are votes compared to other instruments of political influence, the greater the spending agenda's vulnerability to manipulation by bureaucratic agents.

A second instrument of political influence is *persuasion*. Agents may lobby public officials or attempt to shape public opinion on spending issues. To the extent that agents have special expertise about the public undertaking involved, they will be especially well-positioned to influence both officials and the public. It may be difficult to distinguish between spending recommendations based on expert assessments of public needs and those based on agents' self-interest.

A third instrument is *campaign support*. Agents can attempt to influence the spending positions of public officials and candidates or to affect the electoral prospects of sympathetic contenders, through their donations of time or money or other resources. Campaign support, unlike voting, can be calibrated to match the intensity of a donor's interest in an election. A citizen with a moderate preference for one candidate can wear a lapel pin or display a bumper sticker. As the intensity of her preference rises, she can attempt to influence the votes of her friends and relatives, work on phone banks at campaign headquarters, canvass door to door, and so on.

Financial contributions can be varied with even greater precision according to the donor's stake in the outcome.

How should we expect the two types of agents to differ in their campaign contributions? The logic underlying Proposition 9 suggests that a large number of bureaucratic agents will each be inclined to make modest efforts to promote their budgetary interests. There will be *fewer* contributions from profit-seeking agents (if only a minority of the members of a profit-seeking entity collect rents from public contracts) but each contribution is likely to be larger, in line with the rents at stake. Since there are physical limits on the time any one person can donate to a campaign (and since the owners of firms involved in government contracts may tend to place relatively high values on their time) contributions from profit-seekers will usually be in the form of money.

The Hatch Act and comparable state and local laws generally limit the amount of time bureaucrats can donate to campaigns, while campaign finance laws limit the amount of money profit-seekers can contribute. The influence agents can exert on spending decisions through campaign support depends on the relative effectiveness of these constraints, on politicians' willingness to tailor their spending policies to obtain campaign support, and on the relative political potency of the campaign resources each type of agent can most easily contribute. One particularly interesting question is how politicians perceive the relative political value of *votes* themselves (more of which, I suggest, will be supplied by bureaucratic agents) and *money* to use in search of votes (more of which will be supplied by profit-seeking agents).

Finally agents can seek to shape public spending through *bribery* or other illegitimate forms of influence over public officials. Bureaucratic and profit-seeking agents will differ in their propensity to bribe officials, I suggest, roughly as they differ in their campaign contributions. If a profit-seeking agent has large rents at stake, and if he is undeterred by moral scruples or the threat of discovery, he may be inclined to devote significant sums to induce officials to increase the relevant budget, increase the available rents through looser management, or steer a contract away from lower-bidding or more qualified competitors. *Individual* bureaucratic agents will generally have smaller rents and the amount they will be willing to spend to defend or expand them will be correspondingly modest – probably too little, in most cases, to corrupt a politician. Bureaucratic agents may be motivated to pool their resources into a more impressive bribe, but such an arrangement would be difficult to organize and enforce in secret.

Proposition 10 The more important are campaign donations and bribes compared to other instruments of political influence, the greater the spending agenda's vulnerability to manipulation by profit-seeking agents.

This implies that, task by task, and jurisdiction by jurisdiction, choices between profit-seekers and bureaucrats should be biased away from profit-seeking agency when campaign contributions are important factors in budgetary politics, or where political corruption is difficult to detect or deter. Where corruption is uncommon and campaign finance laws limit the political potency of monetary contributions, conversely, the votes of bureaucratic agents may have the greater potential for warping spending decisions.

NOTES

1. The sanction can be complex and indirect, as with loss of reputation.
2. To be precise, a private monopoly will probably have lower costs than a public bureaucracy, for reasons explained below, but cost savings will generally result in higher rents rather than lower selling prices. It is also worth noting that both actual and *potential* competition can discipline profit-seekers.
3. Williamson (1975, chaps 2 and 4) discusses the perils of recontracting.
4. A degree of discretion and initiative is obviously required in the event of an actual attack, and agents must somehow be motivated to achieve results and not simply follow a necessarily incomplete set of standard procedures; see the later section on bureaucratic honour.
5. March and Simon (1958) propose an analogous set of guidelines for the choice between 'product specifications' (here, parallel to pure profit-seeking agency) and 'activity specifications' (corresponding to pure bureaucratic agency). Contracts are best defined by 'specifications of quality and quantity of output to the extent that: (a) the activity pattern is difficult to observe and supervise; (b) the quantity and quality of output are easily observed and supervised; (c) the relations between activity pattern and output are matters of common sense, are matters of skill in the specific occupation for which the operatives are trained, or are highly variable, depending upon circumstances of the individual situation that are better known to the operatives than to supervisors and specialists'. Conversely, contracts are best defined by 'activity specifications in preference to product specifications to the extent that; (a) the activity pattern is easily observed and supervised; (b) the quantity and quality of output are not easily observed and supervised; (c) the relations between activity pattern and output are highly technical, and are matters of scientific and engineering knowledge, better known to specialists than to the operatives' (p. 145).
6. Niskanen (1971, pp. 201–9) calls for such a system of competition and rights to cost savings as remedies for the ills of bureaucracy.
7. Cited in Lindblom (1977, p. 71).
8. It is worth noting that these points apply to private as well as public bureaucracies. March and Simon (1958, pp. 147–8) discuss four kinds of circumstances (paraphrased here) where subordinates exercise discretion: first, when mandates are conditional and specific choices must be based on assessments of alternatives; second, when mandates must be adapted to specific circumstances; third, when the agent has expertise that the principal invokes but has not imparted; finally, when the mandate includes only general goals and requires specifications to have operational meaning.
9. Jay's role in the negotiations is discussed in Morris (1985) pp. 78–93.
10. Long-term relationships and repeat dealings, by instilling incentives to good performance, may help to overcome one disadvantage of profit-seeking agency. Indeed this is probably one of the most important mechanisms of accountability in private-sector

exchanges. When regulations require public officials to accept the lowest bid, however – as is generally the case – reputation cannot be taken into account. There are real dangers to allowing public officials to award contracts on the basis of intangible factors like reputation, limiting the potential for this incentive to efficient judgement in the public sector.
11. Mill (1929, p. 139) argued that efficient management

> requires two quite distinct qualifications: fidelity, and zeal. The fidelity of the hired managers of a concern it is possible to secure. When their work admits of being reduced to a definite set of rules, the violation of these is a matter on which conscience cannot easily blind itself, and on which responsibility may be enforced by the loss of employment. But to carry on a great business successfully, requires a hundred things which, as they cannot be defined beforehand, it is impossible to convert into distinct and positive obligations. First and principally, it requires that the directing mind should be incessantly occupied with the subject; should be continually laying schemes by which greater profit may be obtained, or expense saved. This intensity of interest in the subject it is seldom to be expected that any one should feel, who is conducting a business as the hired servant and for the profit of another.

It is only stretching my logic slightly to argue that bureaucracies are generally superior in fidelity but lacking in zeal, while profit-seekers' greater zeal for efficiency is often difficult to harness to the public interest.
12. The success of profit-seeking agency relationships, from the public's point of view, depends heavily on how much meaning is preserved in the course of this translation.
13. This distinction is a matter of degree; there *are* points throughout public agencies where incentives and authority are concentrated to some extent.
14. A sense of honour or duty is a further, intrinsic force.
15. Louis De Alessi (1974, p. 647) has observed that, since the salaries of government managers are usually constrained, the opportunity cost of non-pecuniary sources of utility is lower'.
16. Orzechowski (1977, p. 239).
17. This suggests that bureaucrats' rents in general will tend to change with the state of the private economy, varying inversely with the business cycle.

REFERENCES

De Alessi, Louis (1974), 'Managerial Tenure Under Private and Government Ownership in the Electric Power Industry', *Journal of Political Economy*, vol. 82, no. 3.
Downs, Anthony (1967), *Inside Bureaucracy*, Boston: Little, Brown and Company.
Lindblom, Charles E. (1977), *Politics and Markets*, New York: Basic Books.
March, James G. and Herbert A. Simon (1958), *Organizations*, New York: John Wiley & Sons.
Mill, John Stuart (1929), *Principles of Political Economy*, London: Longmans, Green and Co.
Morris, Richard B. (1985), *Witnesses at the Creation: Hamilton, Madison, Jay, and the Constitution*, New York: New American Library.
Niskanen, William J. (1971), *Bureaucracy and Representative Government*, Chicago: Aldine-Atherton.
Olson, Mancur (1965), *The Logic of Collective Action: Public Goods and the*

Theory of Groups, Cambridge, Mass.: Harvard University Press.
Orzechowski, William (1977), 'Economic Models of Bureaucracy: Survey, Extensions, and Evidence', in Thomas E. Borcherding (ed.), *Budgets and Bureaucrats: The Sources of Government Growth*, Durham: Duke University Press.
Schmidt, William E. (1986), 'No More Selling of Votes? County is a Little Wary', *The New York Times*, 15 October.
Tullock, Gordon (1977), 'What is to be Done?' in Thomas E. Borcherding (ed), *Budgets and Bureaucrats: The Sources of Government Growth*, Durham: Duke University Press.
Weber, Max (1946a), 'Politics as a Vocation', reprinted in H.H. Gerth and C. Wright Mills, *From Max Weber: Essays in Sociology*, New York: Oxford University Press.
Weber, Max (1946b), 'Bureaucracy', reprinted in Gerth and Mills, *From Max Weber*.
Williamson, Oliver (1975), *Markets and Hierarchies*, New York: The Free Press.

11. Public and Private Sector Relationships in the Age of Privatization

Ronald C. Moe

One element in the appeal of privatization as a theory and as a political strategy is the belief that privatization, however it is defined, necessarily results in a substantial reduction in governmental involvement in the national economy and that this is a good thing. Less involvement means that the government, in this case the federal government, will not require the same degree of managerial authority and capacity. Thus privatization has come to be associated not only with less government, but with less effective government as well.

This chapter takes issue with both the explicit and implicit assumptions that inhere in this view of the purpose and consequences of privatization. While it is true that occasionally an entire activity or entity is transferred ('load shedding' or 'divestment') to the private sector, thus truly 'privatizing' that activity or entity, the typical privatization effort is not of this character. In popular parlance, privatization is considered to have occurred whenever the provision of a public good or service is assigned, usually by contract, to a third party. The assignment of public functions to third parties, while it may decrease the need for direct government employment, does not eliminate, or even substantially reduce, the requirements of government management; it simply changes the character of this management.

Privatization, contrary to conventional wisdom, often results not in less, but in new and more sophisticated demands being placed upon public management, demands presently little recognized or appreciated by either privatization advocates or the public sector management community itself.

The purpose of this discussion is to acquaint the reader with some of the dimensions of the public management of privatization. The working assumption behind this analysis is that the public and private sectors are fundamentally distinctive, yet interdependent. The relationship is symbiotic, not adversarial, with the effectiveness and prosperity of the two sectors being positively linked.

THIRD-PARTY GOVERNMENT

In the United States, it has been a major political value since the founding of the Republic that officers and employees of the federal government should be held accountable for their actions to elected officials and through these officials to the public. This hierarchical model of administrative organization and accountability has remained the norm for two centuries and is supported by a system of Constitutional requirements, statute law and court decisions.

We distinguish in the US between the public and private sectors and this distinction is recognized in law. The federal government possesses the rights and immunities of the sovereign; organizations functioning in the private sector do not, or at least ought not, possess such rights and immunities. The public sector is governed by public law, the private sector largely by private law. Thus officers of the US, in performance of their duties, must adhere to the Constitutional requirement of providing 'due process' to their actions and decisions, a requirement not imposed upon an officer of a private corporation. The assignment of functions between the public and private sectors must take into account the fundamental legal distinctions between the sectors.[1] All too often, however, the assignment process is based largely, if not solely, upon economic factors.

In recent decades, two contradictory trends have emerged to influence the course of federal government management. The first trend is a reflection of the anti-government bias prevalent throughout the political community generally and takes the form of deliberately limiting the internal capacity of the federal government to perform its functions and responsibilities. This trend is most obvious in the arbitrary ceilings imposed by both the President and Congress upon management expenditures, personnel and compensation. The second trend, at odds with the first, is the continuing pressure to involve the federal government in more activites, such as the 'bail-out' of the savings and loan industry, environmental protection and hazardous waste clean-up, or AIDS research, activities which by their nature require substantial commitments of resources: managerial, financial and personnel.

The principal means employed to bridge the gap between these two opposing trends has been to utilize the services of third parties. These may be other governments, new quasi-governmental bodies of indeterminate legal status, instrumentalities, non-profit organizations or for-profit corporations.[2] Except in the case of utilizing the services of other governments, such as states and cities, the use of third parties is generally viewed as a form of privatization.

As the functions demanded of government have increased and become more complex, so the contracting process for these goods and services has become more complex and troublesome to the political leadership and the career management leadership of the country. Elected and appointed officials have found that, while they can assign responsibility for producing goods and services to third parties, they are still held accountable by the public for the actual performance of the public function.[3]

CONTRACTING OUT: WHERE ARE THE LIMITS?

While governmental contracting for services is a practice of longstanding, indeed one predating the formation of the Union, there has been a substantial increase both in the amount and in the types of activities being contracted for in recent decades. Scholars and journalists are beginning to write of the 'shadow government'[4] and the 'hollow government',[5] terms referring to the decline in the capacity of the federal government to manage its own affairs and the increasing (and presumably undesirable) reliance upon third-party contractors. Although the term is not generally used in this context, these commentators are also questioning whether privatization has gone too far.

Promoters of privatization tend to emphasize economic criteria, almost to the exclusion of other criteria, in the decision-making process as to whether a particular function should be performed by the public or the private sector. Not surprisingly, therefore, they generally find it difficult to locate many activities that should remain the sole prerogative of government or that should be performed by government managers or employees.[6]

The theoretical foundation for privatizing most functions of a public character is furnished in large measure by the tenets of the public choice school of economics. In essence, the public choice theorists contend that the public and private sectors have much in common and that their behaviour is largely explained in terms of economic incentives. Given what is alleged to be the monopolistic character of the public sector, the need for efficiency and cost-effectiveness is largely absent from policy and administrative decisions of public sector managers. What is necessary, according to privatization promoters, is to alter the incentive system of public institutions and managers so that market competition can be brought to bear on both decisions and operations. The litany of their presentation is then to cite numerous instances where privatizing services, such as garbage collection and prisons, have led to 'better operations' at less cost to the taxpayer.[7]

The contracting process is portrayed as a relatively simple, straightforward process in which a government agency seeks out would-be providers who submit competitive bids to provide the desired product or service at the least cost. The model presupposes the working of a relatively free and competitive market mechanism where there are a number of potential bidders, a presupposition frequently absent from real-life conditions.

Harold Seidman, in recent Congressional testimony observed:

> The assumption that competition and market discipline are all that are required to produce optimal [governmental] performance is an illusion. When the government is contracting for intangibles such as policy analysis, management services and research and development, opportunity for competition among qualified suppliers is often limited or non-existent. Success or failure of the many companies whose principal – and sometimes only – customer is the U.S. Government depends more on their skill in manipulating the political system than in competing in the market place.[8]

At the federal government level, the policy governing the contracting-out process is to be found in Office of Management and Budget (OMB) Circulars No. A-76 (4 August 1983) and No. A-120 (4 January 1988). Circular A-76 'establishes federal policy regarding the performance of commercial activities' and then lists 'examples' of those activities considered commercial in character and thus likely candidates for being contracted out. The circular also states that certain functions are 'inherently governmental in nature' and hence are not appropriate for the contracting process. Circular A-76 defines an 'inherently governmental function' as:

> a function which is so intimately related to the public interest as to mandate performance by Government employees. These functions include those activities which require either the exercise of discretion in applying Government authority or the use of value judgment in making decisions for the Government ...[9]

The Office of Management and Budget and a number of departments and agencies have promoted a relatively broad interpretation of what constitutes a 'commercial' activity and, conversely, a relatively narrow definition of what constitutes an 'inherently governmental function'. This attitude has been reinforced by externally imposed limits placed upon management and operations capabilities of departments and agencies. These limitations include such devices as budgetary restrictions, arbitrary administrative cost ceilings, personnel and compensation 'caps'. Programme managers, faced with these externally imposed regulations and limitations, seek relief in order to accomplish their mandated mission and this relief is generally provided through turning to third parties in contractual arrangements. Increasingly decisions to rely on the contracting process have not been driven by theory, but by the sheer absence of any other reasonable option.

Circular A-120 is designed to provide guidelines for the use of "advisory and assistance" services, better known as consulting. The circular identifies those functions for which advisory and assistance services may not be utilized. The prohibited functions include 'work of a policy, decision-making or managerial nature which is the direct responsibility of agency officials'.[10]

While the guidelines may be helpful in a general way in determining the limits of contracting out, it requires specific cases to give meaning to the general prohibition. For instance, can statutorily required auditing of the expenditure of public funds be contracted with a private party if the auditing process permits discretionary disposition of disputed monetary claims against the government? Or can the selection of candidates for participation in a federal programme be assigned to a contractor?

Recently a Senate Subcommittee requested the General Accounting Office (GAO) to investigate several specific contracts to determine whether these contracts involved the transference of an 'inherently governmental function' to a private party. One contract by the Department of Energy (DOE) called for the contractor to provide Hearings Officers to conduct hearings and Personnel Security Review Examiners to review findings concerning the eligibility of individuals for DOE security clearances. The GAO concluded that these functions are inherently governmental in nature and should be performed only by federal employees.[11]

What these instances illustrate is an important fact generally overlooked by those discussing privatization: that there are fundamental distinctions between the governmental and private sectors and that these distinctions are based on legal principles, not economic theory. Ultimately there are limits to what public sector services are *permitted* to be contracted out to private parties.

There are also limits, more subtle and less easily defined, as to what services *ought* to be contracted out. Services in support of management are a case in point. Agency libraries are sometimes put to contract, but from a public sector management standpoint this is a questionable practice. Contemporary libraries are more than simply depositories for books, they are also critical data and information centres whose function is to support management. Private contractor personnel understandably have their primary loyalty, not to the head of the agency, but to the private firm that pays their cheque and seeks a profit. The agency head can only indirectly have an impact on the management and priorities of the library and its personnel. Threats of cancelling contracts are not a practical method of providing coherent managerial leadership. Thus, while libraries may not be legally considered an 'inherently governmental function', it is probably correct to state that they constitute a function integral to the management requirements of a properly managed and accountable agency of government.

The notion that somehow privatization necessarily 'shrinks' the size of government, as measured in financial terms, and that most functions of the federal government could best be performed by private contractors simply misses the mark. Anyone familiar with American politics today knows that it is not generally persons in the government who are seeking new government programmes, new and better entitlement schemes, new forms of government guarantees against the risks of the market-place, or new defence weapons systems; it is the private contractors and interest groups who have formed the largest and most effective lobbies for more interventionist, and less accountable, government.[12]

THE CHANGING ROLE OF PUBLIC MANAGEMENT

Public management of third-party relationships is generally more complex and subtle than management relationships associated with the traditional hierarchical public sector. Even the strategic options available to public managers are substantially altered, as Don Kettl observes:

> The point is simple yet often overlooked. Third-party strategies are not self-executing and often replace one set of administrative problems with another. If directly administered government programs must deal with self-interested bureaucrats, third-party programs must deal with self-interested proxies, each seeking to maximize their own interest, sometimes at government's expense. Contracts must themselves be administered to insure high accountability and performance. The role of administrators is different, but it does not disappear.[13]

Indirect provision of services by third parties alters the management incentive structure of government.[14] Substantive programme results, once the principal basis for judging managerial performance, are being gradually displaced by process managerial standards. Programme managers tend to become 'risk averse' as they find their political superiors are more interested in whether appropriated monies have been committed in a timely manner and contracts awarded in a politically acceptable mix, rather than in programme results. Substantive programme knowledge gradually erodes within agency management as managers are evaluated on how well they adhere to procedures rather than how well they are serving the mission of the agency.[15]

Many public managers are originally attracted to public service in general and an agency in particular because of the mission of the agency. Mission fulfilment, such as being involved in the management of the nation's space programme in a 'hands on' capacity, is an important attraction to public sector management and helps compensate for comparatively low salaries. But privatization can often result in the transference to the private sector of important management decisions and even of much policy making. Programme managers see that the interesting work is being done by others while they are left with accountability to political leaders for the programme and with the routine tasks of contract management.

Harold Seidman and Robert Gilmour contend that the reduction in federal agency responsibilities for direct provision of services has resulted in the emergence of a new type of career executive.

> Administration through third parties has converted the roles of senior career executives to those of grant and contract administrators, paymasters and regulation writers and enforcers. Emphasis has inevitably shifted from delivering services and evaluating results to complying with rules and regulations.[16]

Assume for the moment that an activity is selected for assignment to third parties with public sector managers retaining residual authority. What are some of the changes likely to be encountered as management is shifted from a command to a negotiations mode?

The most important change is that contract writing becomes a critical tool of public management. In a hierarchical organization, managers can accept a general programme objective and make incremental corrections in operations as the programme evolves. They can interact directly with field personnel. In a contract relationship, however, the public manager must negotiate with private managers, thus making subsequent incremental corrections more difficult. Public sector mangement in a privatized environment must be heavily front end-loaded. That is, a premium is placed on planning, on anticipating problems in advance, and being able to correct these problems conceptually within the contract-writing process. Contract writing, now principally viewed as a technical task performed by mid-level managers, must become one of the principal tools of the new public management.

Congress and the President have both found the contracting process a convenient tool to which to attach certain social objectives that would have difficulty being accepted on their own merits in the legislative process. As a result, private contractors often find themselves required to implement certain political objectives as a condition for obtaining a contract. Perhaps in seeking to maximize the contracting-out process we are governmentalizing the private sector more than we are privatizing the public sector.

The potential dangers of mixing governmental powers with privately owned corporations is most evident in the financial area. Government-sponsored enterprises (GSEs), such as the Federal National Mortgage Association ('Fannie Mae'), partake of the best of both the private and public worlds. They are able to pursue private profit under private management, yet are shielded from major financial risk because their obligations are implicitly guaranteed by the federal government. We have yet to develop an effective theory or practice of public management of these GSEs.[17] Privatizers themselves tend to be ambiguous about them and contribute little to the management dialogue.

It is critical to the management of third-party contracts that the agency itself retain the capacity to produce the goods, perform the research or deliver the services. Only by keeping this capacity will the necessary 'in-house' capability be assured, not only to replace the contractor, if necessary, but also to permit the qualitative evaluation of the product, findings or service from the contractor. If this is not done, the evaluation process may become simply an auditing process providing information on how well the procedures have been followed for expending funds in a legal manner.

The introduction of market-oriented thinking has already profoundly affected public sector financial strategies and managment. Market mechanisms, such as user fees, are being imposed in a number of areas and this has important implications for public management.[18] User fees tend to shift the burden for paying for certain activities from the general public to the specific beneficiaries. User fees also tend to discourage indiscriminate use or overuse of certain resources.

This shift of costs from the general treasury to the beneficiary has implications for agency management because political power tends to be related to the source of agency financing. If there is a shift away from financing through appropriations towards user financing, the ability of Congress and central management agencies to supervise the agencies decreases. From a congressional and presidential perspective, therefore, user fees are not simply a convenient and politically neutral form of financing, but rather a major political decision. Indeed privatization has already been a major contributing force in disaggregating the organization of the executive branch and in weakening the President's managerial capacity.[19]

THE COSTS OF GOVERNMENT DISINVESTMENT

Privatization, properly understood and managed, is a valuable option for the provision of public goods and services. In the US we have utilized the private sector to a greater extent than any other nation. But there are limits to the legality and utility of privatization. When privatization is improperly used it is costly, not only to the capacity of government to perform its mission, but to the private economy as well.

In 1989, a new Secretary of Energy, James D. Watkins, was shocked to find out how little capacity for supervision and oversight was available internally for managing the vast array of Departmental programmes and responsibilities and how dependent the Department (DOE) had become on private contractors. He found, to his dismay, that his Congressional testimony was drafted by a contractor. He found contractors were supervising other contractors. Arbitrary personnel ceilings, inadequate compensation and OMB pressure had denuded the Department of its managerial capacity and institutional memory. The Department itself noted that its workforce is 16 000 as against a contract force of well over 100 000. A recent Senate report on the Department concluded:

> DOE relies on private workforce to perform virtually all basic governmental functions. It relies on contractors in the preparation of most important plans and policies, the development of budgets and budget documents, and the drafting of reports to Congress and Congressional testimony. It relies on contractors to monitor arms control negotiations, help prepare decisions on the export of nuclear technology, and conduct hearings and initial appeals in challenges to security clearance disputes...
>
> DOE top management does not have the basic information it needs to understand the dimensions of its reliance on a contractor workforce. Available data indicates that the private workforce may approach or even exceed the number of federal employees in offices responsible for highly sensitive activities.[20]

The situation found in the Department of Energy is replicated throughout the federal government. The Securities and Exchange Commission, for lack of attorneys, is unable to bring necessary suits to maintain the integrity of private securities markets.[21] The Food and Drug Administration, its personnel severely reduced, is unable to conduct all the testing required by law.[22] The Navy, forced to rely on private contractors to run some of its ships, is now criticized by its own Inspector General for assigning sensitive governmental functions to private parties.[23] Finally, the Internal Revenue Service (IRS), unable to attract or retain auditors and underfunded for systems development, is rapidly becoming antiquated.[24]

Speaking to the latter point, the IRS, once the envy of the world, has been permitted to decline to the point where the Comptroller General, Charles Bowsher, estimates that $87 billion in taxes owed in 1988 were not paid. Antiquated systems are extremely costly. 'But better systems alone won't solve the IRS's problems,' states the Comptroller General, 'the agency must also invest in people. The IRS must attract top graduates in accounting, legal and computer fields ... a task that is increasingly difficult as federal pay in these jobs lags behind the private sector more every year. While all government agencies face problems in competing for qualified people, the need is especially acute at IRS.'[25]

Disinvestment in governmental institutions is costly in monetary terms, but is also costly in terms of supervising the vast 'indirect work force' so as to protect the public interest. This so-called indirect work force of contractors, consultants, grantees and others is estimated to be as high as eight million.[26] Much of this bureaucracy is a product of efforts to assign as many functions as possible to the private sector. Privatization, rather than being short-changed by the federal government, as frequently charged by privatization advocates, in many areas and agencies may well have gone beyond what is sensible or legal.

Deregulation, like privatization, is a concept and term subject to many definitions and interpretations. It is generally conceded that deregulation which resulted in eliminating price controls, restrictive market entry requirements and restraints on competition has been beneficial to the economy and the consumer. In many instances, however, deregulation was interpreted as simply less governmental regulatory capacity in fields where government regulation is necessary to ensure honest transactions, the safety and soundness of financial institutions and the interests of the general public as against private interests. Thus it is estimated that cuts made in the budgets of key regulatory agencies during the 1980s will cost the economy many tens of billions in the 1990s. Comptroller General Charles Bowsher in November 1989 observed: 'When you look at what happened in the S&L crisis and look at the situation at H.U.D. and things like that, if we had adequate financial reporting, if we had the right number of auditors to go out and check on this, we would have saved billions of dollars. In other words, we have been penny-wise and really pound-foolish here.'[27]

Disinvestment in the capacity of government to perform the functions citizens expect of their government is a high-risk strategy where the negative consequences tend to be cumulative and difficult to reverse. The anti-government bias of most public choice theorists and privatization advocates is both misdirected and unnecessary. Regulation is not bad *per se*; there is useful and appropriate regulation just as there is costly and inappropriate regulation. The challenge is to decide where regulation and oversight is useful and appropriate and then assure that the government is provided with authority and resources sufficient to perform its function effectively.

Similarly the answer to the problem of unwise assignment of governmental functions to private parties is not to launch an attack on privatization in general. The appropriate response is to raise anew what Charles Wolf correctly calls 'one of the cardinal issues of public policy: namely, "who should do what?", as between government and the private sector'.[28]

PUBLIC AND PRIVATE SECTORS: ALLIES OR ADVERSARIES?

Today a single, highly competitive world economy is emerging. National boundaries are less effective barriers as ideas, monies and people flow rapidly and easily from one country to another. All nations, including the Communist nations, are adapting to this new market-oriented economic order. The US, thanks in part to the privatization movement, is well under way in its own adjustment to new economic realities.

Those promoting privatization in the United States tend to accept the premise that the interests of the public and private sectors are in inevitable conflict. Although rarely stated directly, the assumption appears to be that this international competition is largely and properly between the private sectors of the respective countries.

With respect to the US, the prevailing political model is akin to a zero-sum game. That is, the smaller and less effective the federal government, the larger and more effective the national private sector. The public and private sectors are viewed as natural adversaries where the prosperity of one sector is achieved largely at the expense of the other sector.

The author rejects the zero-sum game model as the model most likely to make the US competitive in the new world economic order. Competition between nations is not confined to private sectors, but is equally pervasive between public sectors. Public sectors are responsible for developing and protecting the infrastructure that permits private sector growth and stability. For instance, private securities markets must be kept honest and efficient through governmental supervision, or capital transactions will take place in other national markets. Private security interests, therefore, have a stake in building the capacity of the Securities and Exchange Commission to regulate their activities. Similarly, if foreign airlines are going to have confidence in the safety of American-made passenger planes, the domestic aircraft industry has a stake in building the capacity of the Federal Aviation Administration to monitor its activities. The list of private and public congruence of interests is endless.

The private sector does not benefit from an adversarial attitude towards the public sector. The two sectors, although fundamentally different, are nonetheless tied together in a symbiotic relationship. Neither sector can prosper while the other is weakened. The prosperity of both is linked in a mutually beneficial relationship. Privatization, however defined, will require energetic and creative public sector management and oversight to be successfully implemented.

The US is reviewing many of its public functions to determine where these functions, in whole or in part, are best assigned to contribute to the growth of the nation's competitive position. This assignment process is critical to America's future and should be guided by theory leavened with experience.[29] The choice is not whether there will be public management of privatization; such management is a given as long as public (governmental) authority or public funds are necessary to implement a public policy or programme. The choice is whether or not that management will be enlightened by sound doctrine and implemented by public managers endowed with adequate resources and discretion to ensure that the objectives are achieved. To complete the assignment process successfully, the two sectors must be viewed as allies, not adversaries.

NOTES

1. Ronald C. Moe, 'Exploring the Limits of Privatization', *Public Administration Review*, **47**, November/December 1987, pp. 453–60.
2. Harold Seidman, 'The Quasi World of the Federal Government', *The Brookings Review*, **6**, Summer 1988, pp. 23–7.
3. National Academy of Public Administration, *Privatization: The Challenge to Public Management*, Washington: National Academy of Public Administration, 1989, p. x.
4. Daniel Guttman and Barry Wilner, *The Shadow Government: The Government's Multi-Billion-Dollar Giveaway of Its Decision-Making Powers to Private Management Consultants, 'Experts,' and Think Tanks*, New York: Pantheon Books, 1976. Daniel Guttman, 'Organizational Conflict of Interest and the Growth of Big Government', *Harvard Journal on Legislation*, **15**, Spring 1978, pp. 297–364.
5. Mark L. Goldstein, 'Hollow Government: The Incapacitating Consequences of Continuing Austerity', *Government Executive*, **21**, October 1989, pp. 12–22.
6. Alan Pifer and Forrest Chisman, 'Putting Out a Contract on the Government', *Wall Street Journal*, 15 October 1984, p. 28.
7. A recent book in this genre is: Randal Fitzgerald, *When Government Goes Private: Successful Alternatives to Public Service*, New York: Universe Books, 1988.
8. Harold Seidman, testimony before the Subcommittee on Human Resources of the House Committee on Post Office and Civil Service, 5 December 1989, pp. 3–4. The hearings will be published in 1990.
9. OMB Circular No. A-76, para. 6e.
10. OMB Circular No. A-120, para. 7B.
11. Letter from Comptroller General Charles Bowsher to Senator David Pryor, Chairman, Federal Services, Post Office and Civil Service Subcommittee, Senate Committee on Governmental Affairs, B-237356, 29 December 1989.

12. For an insightful discussion of how this process works, called by some 'interest group liberalism', consult Theodore Lowi, *The End of Liberalism*, New York: Norton, 1979.
13. Donald F. Kettl, 'Third-Party Government and the Public Manager: The Changing Forms of Government Action, *NAPA Proceedings*, Washington: National Academy of Public Administration, 1986, p. 33. See also by the same author: *Government By Proxy: (Mis?) Managing Federal Programs* Washington: CQ Press, 1988.
14. Lester M. Salamon, 'Rethinking Public Management: Third-Party Government and the Changing Forms of Government Action', *Public Policy*, **29**, Summer 1981, pp. 255–75.
15. US Library of Congress, Congressional Research Service, *Privatization From a Public Management Perspective*, 89–160 Gov (Ronald C. Moe), March 1989, pp. 75–6.
16. Harold Seidman and Robert S. Gilmour, *Politics, Position and Power: From the Positive to the Regulatory State*, 4th edn, New York: Oxford University Press, 1986, pp. 134–5.
17. Thomas H. Stanton, *Government-Sponsored Enterprises: Their Benefits and Costs as Instruments of Federal Policy*, Washington: Association of Reserve City Bankers, 1988. Ronald C. Moe and Thomas H. Stanton, 'Government-Sponsored Enterprises: Reconciling Public Law With Private Management', *Public Administration Review*, **49**, July/August 1989, pp. 321–9.
18. Clayton P. Gillette and Thomas P. Hopkins, 'Federal User Fees: A Legal and Economic Analysis', *Boston University Law Review*, **67**, November 1987, pp. 451–531. Michael W. Bowers, 'The Expansion of User Fees to Finance Government Programs: An Area to Watch,' *Federal Bar News and Journal*, **34**, January 1987, pp. 21–36.
19. For further discussion by this author of the current status of the President's managerial capacity, consult: 'Traditional Organizational Principles and the Managerial Presidency: From Phoenix to Ashes', *Public Administration Review*, **50**, March/April 1990, pp. 129–40.
20. US Congress, Senate, Committee on Governmental Affairs, Subcommittee on Federal Services, Post Office and Civil Service, Report to the Subcommittee Chairman by Majority Staff, 'The Department of Energy's Reliance on Private Contractors to Perform the Work of Government', in *Use of Consultants and Contractors by the Environmental Protection Agency and the Department of Energy*, S.Hrg. 554, 101st Congress, 1st session, Washington: US Govt. Print. Off., 1990, p. 65.
21. US Securities and Exchange Commission, *Self-Funding Study*, Washington: Securities and Exchange Commission, January 1989.
22. Philip J. Hilts, 'A Guardian of U.S. Health is Failing Under Pressure: The FDA and Safety', *New York Times*, 4 December 1989, p. A-1. Enrique J. Gonzales, 'A Rudderless FDA Drifts, Awaits Congressional Action', *Washington Times*, 8 December 1989, p. B-6.
23. Peter Grier, 'Has Privatization Gone Too Far?', *Military Forum*, **5**, April 1989, pp. 30–5.
24. Louise D. Walsh, 'IRS Loses 2 Million Tax Documents Yearly', *New York Times*, 19 February 1989, p. A-16.
25. National Academy of Public Administration, Charles A. Bowsher, The James E. Webb Lecture, 'An Emerging Crisis: The Disinvestment of Government', Washington: National Academy of Public Administration, 1988, pp. 6–7.
26. '[A]ccording to a [1979] *National Journal* survey, their [DOD, HEW] budgets support four workers who do not work directly for the federal government for every one who shows up on the payroll.' Barbara Blumenthal, 'Uncle Sam's Army of Invisible Employees', *National Journal*, 5 May 1979, p. 730.
27. Jeff Gerth, 'Regulators Say 80's Budget Cuts May Cost U.S. Billions in 1990s', *New York Times*, 19 December 1989, p. 1.
28. Charles Wolf Jr., in the Preface to Randy L. Ross, *Government and the Private Sector, Who Should Do What?*, New York: Crane Russak and Co., 1988, p. x.
29. John D. Donahue, *The Privatization Decision: Public Ends, Private Means*, New York: Basic Books, 1989.

Name Index

Adelman, Irma, 136, 137, 138, 140, 142, 151
Alesina, Alberto, 33
Apter, David E., 138, 141

Balassa, Bela, 146, 151, 155
Baldwin, Richard E., 182
Barnet, Richard, 36
Bergevin, J., 8, 10
Bernheim, B. Douglas, 179
Blair, Margaret M., 173
Blecker, Robert A., 161, 168, 180
Block, Fred C., 168
Bosworth, Barry, 168
Bowsher, Charles, 228
Brada, Josef C., 145, 148
Bresciani-Turroni, C., 78
Bresser Pereira, Luiz, 43, 52
Bresser Pereira, Sylvio, 58
Brown, Brendan, 31, 33
Bruno, M., 81

Cantor, Richard, 168
Carroll, Chris, 168
Carter, Jimmy, 94
Carvalho, Fernando, 72
Chenery, Hollis B., 153
Choksi, A., 63
Christian, James W., 168
Cline, William R., 178
Cobb, John B., 161
Cooper, Ronald S., 164
Cumby, Robert, 32

Daly, Herman E., 161
Dasgupta, Partha, 142
Davidson, Paul, 69
Diakosavvas, D., 7, 11
Dooley, Michael, 33
Dornbusch, Rudiger, 47, 178, 181
Downs, Anthony, 203

Duvalier, Jean Claude 'Baby Doc', 36

Eisner, Robert, 164
Emmanuel, A., 12

Fei, John C., 135
Findlay, R., 6
Fischer, S., 47
Franzmeyer, F., 109
Frenkel, Roberto, 75, 76, 78
Friedman, Milton, 85

Gibson, H., 21
Gierek, President, 145
Gilmour, Robert, 225
Gomulka, President, 145
Grilli, E. R., 7, 13

Haile Selassie, Emperor, 36
Hatsopoulos, George N., 168, 170, 180
Helkie, William L., 179, 180
Helpman, E., 57
Hihn, J. M., 139
Hirschman, Albert, 142
Hochman, Sergio, 35
Hooper, Peter, 179, 180
Huntington, Samuel P., 138
Hussain, M. N., 16, 18

Jain, Arvind, 36
Jay, John, 202–3
Jenkins, Roy (now Lord), 107
Johnson, H. G., 18

Kaldor, Nicholas, 13, 80
Kalecki, Michal, 183
Kanbur, R., 26
Kaunda, Kenneth, 36
Kettl, Donald F., 224
Keynes, John Maynard, 5, 20, 25–8,

Name Index

69, 72, 73, 80–81, 87–90
Khrushchev, Nikita, 201
Kiguel, M., 47, 62
Kindleberger, Charles P., 5, 33
Kloten, Norbert, 118
Kohl, Helmut, 128
Kornai, Janos, 154
Kotlikoff, Laurence J., 162
Krugman, Paul R., 170, 178
Kuznets, Simon S., 136, 140
Leijonhufvud, Axel, 73, 75
Lessard, Donald R., 32–3
Levich, Richard, 32
Lewis, W. A., 5
Litan, Robert E., 173
Liviatan, N., 47, 62

McIntyre, Robert S., 168
Marcos, Ferdinand and Imelda, 36
Mead, Walter Russell, 182
Meese, Richard, 181
Michaely, M., 63
Mill, John Stuart, 5
Mobutu Sese Seko, President, 36
Montias, John M., 145, 148
Moon, Rev. Sun Myung, 37
Morris, Cynthia T., 136, 137, 138, 140
Morrison, J., 8

Nakano, Yoshiaki, 43, 52
Naylor, R. T., 31
Nelson, Joan M., 138
Nguyen, D. T., 7–8
North, Douglass C., 137
Nyers, Rezso, 144

Papageorgiou, D., 63
Parsons, Talcott, 136
Pastor, Manuel, 33, 35–6
Pastore, Afonso Celso, 60
Pechman, Joseph A., 168
Pieper, Paul, 167
Piterman, S., 81
Pöhl, K. O., 117

Poterba, James M., 170
Prebisch, R., 4–5, 6, 10

Ranis, Gustav, 135
Reagan, Ronald, 90, 94
Robertson, Dennis, 5

Sachs, Jeffrey D., 179
Sapsford, D., 6, 7
Sarkar, P., 6, 9–10, 20
Scandizzo, P., 7, 11
Schlote, W., 5
Seidman, Harold, 222, 225
Shackle, George, 71
Singer, H., 4–5, 10, 12, 20
Smelser, Neil J., 136
Soete, Luc, 182
Somosa, General, 36
Spraos, J., 5, 6, 7, 10, 11
Steindl, Josef, 164, 168
Summers, Lawrence, 168

Tabellini, Guido, 33
Thatcher, Margaret, 116–17, 120
Thirlwall, A. P., 8, 10, 13, 16, 18, 21, 98
Toledo, Joaquim Elói, 61
Tullock, Gordon, 203–4

Vines, D., 26
Vujovic, Dusan, 151

Walter, Ingo, 31, 34
Watkins, James D., 227
Wattleworth, M., 8
Weber, Max, 203, 205
Williamson, John, 32–3, 185
Wolf, Charles, 229

Yang, M. C., 7, 13
Yeager, Leland B., 47

Subject Index

Agency of International Development, 153
agencies, theory of *see* privatization; public sector service provision
agriculture
  in economic growth model, 13–16
  reform of, in E. Europe, 144
  and terms of trade, 5, 10
aid and development, 155, 156
Algeria, 23
Argentina, 22, 33, 77, 81, 139
asset management, 34

Bahamas, 24
balance of payments
  and economic growth model, 98–101
  and international payments system, 92–98
  and terms of trade, 4, 16–19
  US deficit in, 90, 94, 162–3, 174–83
Bangladesh, 23
Bank of England, 27–8
banking system(s)
  and capital flight, 31–7
  and European integration, 115, 117–20
  and German unification, 123–32
  and international payments system, 95–6
Barbados, 23
beachhead effect, 182
Benin, 23
Bolivia, 22, 25
Botswana, 23
Brazil, 19, 24, 33, 75, 77
  Collor Plan in, 49–58
    results of, 58–65
  economic debates in, 46–9
  hyperinflation in, 41–6, 78, 81
  political development in, 139, 141

Bresser Plan (Brazil), 58
Bretton Woods Agreement, 28, 89
Britain, 6, 27–8, 111, 115, 116–17
Bulgaria, 145, 147, 151, 152
Bundesbank, Deutsche, 113, 117–20
  and German monetary unification, 122–4, 129–32
bureaucratic agency *see* public sector service provision
bureaucratic authoritarianism, 151
Burkina Faso, 23
Burma, 22, 25
Burundi, 23

Cameroon, 23
capital, 18, 115, 128, 150
  flight of, 31–7, 86
  foreign, and economic development, 150–56
  and savings, 162, 163–6, 171
capital goods, 126–7, 167
Central African Republic, 23
Chad, 23
Chile, 23, 25, 141
China, 24
civil service *see* public sector service provision
classical economic theories, 5, 12
Cold War politics, 93
Collor Plan (Brazil), 49–58
  results of, 58–65
Colombia, 19, 22
'Commod Control' proposal, 26, 27–8
commodity prices
  and debt problems, 19–25, 27, 28
  proposals for control of, 26–8
  terms of trade and, 3, 4–11
communist countries *see* Eastern Europe
Comoros, 24
competition

235

in banking sector, 34–5, 115
and European Single Market, 109–15
and terms of trade movements, 12
see also privatization
competitiveness, measures of, 180–81
Congo, 22
consumption, 14
and Collor Plan, 57–8
in USA, 167–70
contractual systems
and inflation, 69
see also indexation and inflation; privatization; public sector service provision
coordination
in entrepreneurial economies, 71–3
inflation as failure of, 73–82
corruption, 36, 215–16
Costa Rica, 19, 22
Cruzado Plan (Brazil), 43, 48, 56, 58
currencies
European, proposal for, 119
German, unification of, 122–9
reforms of, 49–50, 80–81
see also exchange rates
Cyprus, 19, 23
Czechoslovakia, 145, 147, 148, 151

debt problems of developing countries
and capital flight, 31–7
and commodity prices, 19–25, 27, 28
in E. Europe, 146, 147, 148, 151–2, 153–5
and hyperinflation, 41, 42, 48, 63
and international payments system, 97–8
demand
and economic growth, 27, 91, 98–101
effects of Collor Plan on, 57–8
and terms of trade movements, 12, 13, 17, 18
democracy, 138
depreciation rates, 166–7
deregulation, 228
see also privatization
development *see* economic growth and development
developmental ideologies, 135

diminishing returns in agriculture, 13, 15, 16
dollarization and hyperinflation, 43, 78, 79, 80–82
Dominican Republic, 24

East Germany *see* German Democratic Republic
Eastern Europe, 94
economic reforms in, 144–50
need for structural change in, 150–56
political events in, 143
political participation in, 139, 141, 142
see also individual countries
economic growth and development
constraints on, 27, 91, 98–101
and foreign capital flows, 150–56
history of, in E. Europe, 144–50
and international payments systems, 91–8
models of, 13–16, 98–101
and political development, 134–44
prospects for, in USA, 183–6
and saving rates, 163–6
and terms of trade, 16–19
Economist, The, 86
Ecuador, 19, 24
efficiency, 200–207
Egypt, 23
El Salvador, 22
elites in developing countries
and capital flight, 36–7
and economic/political development, 138–9
embourgeoisement, 139
Ethiopia, 22, 36
Europe, Eastern *see* Eastern Europe
European Community (EC, EEC), 88
creation of single market in, 107–17
monetary union in, 107, 117–20
exchange rates
and capital flight, 31, 33–4
and hyperinflation, 43, 46, 62–3, 78, 79
and international payments system, 91–101

and terms of trade, 4, 20
and US deficits, 178–9
views on determination of, 85–90, 181–2
expectations
formation of, 71–3
inflation as breakdown of, 73–82
exports *see* trade, international

factoral terms of trade, 7
Federal Reserve, 86, 88, 90, 94, 95, 178, 185
Fiji, 23
financial services industry, 108, 114–15
see also banking system(s)
Financial Times, 86
France, 90, 111
free riders, 47

Gabon, 24
Gambia, The, 24
German Democratic Republic, 148
debt problems of, 147
economic reforms in, 144, 145, 146
and reunification, 114, 122–32
Germany, Federal Republic of, 49, 88, 94, 176–7
and European Monetary System, 117–20
and European single market, 109–15
and reunification, 114, 122–32
Germany, pre-1945, 20, 43, 78
Ghana, 23
government(s) and the state
and capital flight, 31–7
deficit spending by, 162, 173–83
and economic development, 134–44, 148, 165
and hyperinflation, 45–6, 48, 64
see also public sector
Great Britain, 6, 27–8, 111, 115, 116–17
Greece, 22
Grenada, 23
groups, economic theory of, 213
growth *see* economic growth and development
Guatemala, 22, 25
Guyana, 24

Haiti, 24, 36

'high inflation', 70, 75, 81
Honduras, 19, 24
honour, bureaucratic, 204–5
hot money and capital flight, 31–7
Hungary, 22, 144–8 *passim*, 151, 152
hyperinflation *see* inflation
hysteresis, 182

imports *see* trade, international
income *see* wages and incomes
indexation and inflation, 43–4, 62, 70, 74–7, 79–80, 82
India, 19, 22, 141
Indonesia, 22
industry *see* manufacturing industry
inertialism, 61–2
inflation and hyperinflation
in Brazil, 41–6
Collor Plan for control of, 49–65
economic debate about, 46–9
in Eastern Europe, 152
post-Keynesian views of, 69–82
institutional change
and inflation, 70, 74–7
and political change, 136–7
in Eastern Europe, 143, 144–50
interest rates, 34, 44–5, 77, 127–8, 168, 184–5
International Clearing Union, proposal for, 27
International Monetary Fund (IMF), 31, 63, 140, 152
international payments systems, 91–101
International Private Banking (IPB), 32, 37
international trade *see* trade, international
International Trade Organisation, proposal for, 28
investment, 14, 113, 127–8, 155–6, 164, 173
Iran, 136, 137
Israel, 23, 37, 81
Italy, 111
Ivory Coast, 24

Jamaica, 19, 22
Japan, 94, 111, 176–7
joint ventures, 155–6

Jordan, 22

Kenya, 19, 22
Keynesianism, 60, 61, 174–5
  see also Post Keynesianism
Korea, South, 23, 137, 139, 140, 153

Latin America, 32, 35–6, 139, 151
  see also individual countries
League of Nations, 5
Lesotho, 23
liability management, 34
Liberia, 24
loan pushing, 34, 35–6, 37
location of industry, 112–14
Luxembourg, 35

Madagascar, 22, 25
Malawi, 23
Malaysia, 22
Maldives, 23
Mali, 22
Malta, 24
mandates, definition of, 201–7
manufacturing industry
  in Eastern Europe, 144, 145, 148
  in economic growth model, 13–16
  and European single market, 109–14
  and German unification, 126–7, 130
  and terms of trade, 5, 10, 13
Marshall Plan, 89, 93
  as model for proposed aid to Eastern Europe, 134, 150–56
Mauritania, 23
Mauritius, 23
Mexico, 19, 22, 33, 94
middle classes and political participation, 139
mineral production, 10, 11
monetarism, 47, 60–61, 123–9
money see capital; currencies; money supply
money supply, 46
  and Collor Plan, 52–7, 60–61, 64
  and inflation, 77
Morocco, 19, 24
multi-party systems, 141–2
Mundell-Fleming model, 175

national income and terms of trade, 3–4
national sovereignty and European integration, 116–17
neo-classical theories
  of exchange rates, 85–6
  of growth, 162, 163–6, 174–5
  of trade, 12
  see also monetarism
neostructuralism, 47, 60, 61
net barter terms of trade see trade, terms of
Nepal, 23
Nicaragua, 24, 36
Niger, 22, 25
Nigeria, 22, 25

oil, 10, 11
Oman, 24
ownership and efficiency, 206–7

Pakistan, 19, 22
Panama, 24
Papua New Guinea, 22
Paraguay, 24
Peru, 24, 25
Philippines, 19, 23, 36, 136
planned economies see Eastern Europe
Poland, 144–8 passim, 151–3 passim
politics
  and agents' behaviour, 211–16
  and capital flight, 33
  and economic development, 134–44
  see also government(s) and the state
population growth, 100
Portugal, 19, 22
Post Keynesianism, 47, 89
  on German unification, 129–32
  on growth, 163, 173
  on inflation, 69–82
prices
  stability of, 69
  see also commodity prices; inflation and hyperinflation
private banking, 34–5
privatization
  in GDR, 125–6
  nature of, 219
  and political behaviour, 211–16 passim
  public sector management of, 224–

Subject Index

6, 229–30
and rent-seeking, 209–11
strengths and weaknesses of, 194–200, 206–7, 221–4, 227–9
product-cycle, 182
productivity, 4, 15, 112–13, 129, 153
profit, 165, 170–73
profit-seeking agency *see* privatization
protectionism, 110
public choice theories, 221
public sector service provision, 220–21
   mandates for, 201–6, 207
   and political behaviour, 211–16
   relations with private sector, 224–6, 229–30
   and rent-seeking, 207–9, 210
   strengths and weaknesses of, 194–200, 222–3

real bills doctrine, 91, 95
reconciliation systems, 141–2
regional policy, 93
rent-seeking behaviour, 207–11
revolutionary governments, 32
risk and capital flight, 32–3
Romania, 23, 145, 147, 148, 151
Rwanda, 23

Sao Tome & Principe, 22, 25
saving rates
   and economic growth, 13, 15, 163–6, 183–4
   and German unification, 127–8
   in USA, 161–3, 166–74
secret banking, 34–5
Senegal, 24
Seychelles, 23
short-term expectations, 72
Sierra Leone, 24
Singapore, 24, 140
socialist countries *see* Eastern Europe
Solomon Islands, 24
Somalia, 22, 25
South Korea, 23, 137, 139, 140, 153
sovereignty and European integration, 116–17
Soviet Union, 94, 143, 144, 147, 201
Spain, 111
Special Drawing Rights (SDRs), 28
speculation, 46

Sri Lanka, 19, 23
stagflation, 26
stagnation, economic, 173
state *see* government(s) and the state
structuralist theories, 12
Sudan, 19, 24
Summer Plan (Brazil), 43–4, 45, 48
supply
   and constraints on growth, 27
   effects of Collor Plan on, 57–8
   and terms of trade movements, 12
Swaziland, 23
Switzerland, 35, 36
symbolism, manipulation of, 136, 141
Syria, 24

Taiwan, 137, 139, 140
Tanzania, 23, 25
Tanzi effect, 77
taxation, 34, 50, 51, 77
   in USA, 167–8, 185–6
technical progress and terms of trade, 13, 16
technocracy, 139
technological gap, 182
tension management, 137–8, 141
Thailand, 19, 22
Togo, 22, 25
trade, international, 63, 155
   and European single market, 109–12
   and international payments system, 92–8
   terms of, 3–4
      causes of movements in, 12–16
      and debt problems, 19–25, 27, 28
      effects on growth of movements in, 16–19, 25–7
      statistics of, 4–11
   see also balance of payments
transfer burden, 20, 154
Trinidad & Tobago, 24
Tunisia, 19, 22
Turkey, 19, 23

Uganda, 22
uncertainty, 80
unemployment, 56, 59, 152
unequal exchange, theory of, 12
Unification Church movement, 37
unionized monetary system (UMS),

92, 95, 98
United Kingdom, 6, 27–8, 111, 115, 116–17
United Nations, 5
United States of America, 101, 202–3
  banking system of, 32, 36
  deficits of, 90, 94, 162–3, 167–8, 173–83, 185
  and exchange rates, 88, 89
  growth in, policy alternatives for, 183–6
  monetary policies of, 86–7, 90
  public service in, 205, 220–21, 227–8, 229–30
  savings rate in, 161–3, 166–74
Uruguay, 22
USSR (Soviet Union), 143, 144, 147, 201

variable proportions, law of, 86
Venezuela, 24, 33

wages and incomes
  and Collor Plan, 56, 57–8, 62, 64
  controls on, 46–7
  and European single market, 112
  and German unification, 128–9
  indexation of, 75
  in public and private sectors, 208–11
  and terms of trade, 12, 13, 15–16
  in US, 183
West Germany *see* Germany, Federal Republic of
Western Samoa, 23
working classes and political participation, 139
World Bank, 8, 63, 140, 155

Yemen, 22, 25
Yugoslavia, 24, 144–8 *passim*, 151, 152

Zaire, 19, 36
Zambia, 24, 25, 36

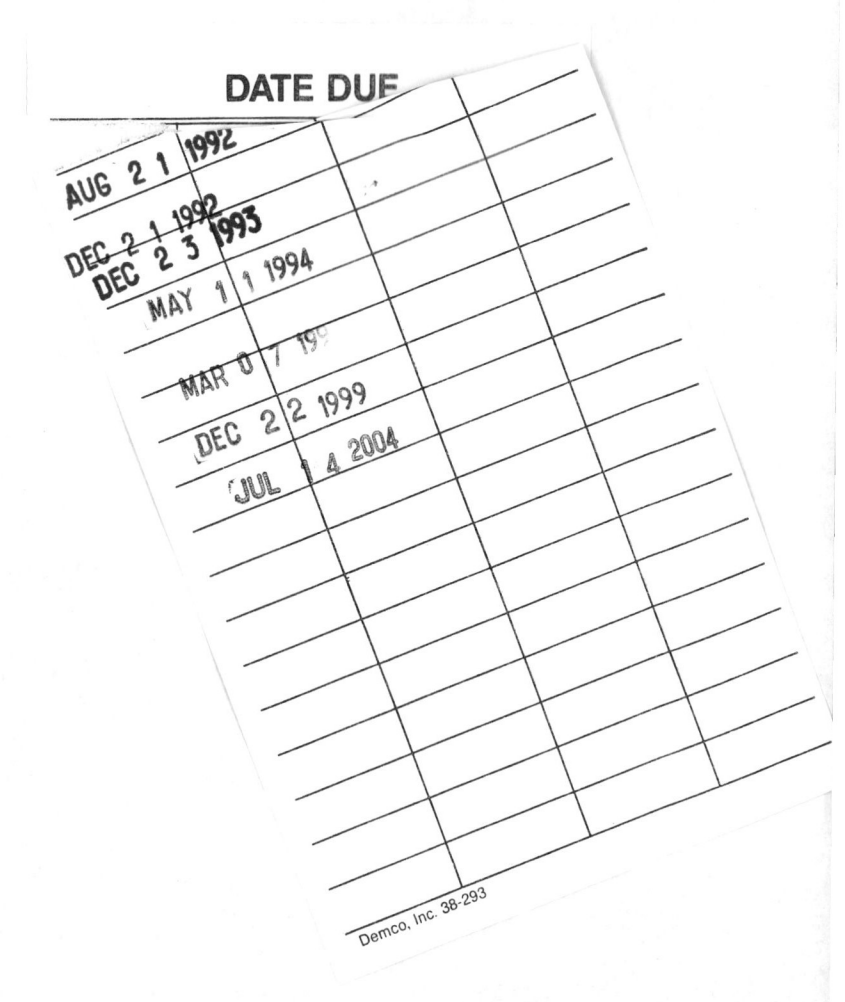